mary

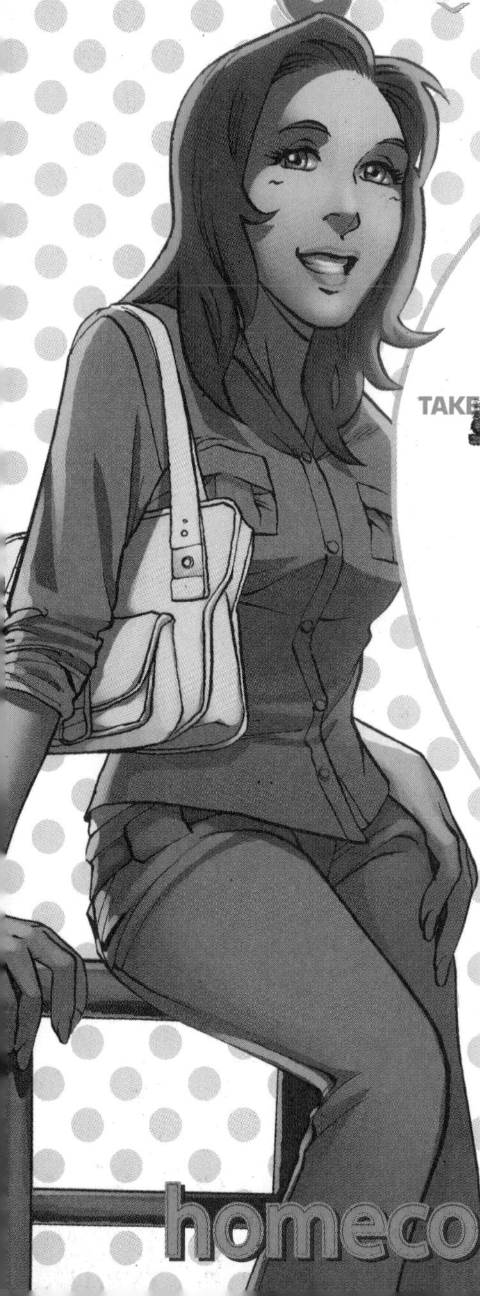

writer
SEAN McKEEVER
art
TAKESHI MIYAZAWA
colors
CHRISTINA STRAIN
letters
DAVE SHARPE
cover art
TAKESHI MIYAZAWA, NORMAN LEE
CHRISTINA STRAIN

editor
MACKENZIE CADENHEAD
consulting editors
C.B. CEBULSKI
& MARK PANICCIA

collection editor
JENNIFER GRÜNWALD
assistant editor
MICHAEL SHORT
senior editor, special projects
JEFF YOUNGQUIST
director of sales
DAVID GABRIEL
production
JERRY KALINOWSKI
book designer
CARRIE BEADLE
creative director
TOM MARVELLI

editor in chief
JOE QUESADA
publisher
DAN BUCKLEY

homecoming

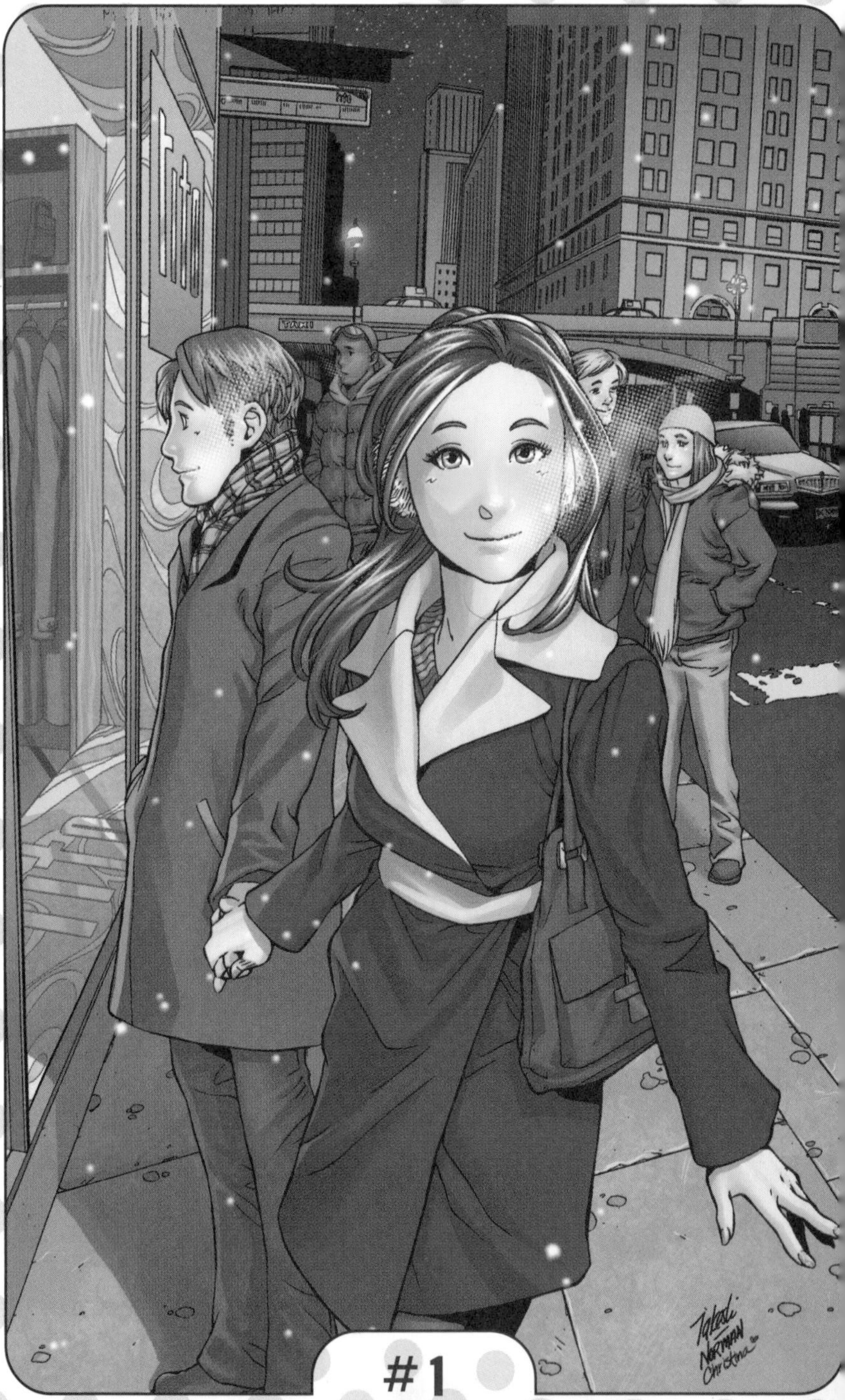

#1

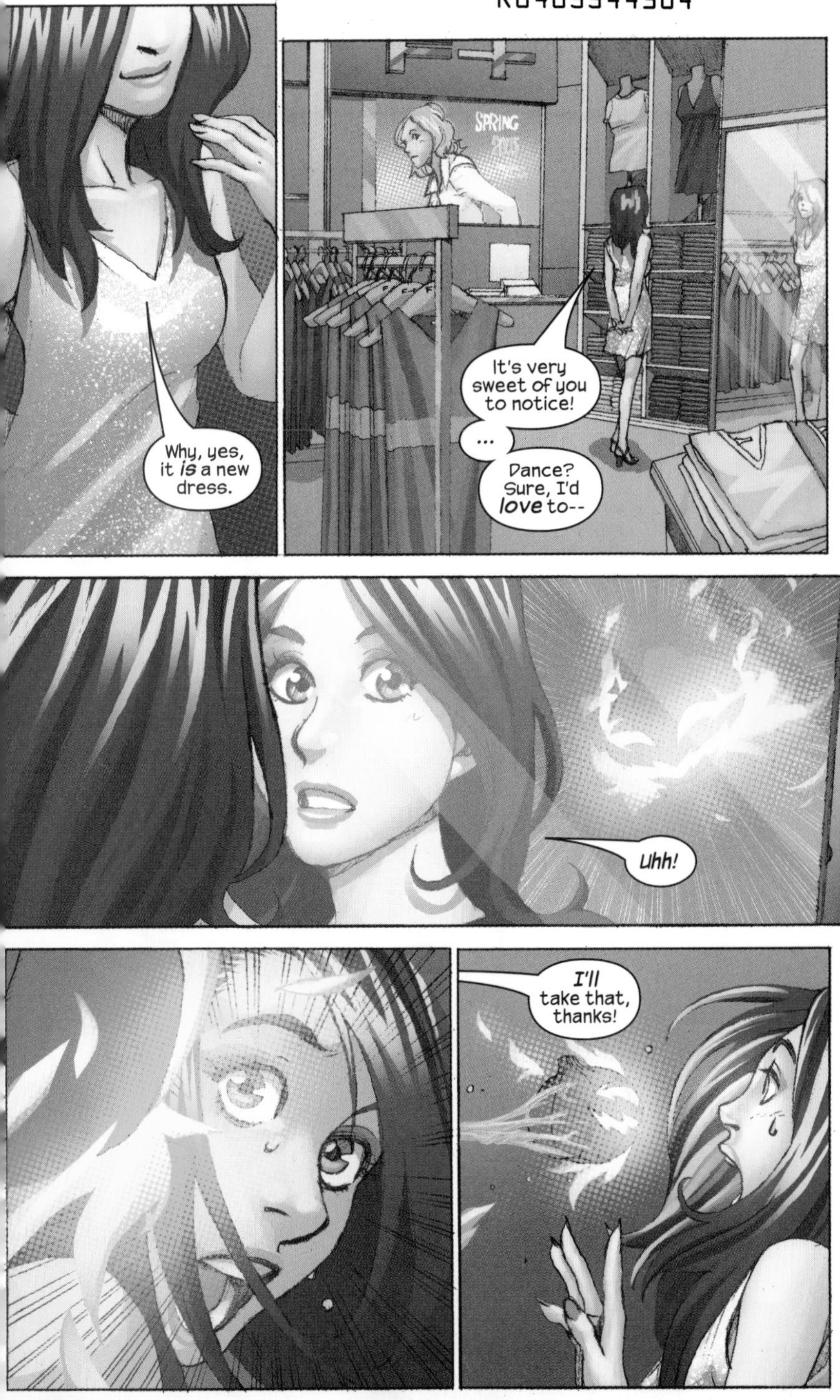
Why, yes, it *is* a new dress.
It's very sweet of you to notice!
...
Dance? Sure, I'd *love* to--
Uhh!
I'll take that, thanks!

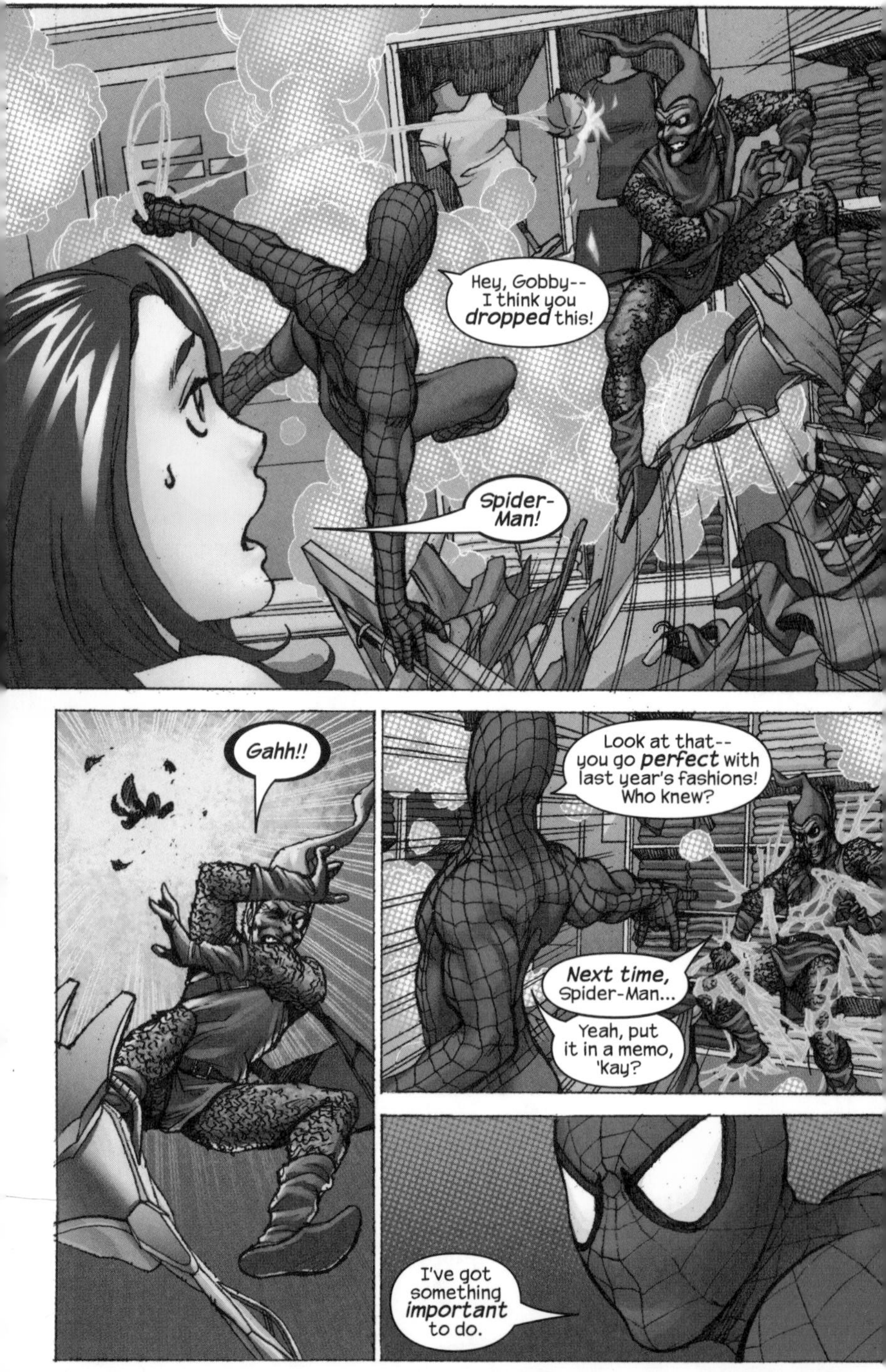
Hey, Gobby--
I think you
dropped this!
Spider-
Man!
Gahh!!
Look at that--
you go perfect with
last year's fashions!
Who knew?
Next time,
Spider-Man...
Yeah, put
it in a memo,
'kay?
I've got
something
important
to do.

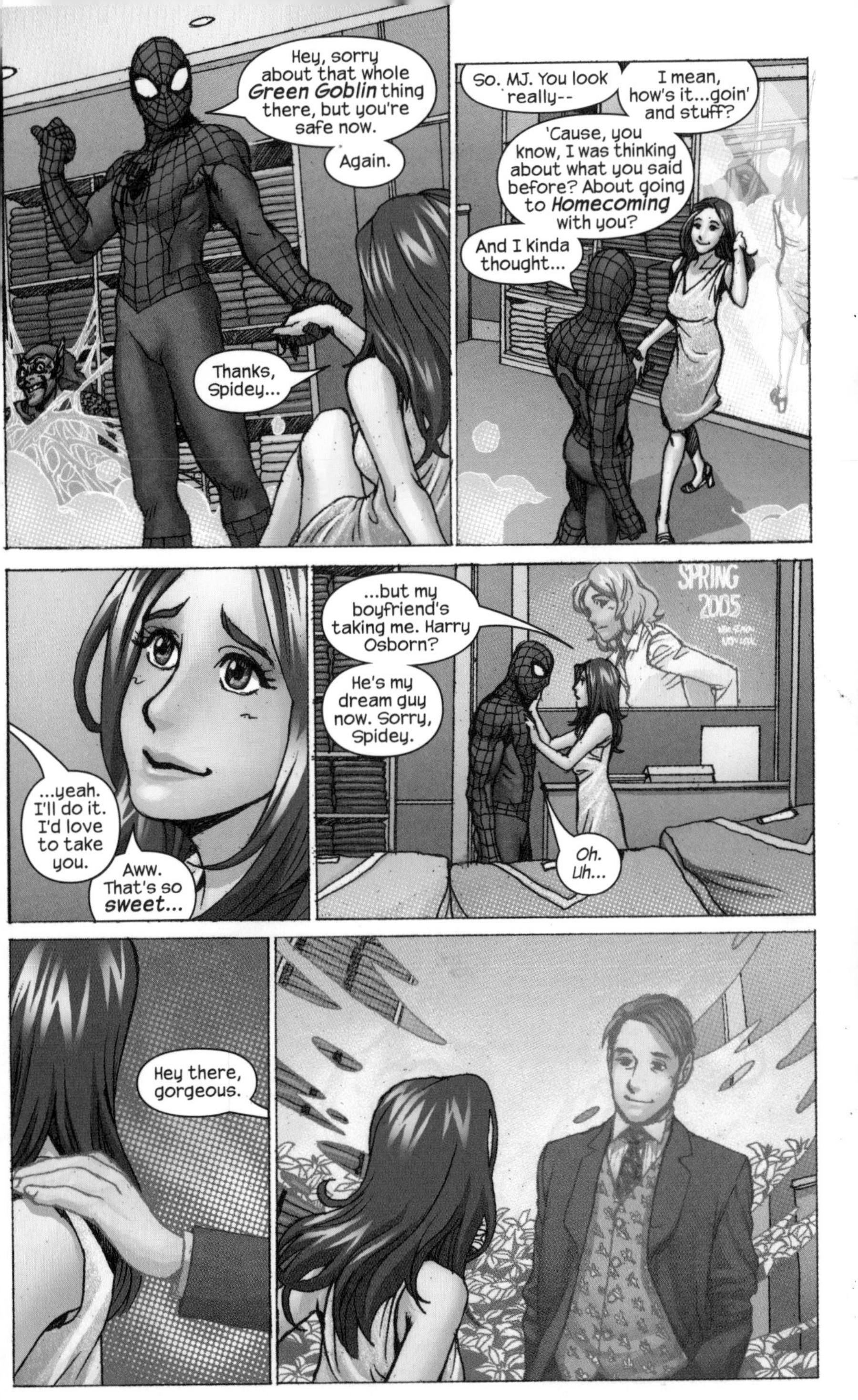

Hey, sorry about that whole Green Goblin thing there, but you're safe now.
Again.
Thanks, Spidey...
So. MJ. You look really--
I mean, how's it...goin' and stuff?
'Cause, you know, I was thinking about what you said before? About going to Homecoming with you?
And I kinda thought...
...yeah. I'll do it. I'd love to take you.
Aww. That's so sweet...
...but my boyfriend's taking me. Harry Osborn?
He's my dream guy now. Sorry, Spidey.
SPRING 2005
Oh. Uh...
Hey there, gorgeous.

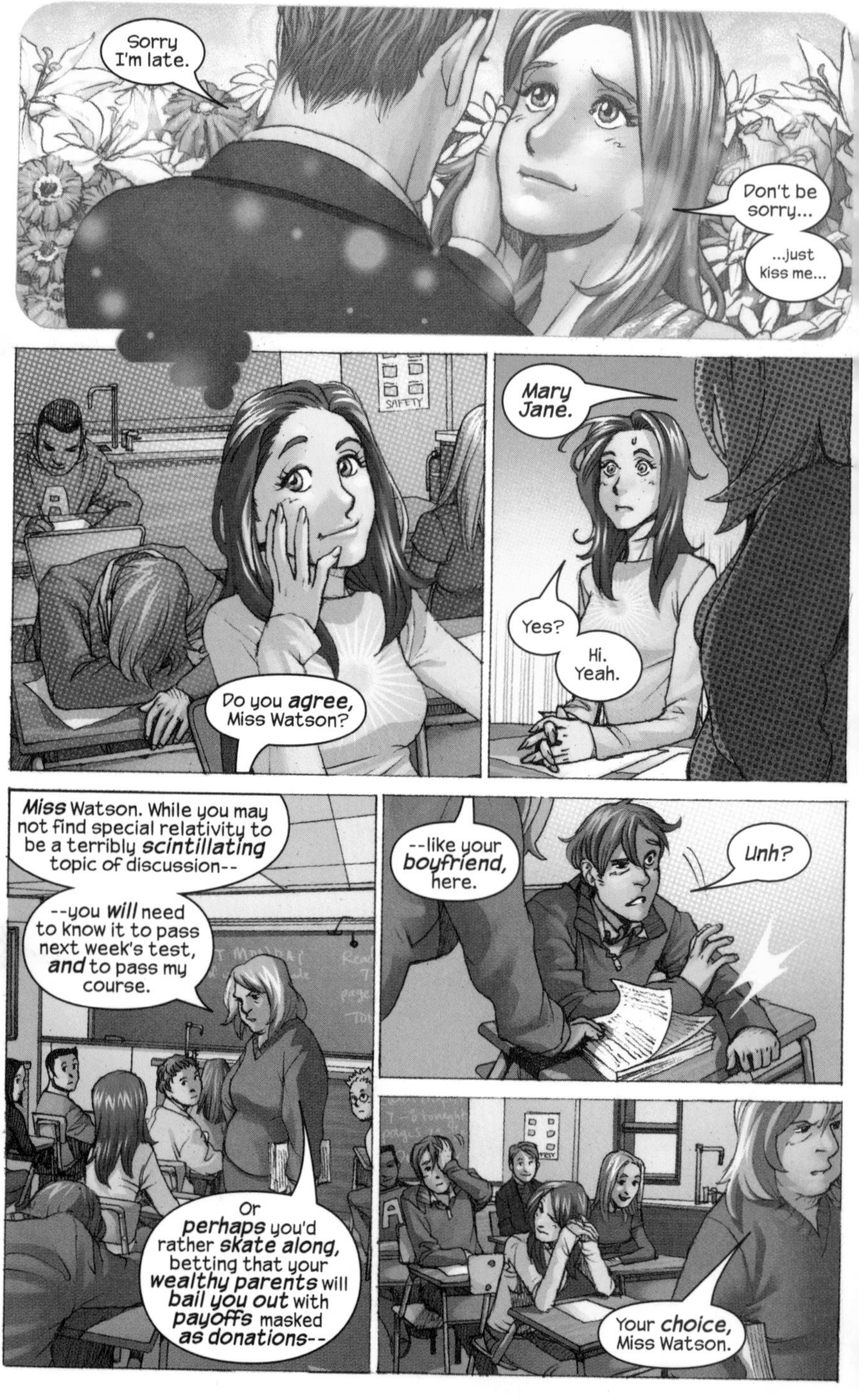

Sorry I'm late.
Don't be sorry...
...just kiss me...
Do you agree, Miss Watson?
Mary Jane.
Yes?
Hi. Yeah.
Miss Watson. While you may not find special relativity to be a terribly scintillating topic of discussion--
--you will need to know it to pass next week's test, and to pass my course.
Or perhaps you'd rather skate along, betting that your wealthy parents will bail you out with payoffs masked as donations--
--like your boyfriend, here.
Unh?
Your choice, Miss Watson.

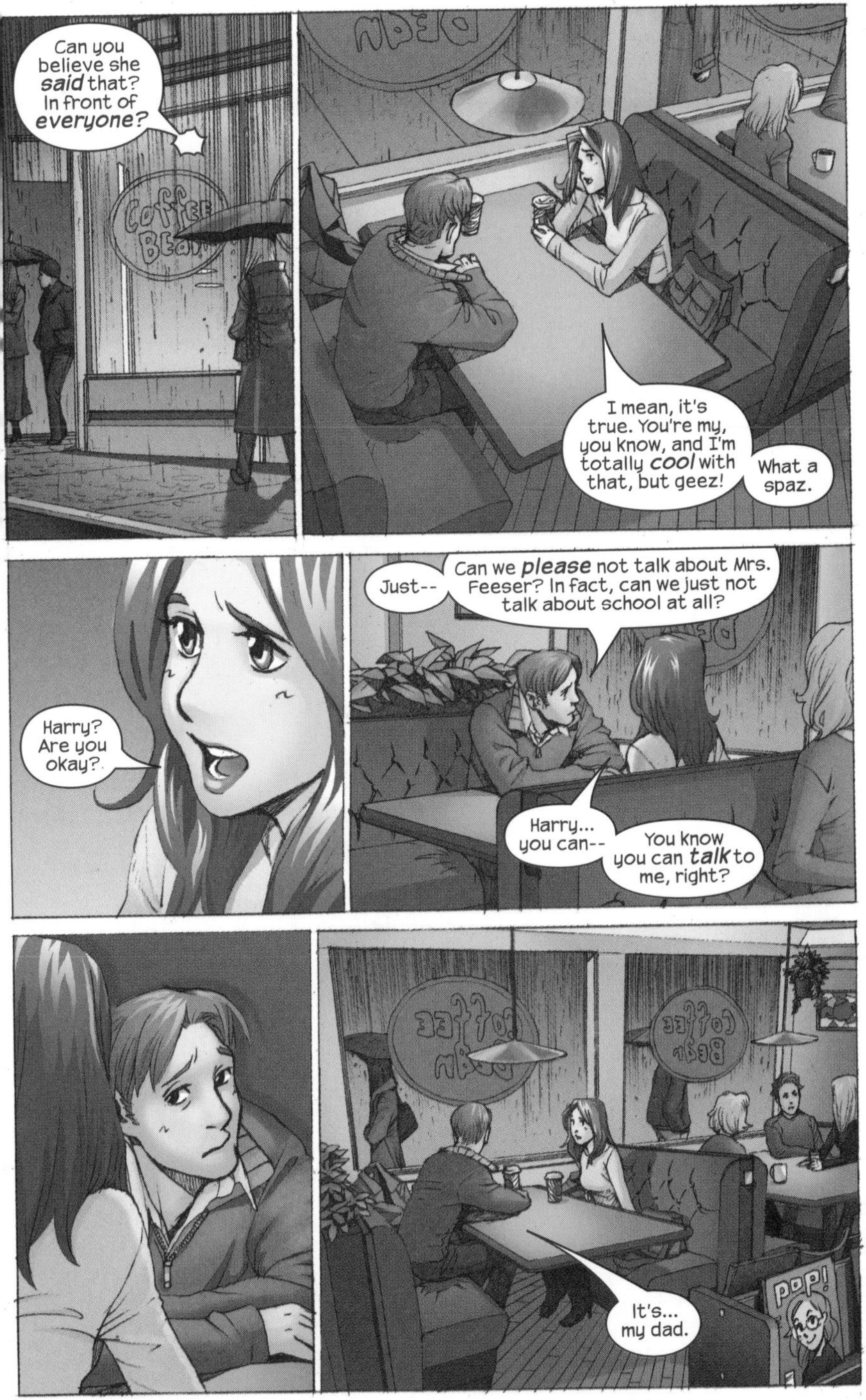
Can you believe she said that? In front of everyone?
I mean, it's true. You're my, you know, and I'm totally cool with that, but geez!
What a spaz.
Harry? Are you okay?
Just--
Can we please not talk about Mrs. Feeser? In fact, can we just not talk about school at all?
Harry... you can--
You know you can talk to me, right?
It's... my dad.

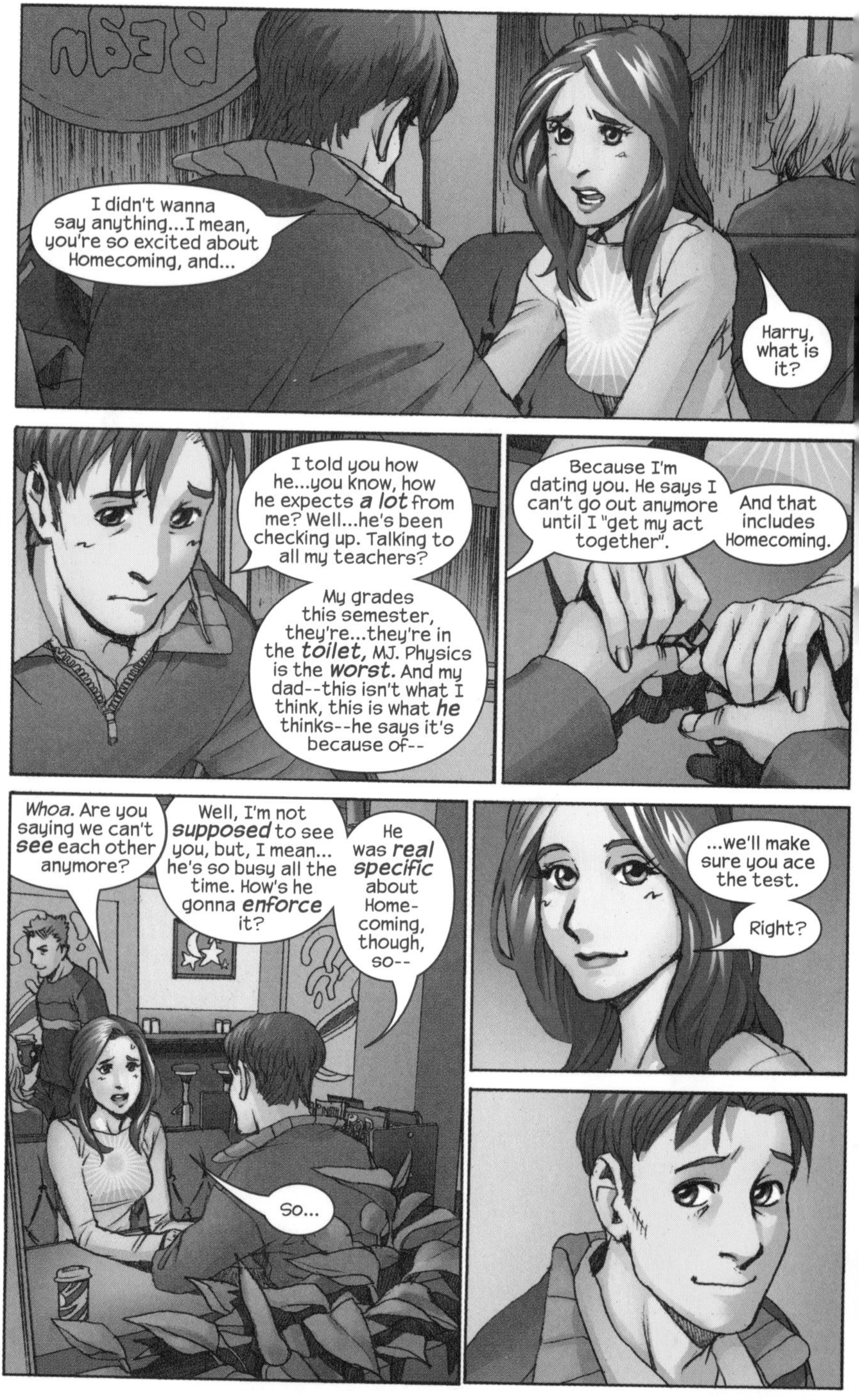
I didn't wanna say anything...I mean, you're so excited about Homecoming, and...
Harry, what is it?
I told you how he...you know, how he expects *a lot* from me? Well...he's been checking up. Talking to all my teachers?
My grades this semester, they're...they're in the *toilet,* MJ. Physics is the *worst.* And my dad--this isn't what I think, this is what *he* thinks--he says it's because of--
Because I'm dating you. He says I can't go out anymore until I "get my act together".
And that includes Homecoming.
Whoa. Are you saying we can't *see* each other anymore?
Well, I'm not *supposed* to see you, but, I mean... he's so busy all the time. How's he gonna *enforce* it?
He was *real specific* about Home-coming, though, so--
So...
...we'll make sure you ace the test.
Right?

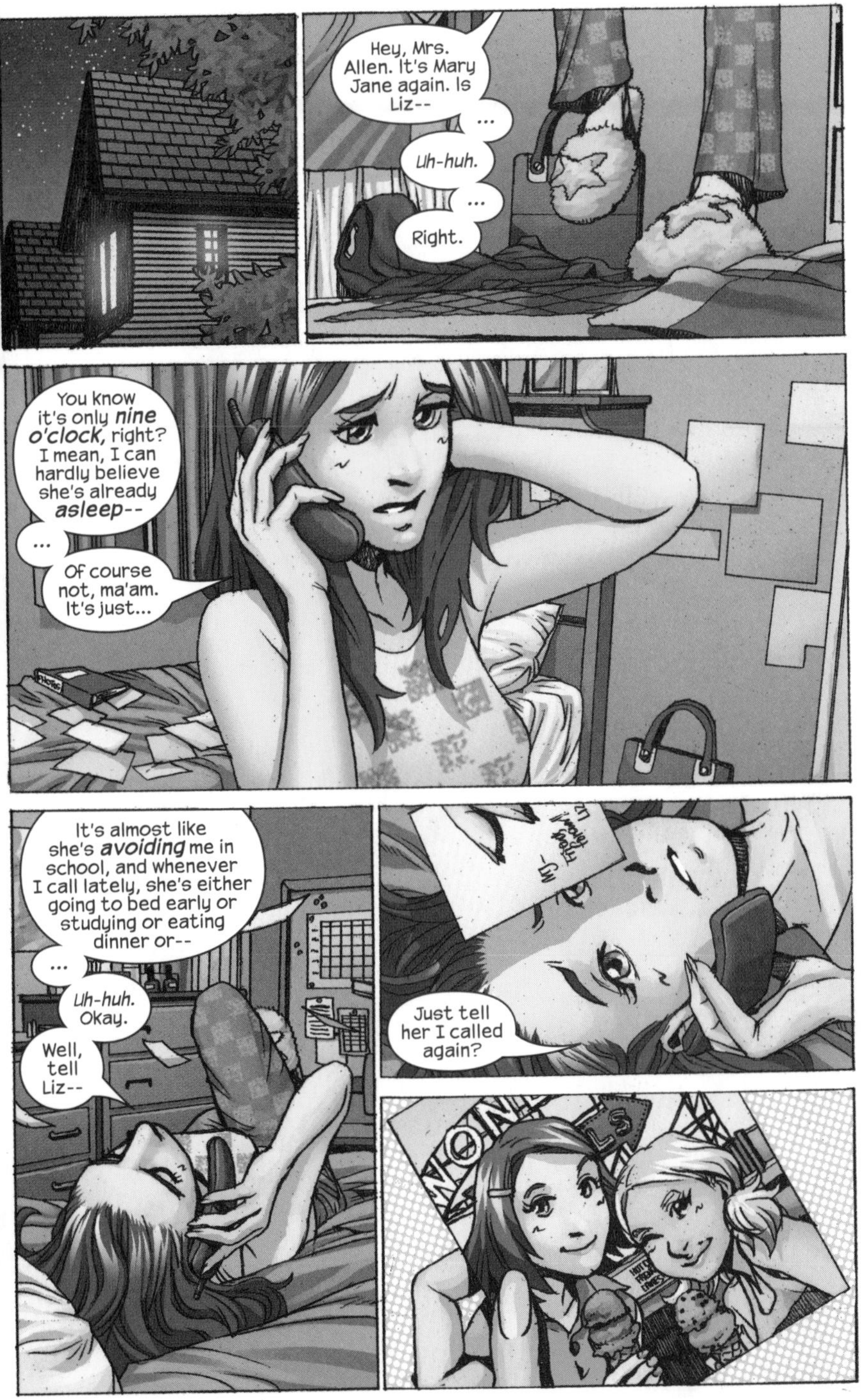
Hey, Mrs. Allen. It's Mary Jane again. Is Liz--
...
Uh-huh.
...
Right.
You know it's only *nine o'clock,* right? I mean, I can hardly believe she's already *asleep*--
...
Of course not, ma'am. It's just...
It's almost like she's *avoiding* me in school, and whenever I call lately, she's either going to bed early or studying or eating dinner or--
...
Uh-huh. Okay.
Well, tell Liz--
Just tell her I called again?

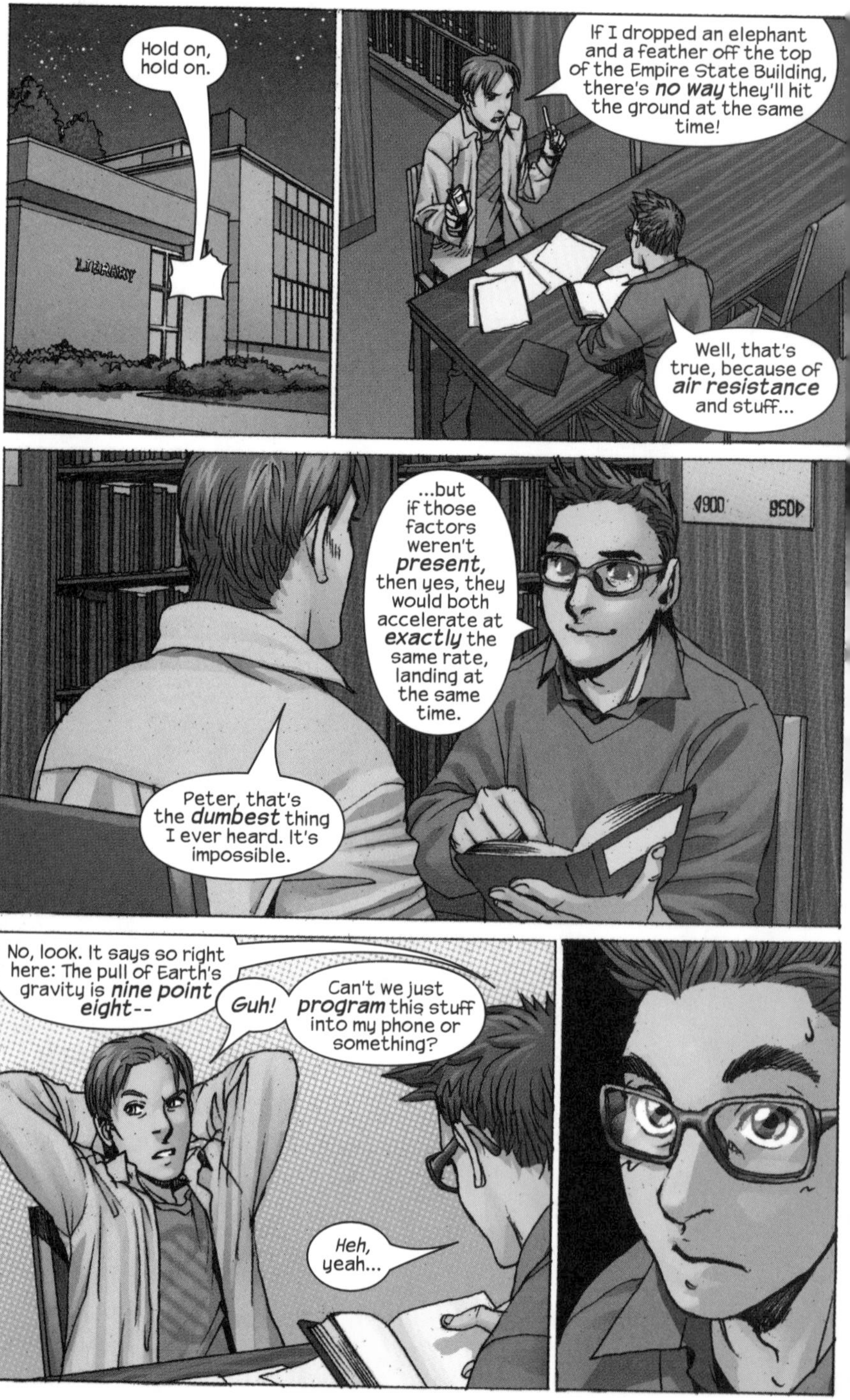
Hold on, hold on.
LIBRARY
If I dropped an elephant and a feather off the top of the Empire State Building, there's no way they'll hit the ground at the same time!
Well, that's true, because of air resistance and stuff...
...but if those factors weren't present, then yes, they would both accelerate at exactly the same rate, landing at the same time.
900
950
Peter, that's the dumbest thing I ever heard. It's impossible.
No, look. It says so right here: The pull of Earth's gravity is nine point eight--
Guh!
Can't we just program this stuff into my phone or something?
Heh, yeah...

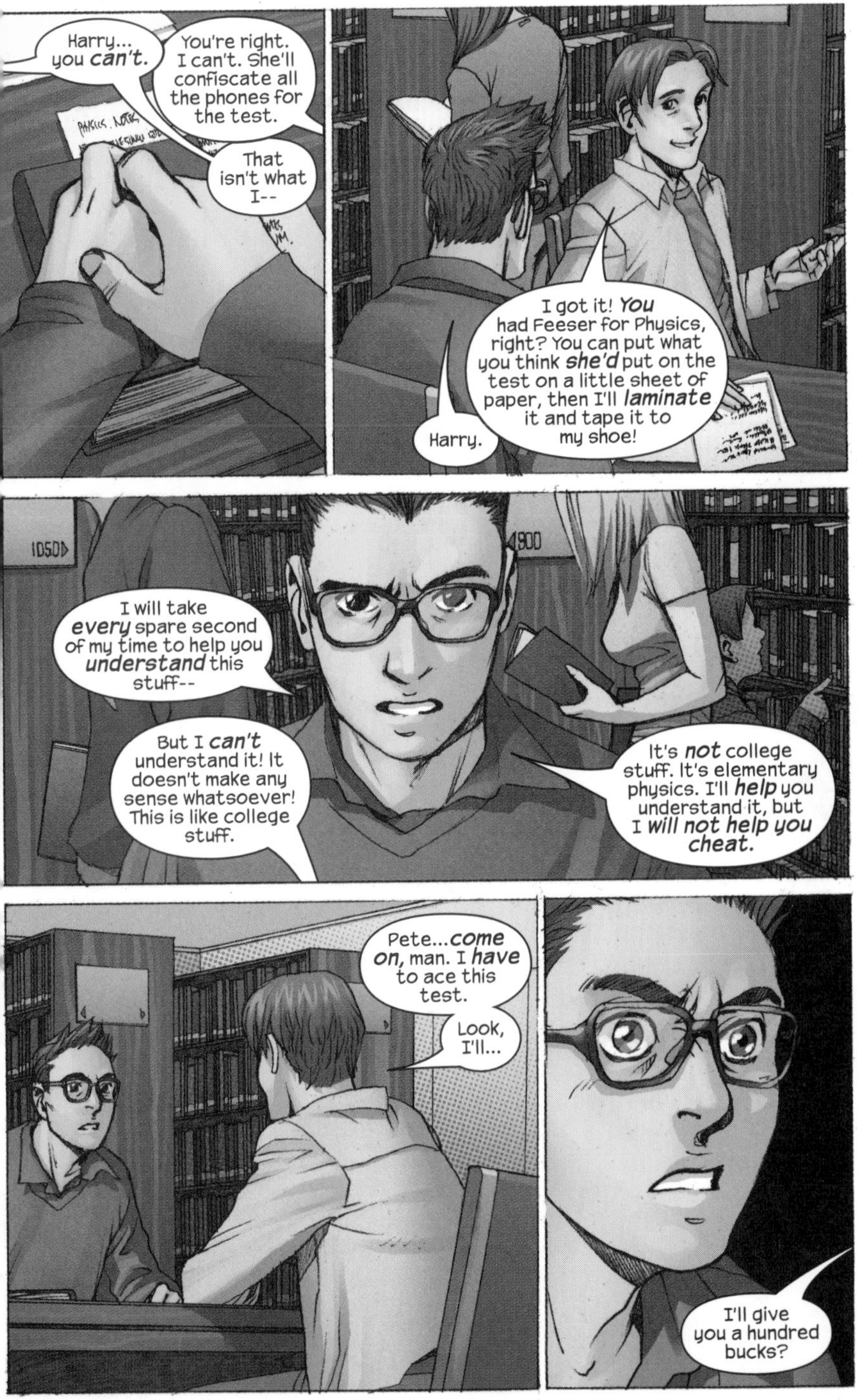
Harry... you can't.
You're right. I can't. She'll confiscate all the phones for the test.
That isn't what I--
I got it! You had Feeser for Physics, right? You can put what you think she'd put on the test on a little sheet of paper, then I'll laminate it and tape it to my shoe!
Harry.
1050
1800
I will take every spare second of my time to help you understand this stuff--
But I can't understand it! It doesn't make any sense whatsoever! This is like college stuff.
It's not college stuff. It's elementary physics. I'll help you understand it, but I will not help you cheat.
Pete...come on, man. I have to ace this test.
Look, I'll...
I'll give you a hundred bucks?

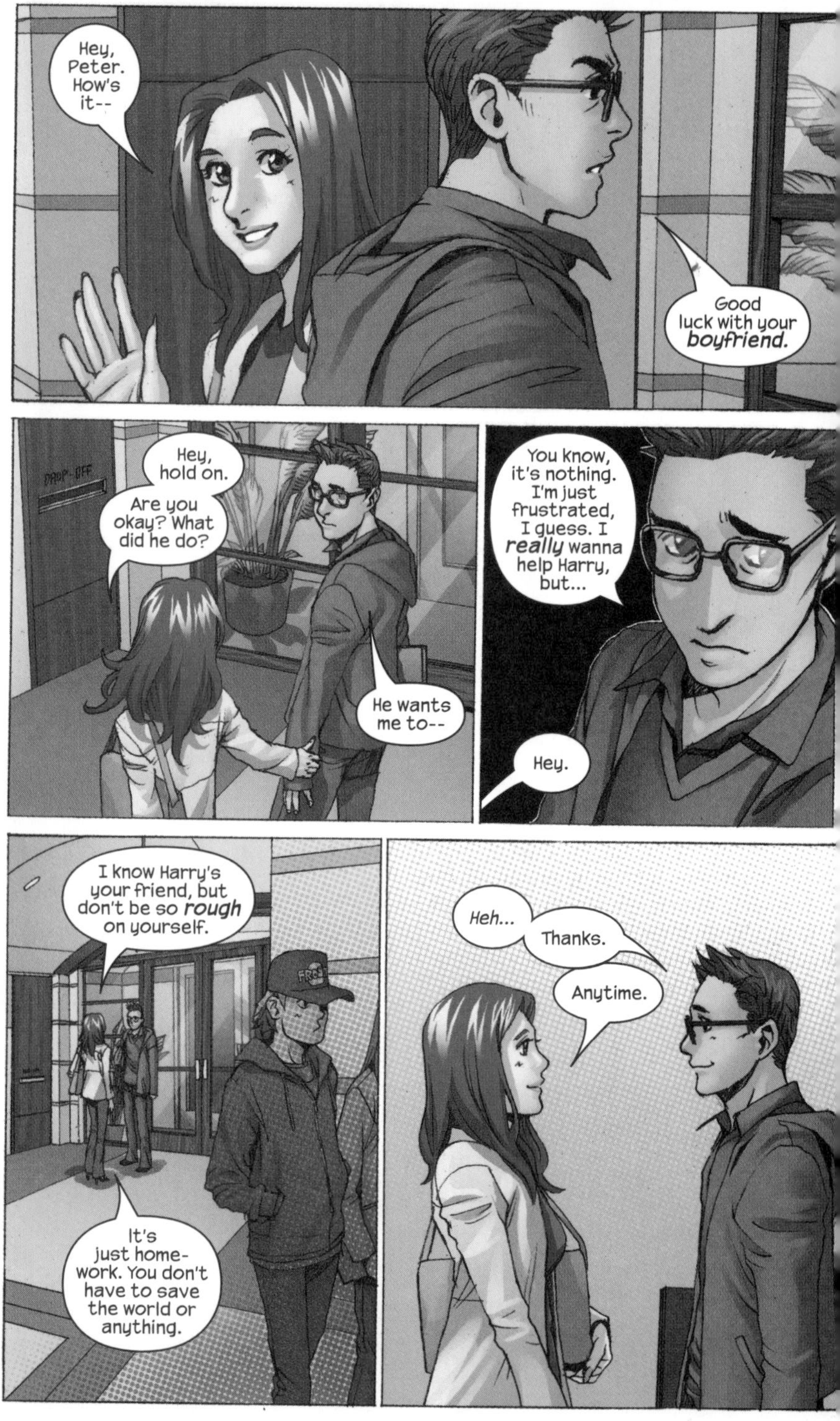
Hey, Peter. How's it--
Good luck with your *boyfriend.*
Hey, hold on.
Are you okay? What did he do?
He wants me to--
You know, it's nothing. I'm just frustrated, I guess. I *really* wanna help Harry, but...
Hey.
I know Harry's your friend, but don't be so *rough* on yourself.
It's just home-work. You don't have to save the world or anything.
Heh...
Thanks.
Anytime.

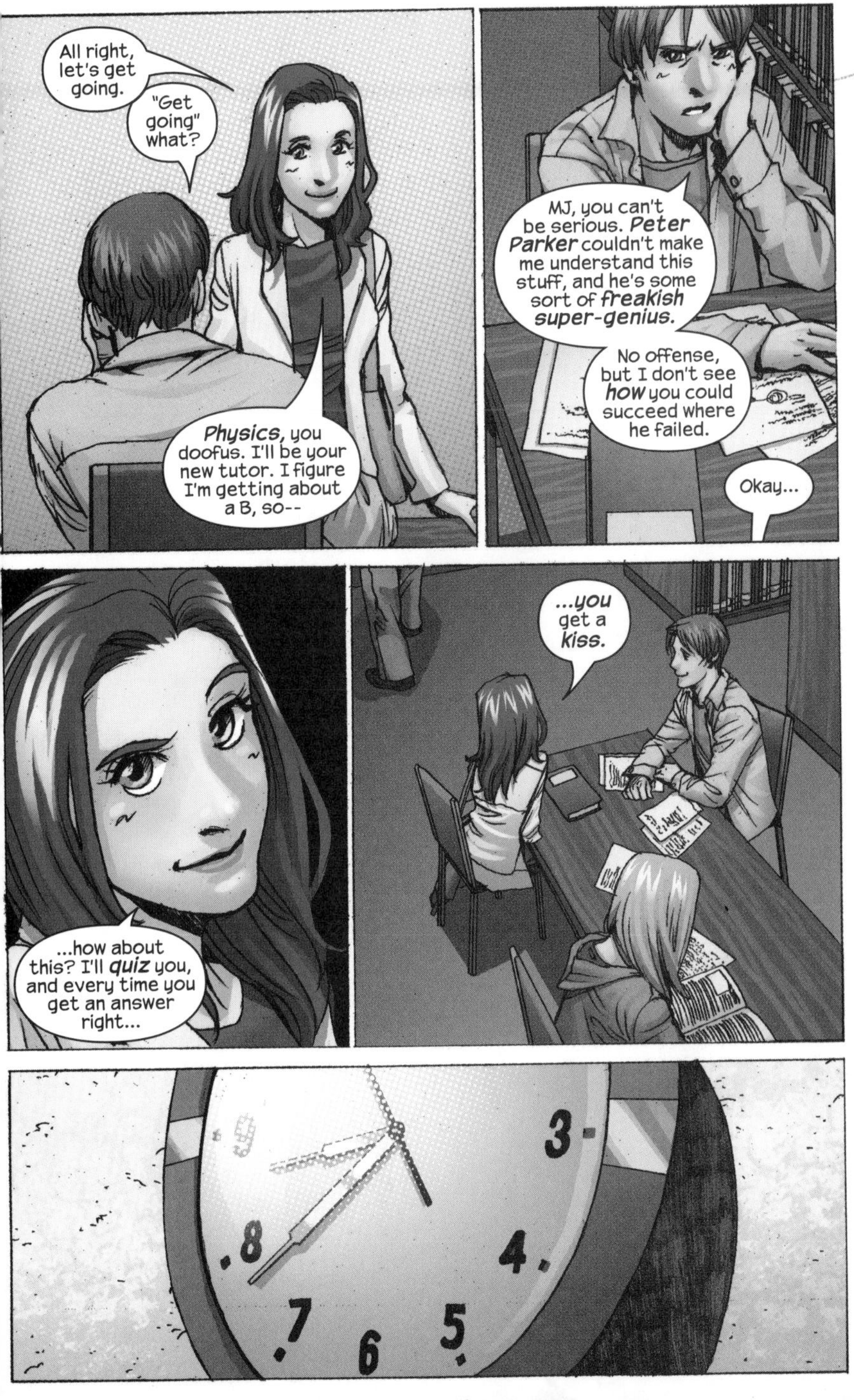
All right, let's get going.
"Get going" what?
Physics, you doofus. I'll be your new tutor. I figure I'm getting about a B, so--
MJ, you can't be serious. Peter Parker couldn't make me understand this stuff, and he's some sort of freakish super-genius.
No offense, but I don't see how you could succeed where he failed.
Okay...
...how about this? I'll quiz you, and every time you get an answer right...
...you get a kiss.
3
4
5
6
7
8

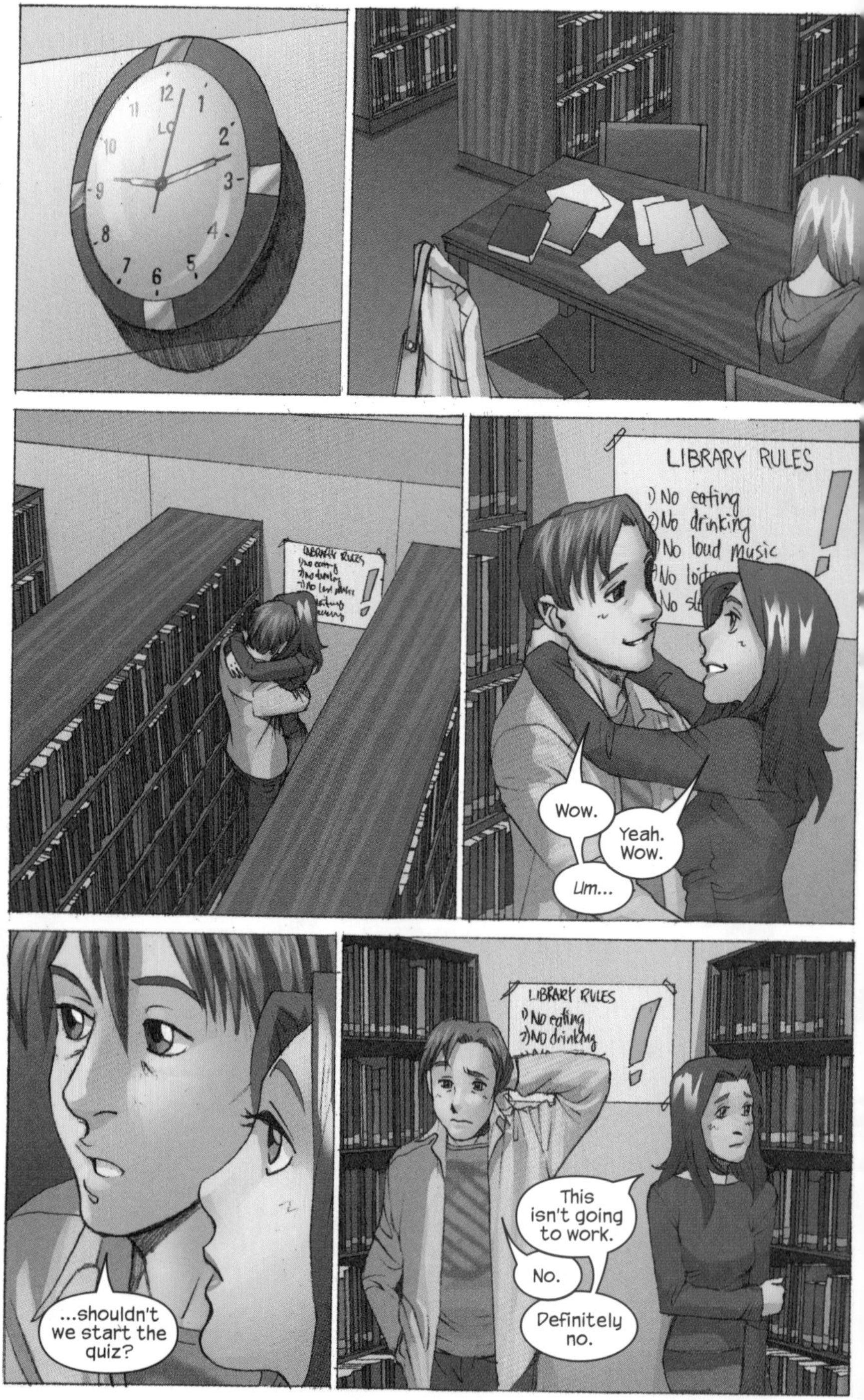
LIBRARY RULES
1) No eating
2) No drinking
3) No loud music
Wow.
Yeah. Wow.
Um...
...shouldn't we start the quiz?
LIBRARY RULES
1) No eating
2) No drinking
This isn't going to work.
No.
Definitely no.

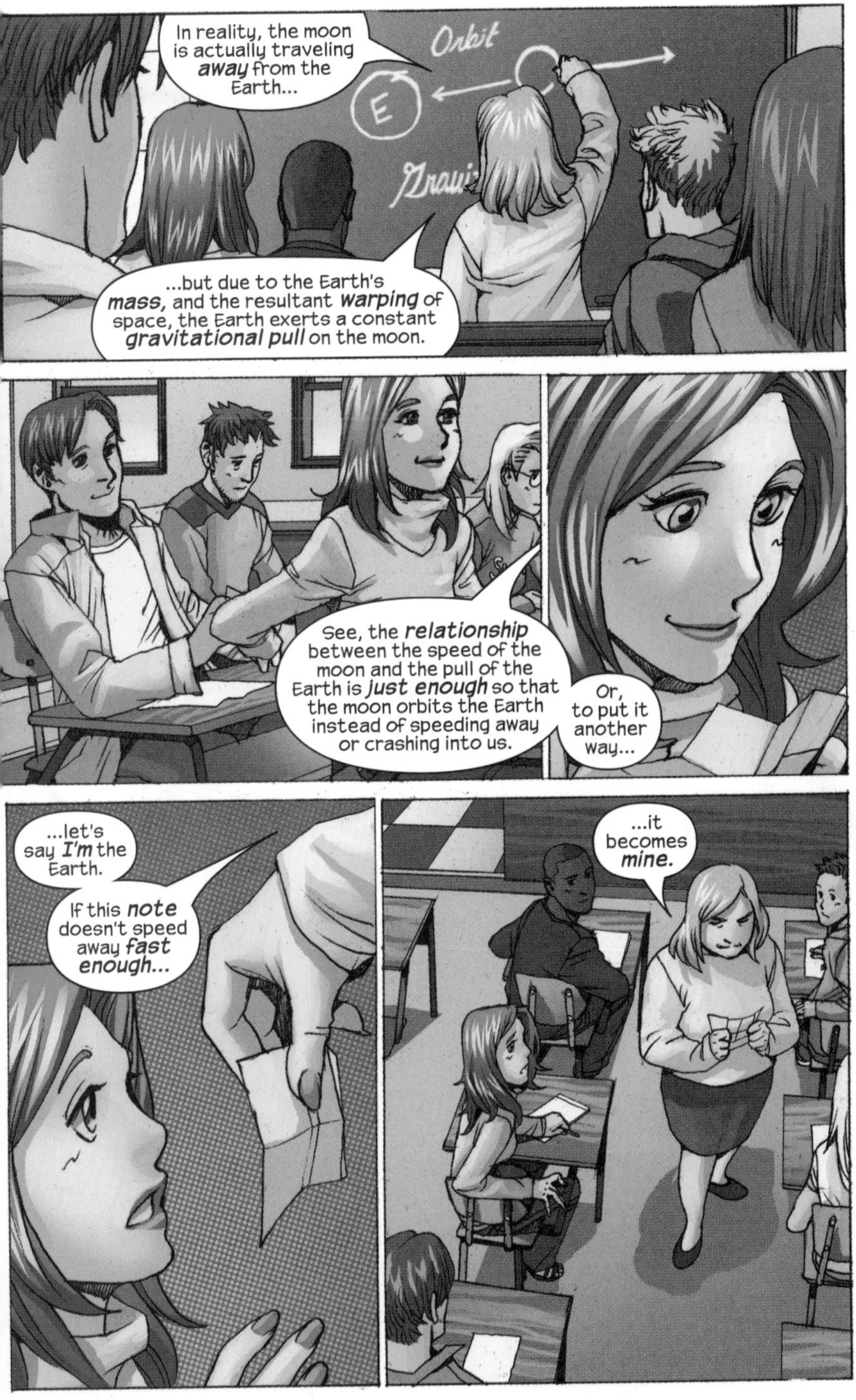
Orbit
In reality, the moon is actually traveling away from the Earth...
E
...but due to the Earth's mass, and the resultant warping of space, the Earth exerts a constant gravitational pull on the moon.
See, the relationship between the speed of the moon and the pull of the Earth is just enough so that the moon orbits the Earth instead of speeding away or crashing into us.
Or, to put it another way...
...let's say I'm the Earth.
If this note doesn't speed away fast enough...
...it becomes mine.

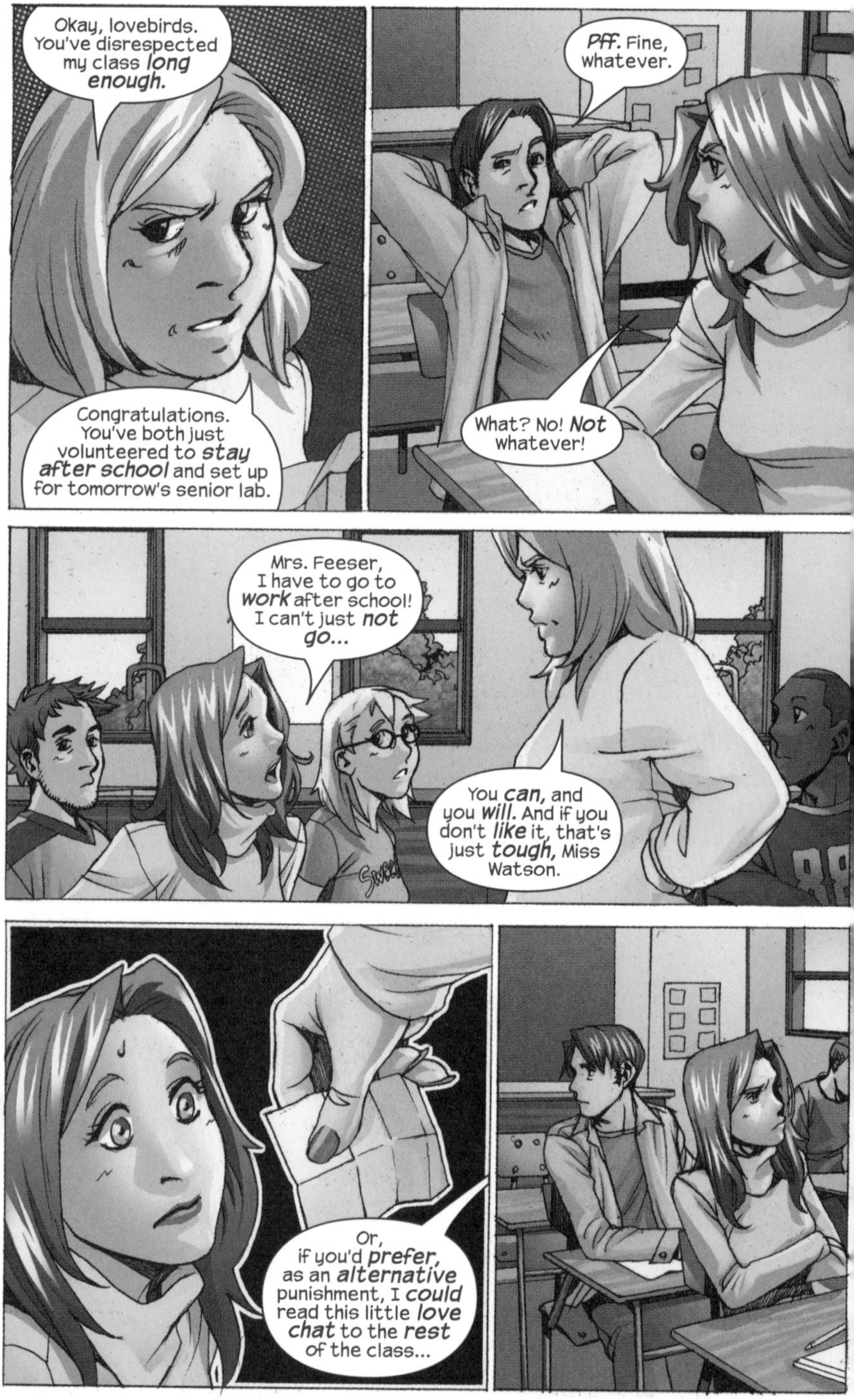
Okay, lovebirds. You've disrespected my class long enough.
Congratulations. You've both just volunteered to stay after school and set up for tomorrow's senior lab.
Pff. Fine, whatever.
What? No! Not whatever!
Mrs. Feeser, I have to go to work after school! I can't just not go...
You can, and you will. And if you don't like it, that's just tough, Miss Watson.
Or, if you'd prefer, as an alternative punishment, I could read this little love chat to the rest of the class...

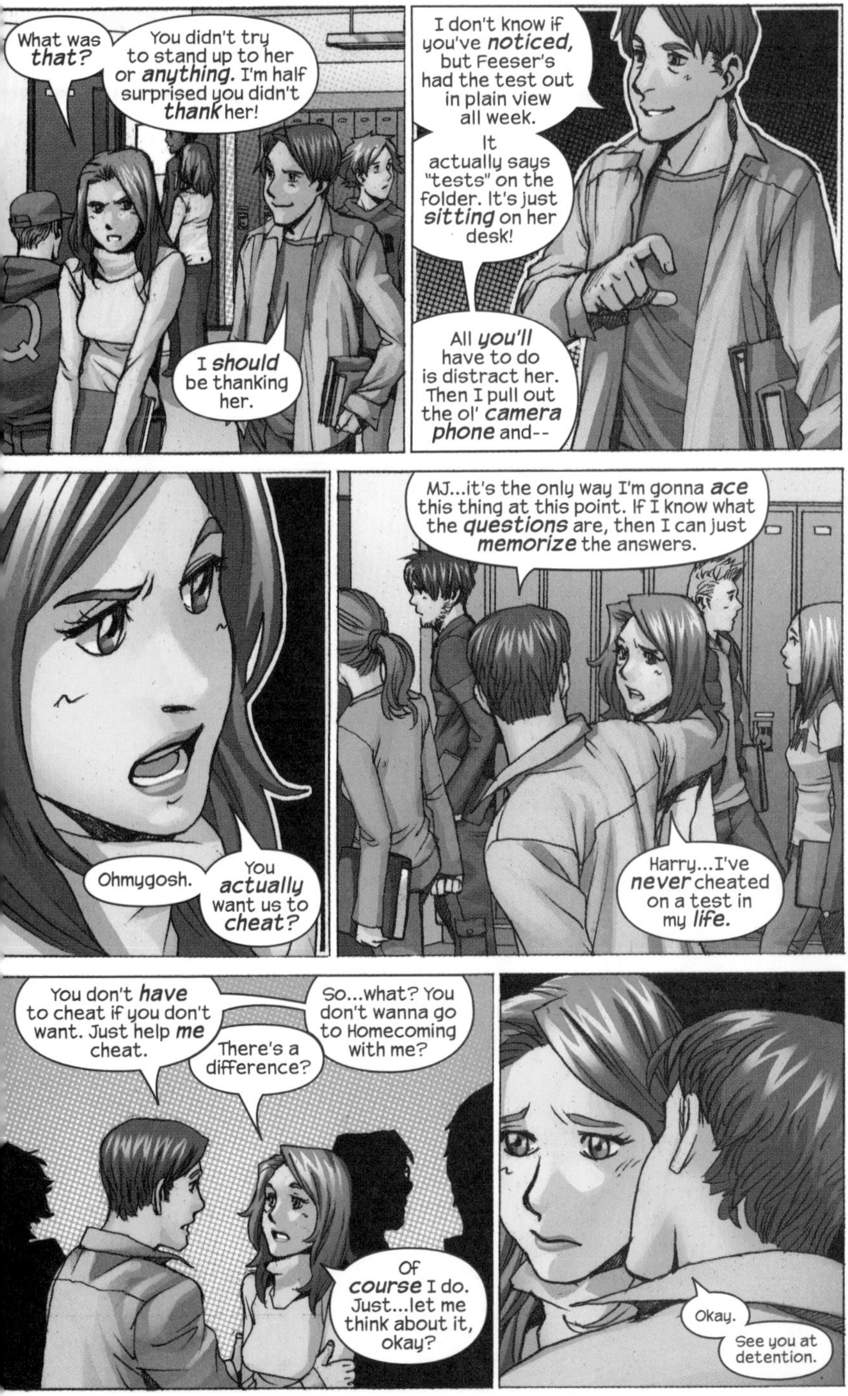
What was *that?*
You didn't try to stand up to her or *anything.* I'm half surprised you didn't *thank* her!
I *should* be thanking her.
I don't know if you've *noticed,* but Feeser's had the test out in plain view all week.
It actually says "tests" on the folder. It's just *sitting* on her desk!
All *you'll* have to do is distract her. Then I pull out the ol' *camera phone* and--
Ohmygosh.
You *actually* want us to *cheat?*
MJ...it's the only way I'm gonna *ace* this thing at this point. If I know what the *questions* are, then I can just *memorize* the answers.
Harry...I've *never* cheated on a test in my *life.*
You don't *have* to cheat if you don't want. Just help *me* cheat.
There's a difference?
So...what? You don't wanna go to Homecoming with me?
Of *course* I do. Just...let me think about it, okay?
Okay.
See you at detention.

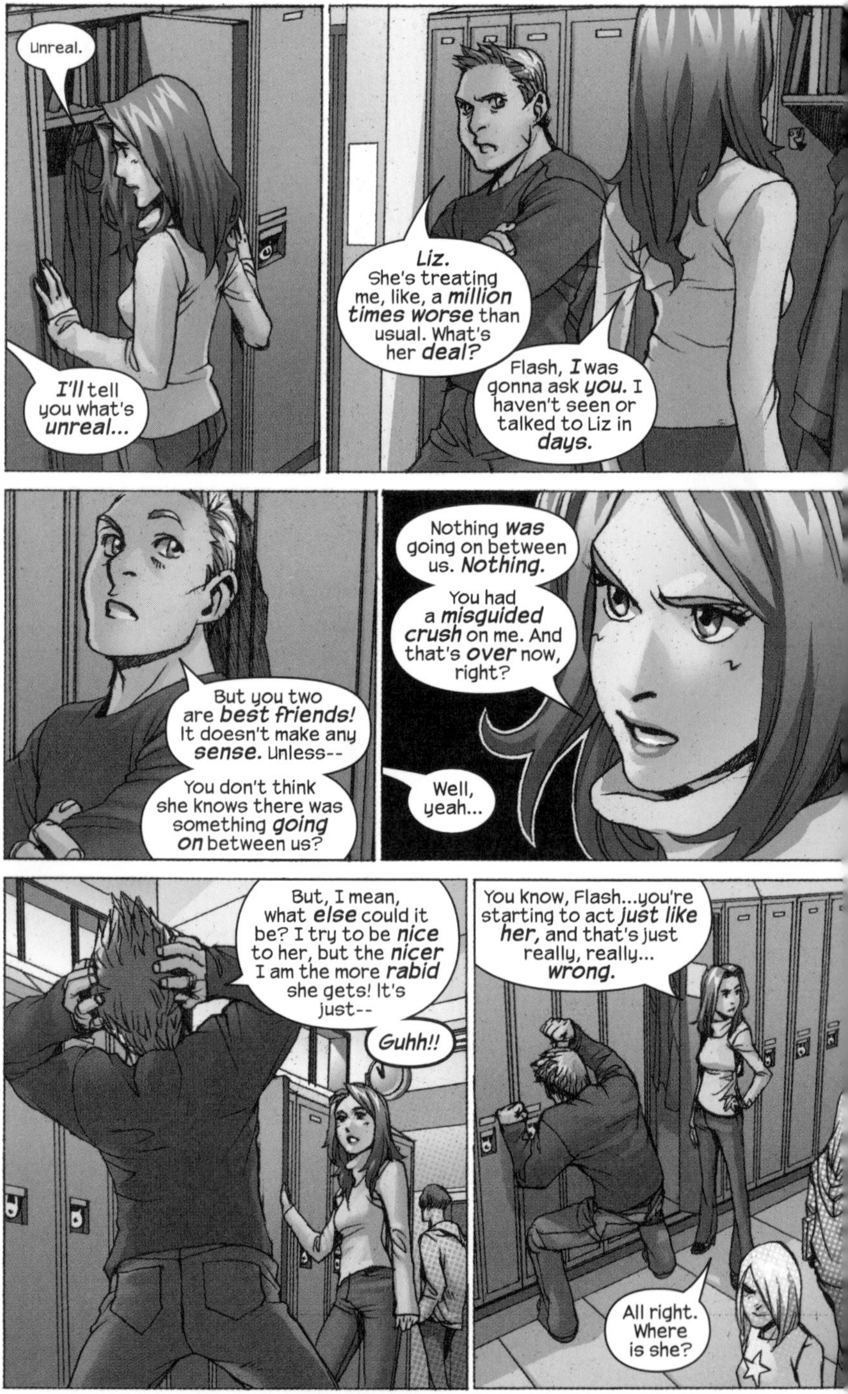
Unreal.
I'll tell you what's unreal...
Liz. She's treating me, like, a million times worse than usual. What's her deal?
Flash, I was gonna ask you. I haven't seen or talked to Liz in days.
But you two are best friends! It doesn't make any sense. Unless--
You don't think she knows there was something going on between us?
Nothing was going on between us. Nothing.
You had a misguided crush on me. And that's over now, right?
Well, yeah...
But, I mean, what else could it be? I try to be nice to her, but the nicer I am the more rabid she gets! It's just--
Guhh!!
You know, Flash...you're starting to act just like her, and that's just really, really... wrong.
All right. Where is she?

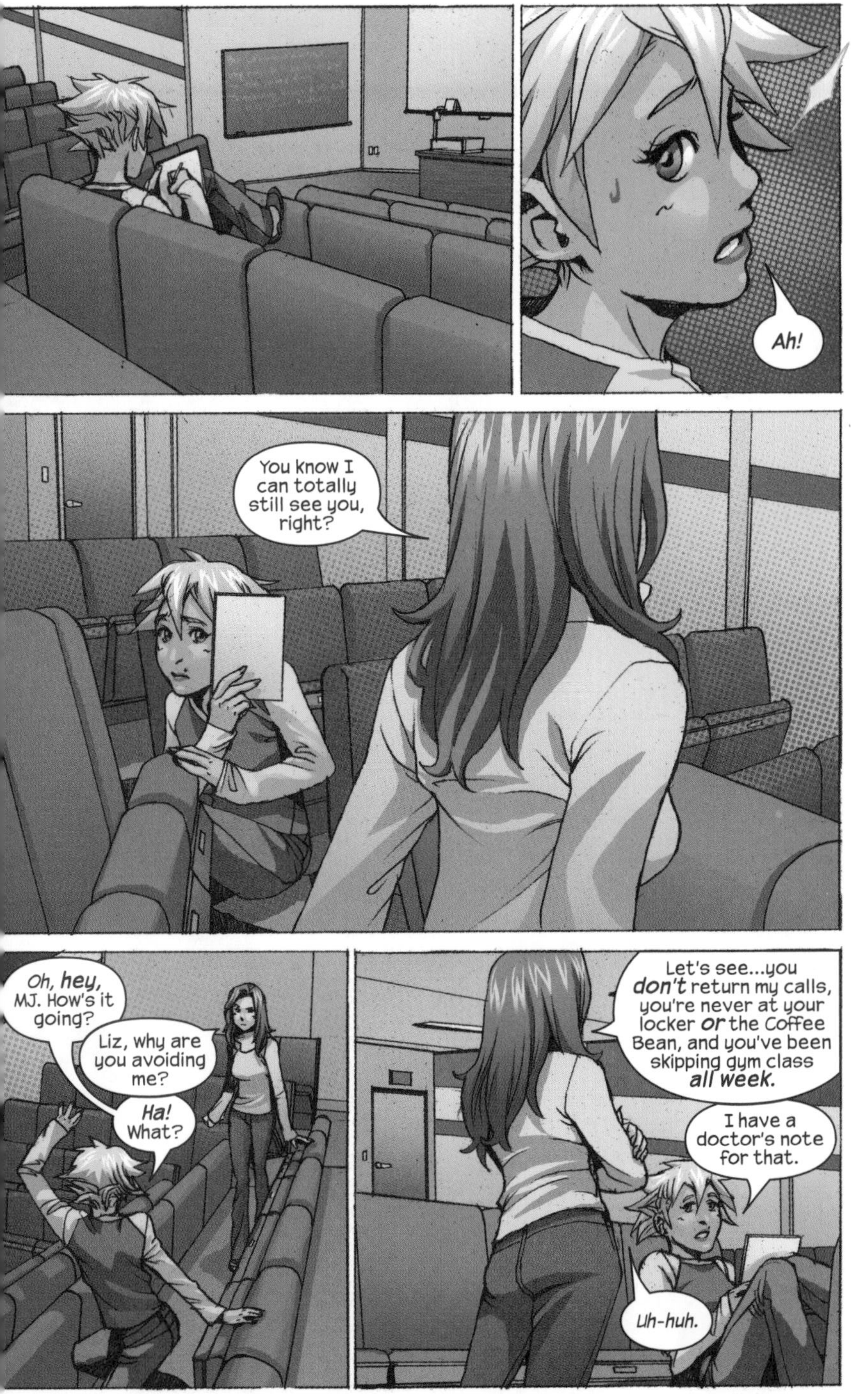
Ah!
You know I can totally still see you, right?
Oh, hey, MJ. How's it going?
Liz, why are you avoiding me?
Ha! What?
Let's see...you don't return my calls, you're never at your locker or the Coffee Bean, and you've been skipping gym class all week.
I have a doctor's note for that.
Uh-huh.

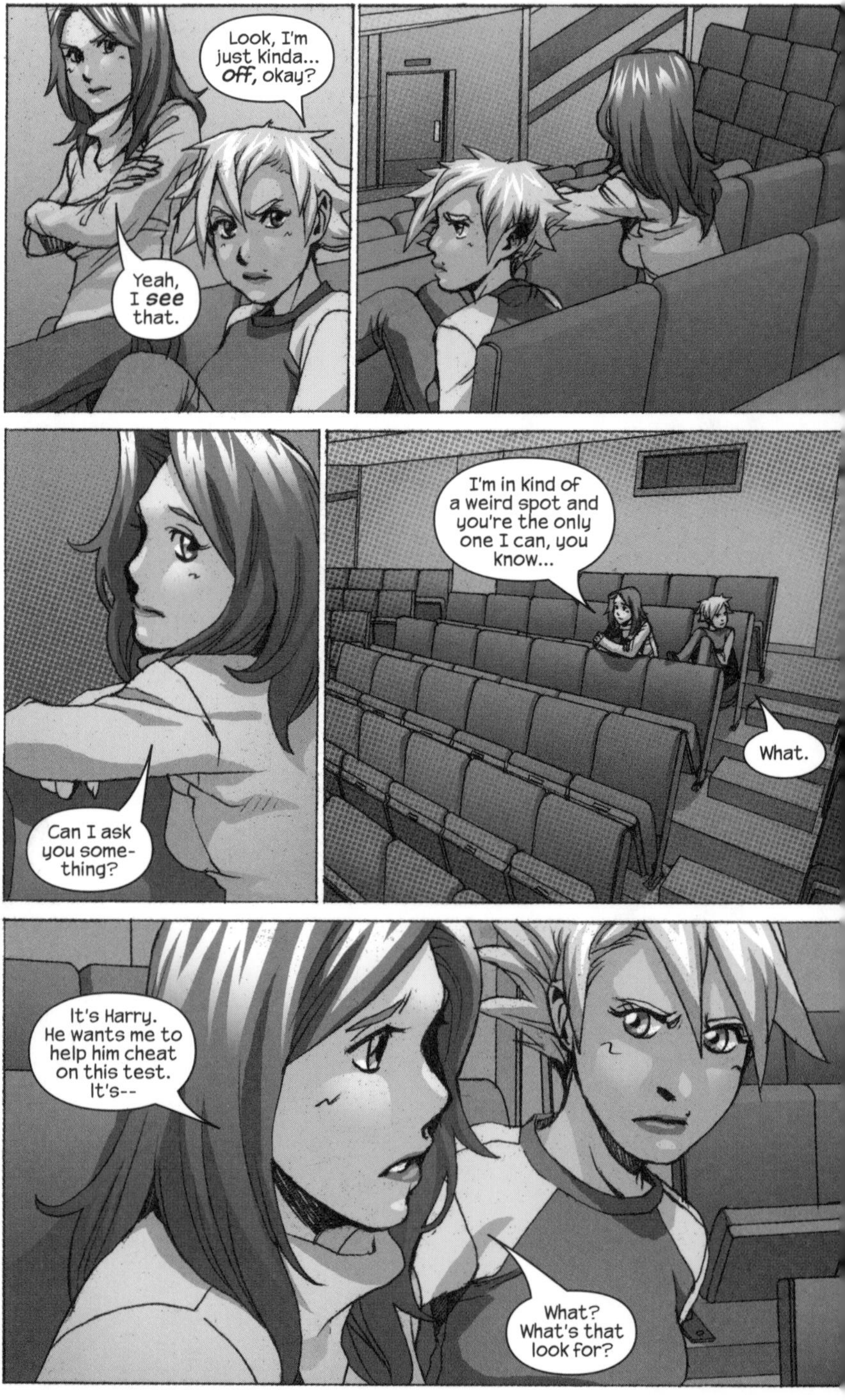
Look, I'm just kinda... *off*, okay?
Yeah, I *see* that.
Can I ask you some-thing?
What.
I'm in kind of a weird spot and you're the only one I can, you know...
It's Harry. He wants me to help him cheat on this test. It's--
What? What's that look for?

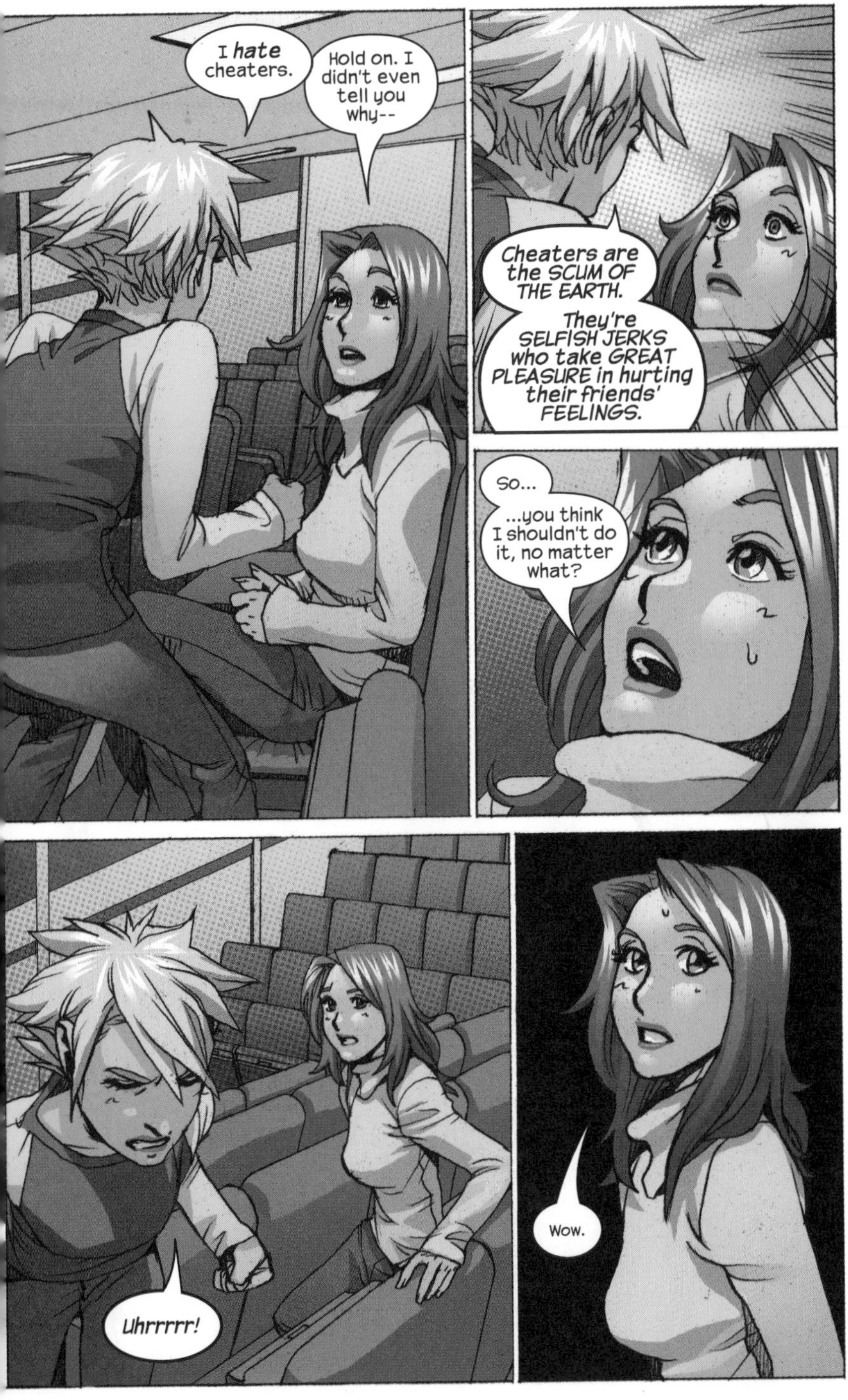
I hate cheaters.
Hold on. I didn't even tell you why--
Cheaters are the SCUM OF THE EARTH.
They're SELFISH JERKS who take GREAT PLEASURE in hurting their friends' FEELINGS.
So...
...you think I shouldn't do it, no matter what?
Uhrrrrr!
Wow.

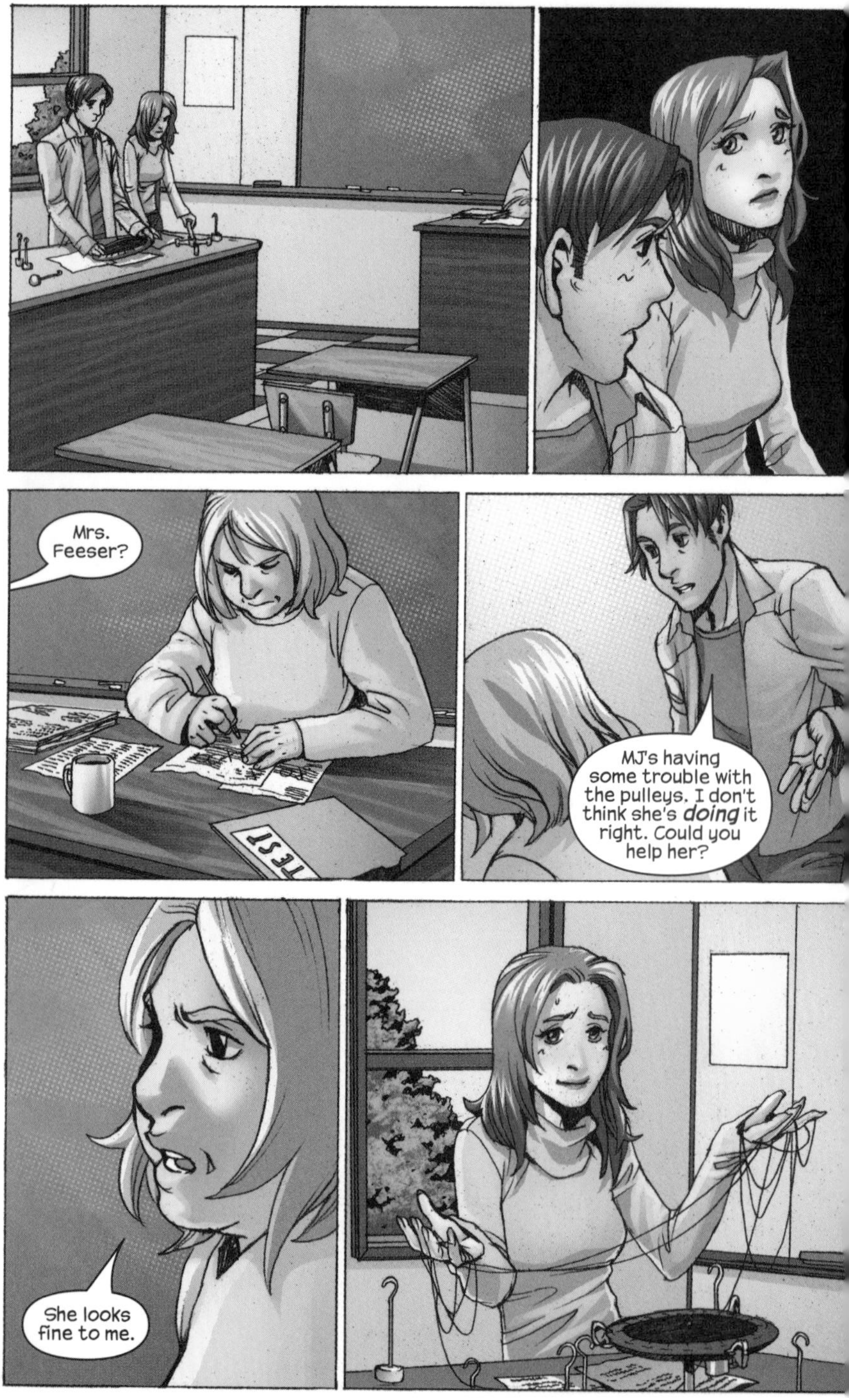
Mrs. Feeser?
MJ's having some trouble with the pulleys. I don't think she's *doing* it right. Could you help her?
TEST
She looks fine to me.

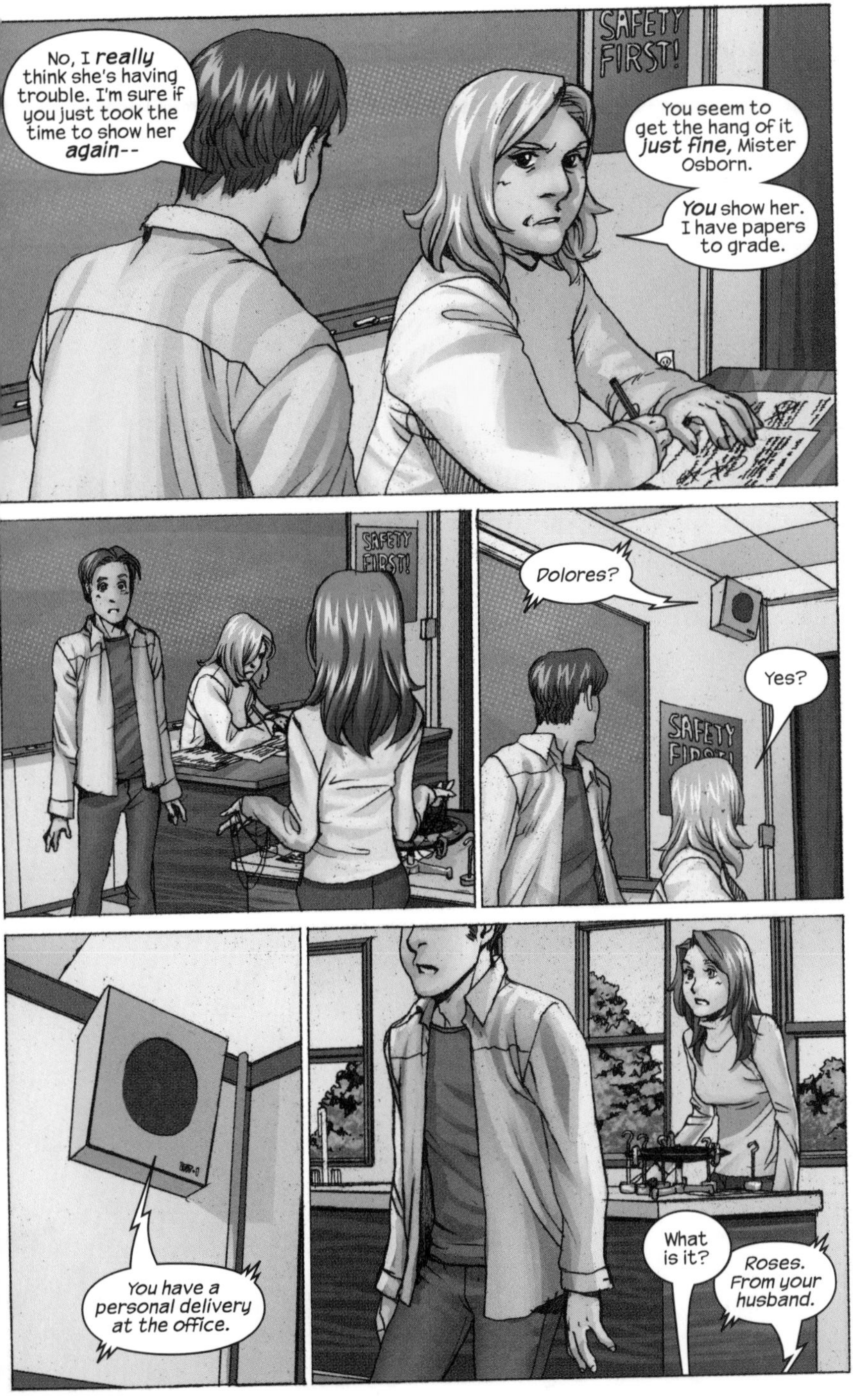
No, I really think she's having trouble. I'm sure if you just took the time to show her again--
You seem to get the hang of it just fine, Mister Osborn.
You show her. I have papers to grade.
SAFETY FIRST!
Dolores?
Yes?
You have a personal delivery at the office.
What is it?
Roses. From your husband.

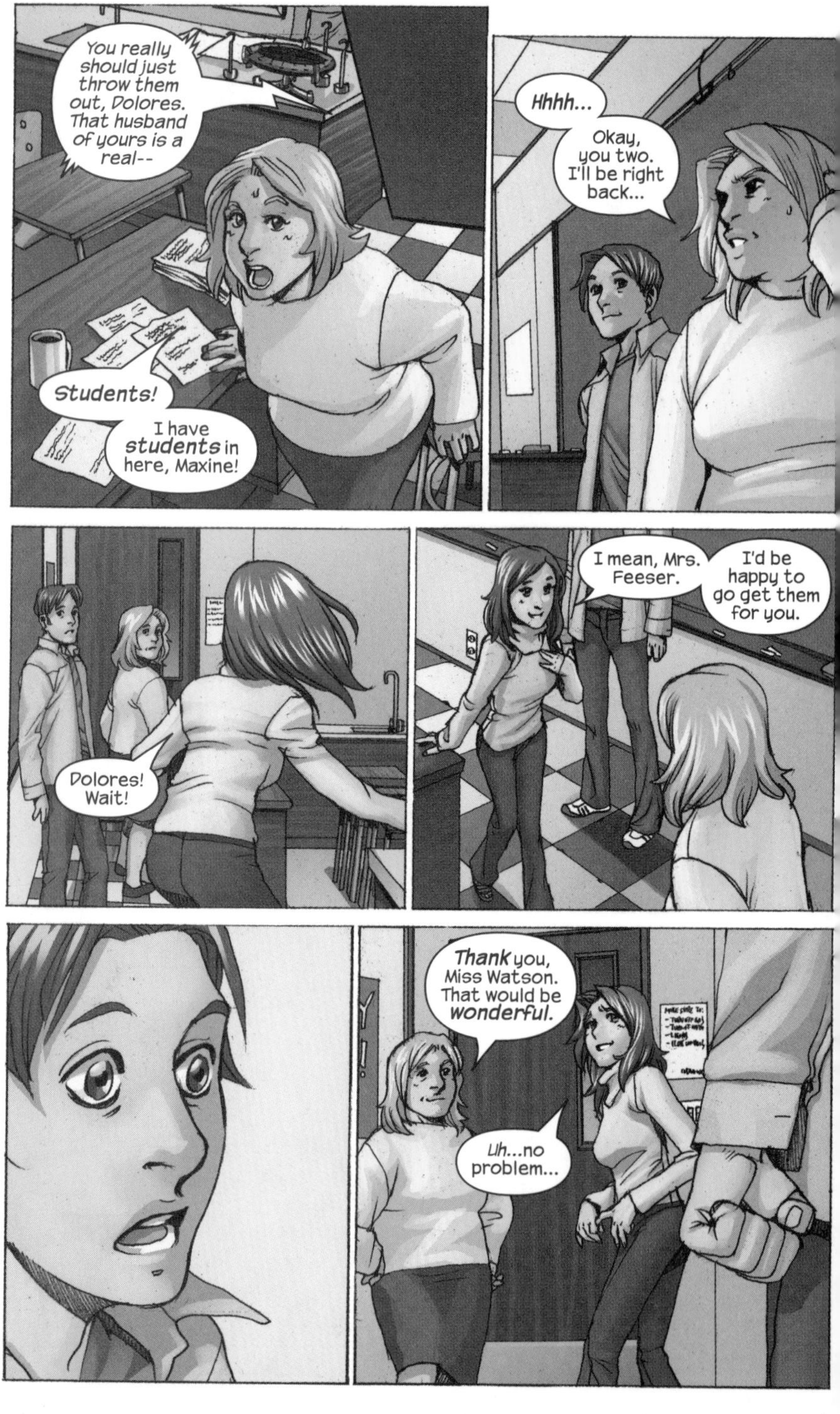

You really should just throw them out, Dolores. That husband of yours is a real--
Students!
I have *students* in here, Maxine!
Hhhh...
Okay, you two. I'll be right back...
Dolores! Wait!
I mean, Mrs. Feeser.
I'd be happy to go get them for you.
Thank you, Miss Watson. That would be *wonderful*.
Uh...no problem...

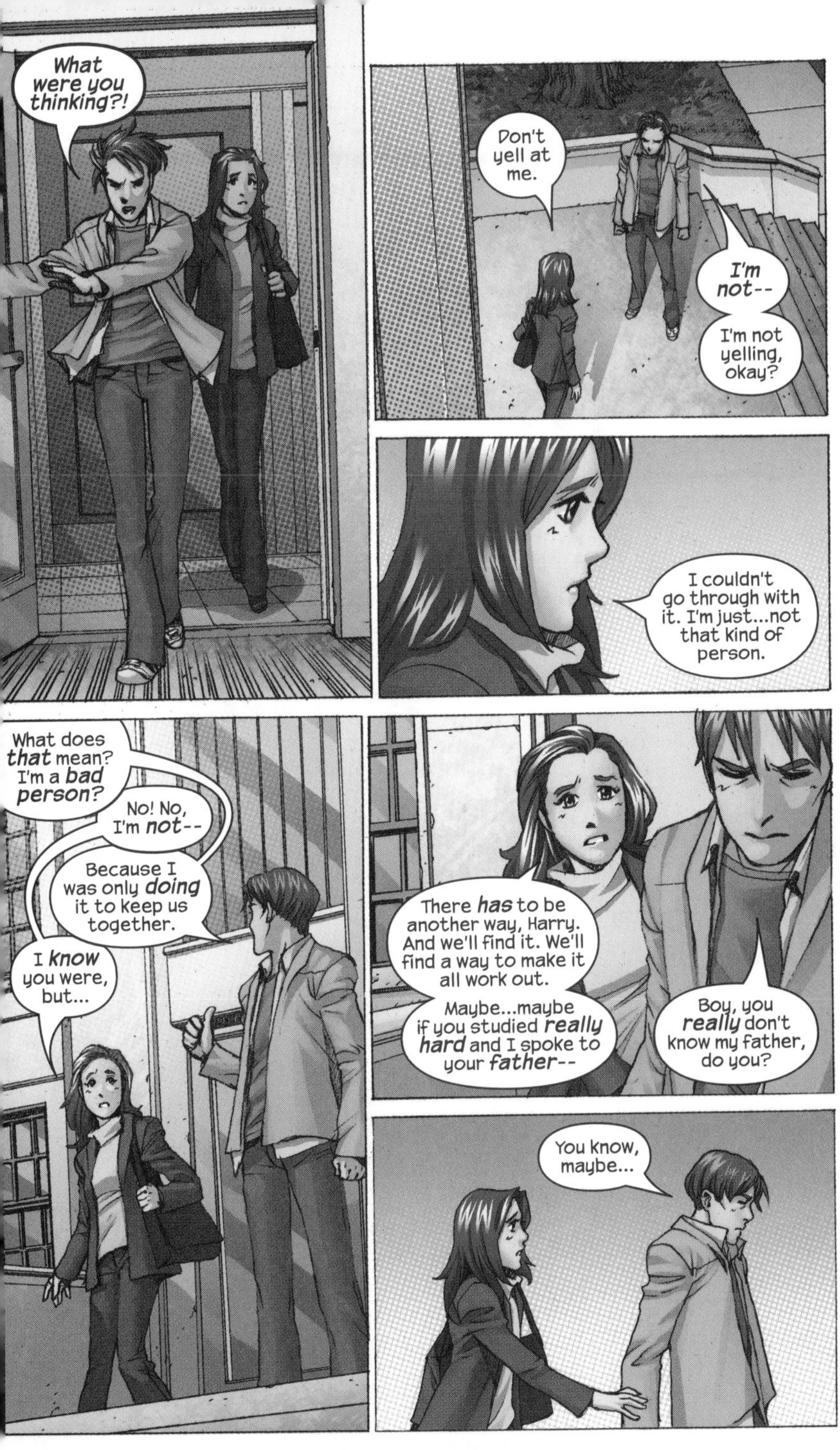
What were you thinking?!
Don't yell at me.
I'm not--
I'm not yelling, okay?
I couldn't go through with it. I'm just...not that kind of person.
What does that mean? I'm a bad person?
No! No, I'm not--
Because I was only doing it to keep us together.
I know you were, but...
There has to be another way, Harry. And we'll find it. We'll find a way to make it all work out.
Maybe...maybe if you studied really hard and I spoke to your father--
Boy, you really don't know my father, do you?
You know, maybe...

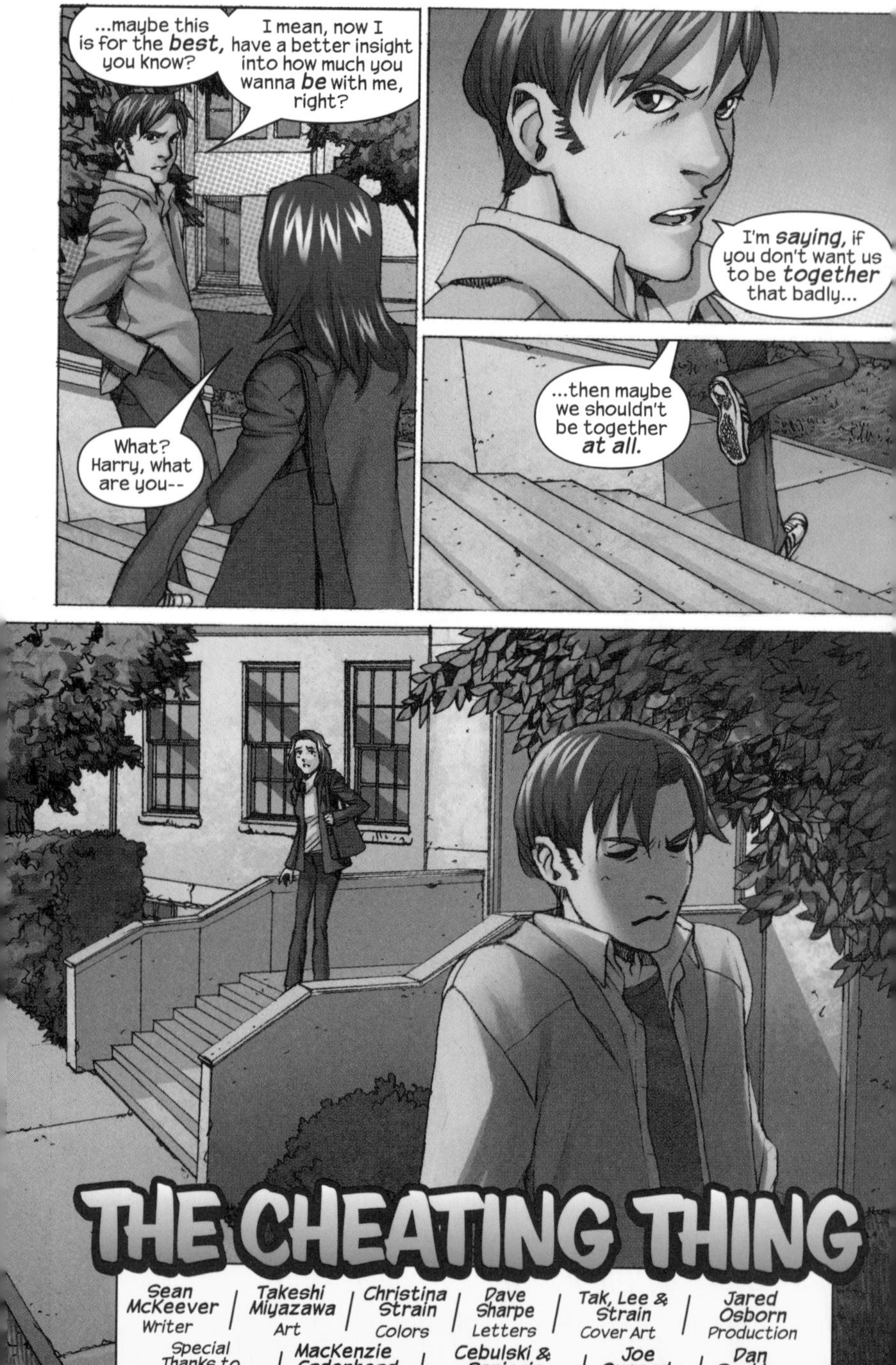

...maybe this is for the best, you know?
I mean, now I have a better insight into how much you wanna be with me, right?
What? Harry, what are you--
I'm saying, if you don't want us to be together that badly...
...then maybe we shouldn't be together at all.
THE CHEATING THING
Sean McKeever Writer
Takeshi Miyazawa Art
Christina Strain Colors
Dave Sharpe Letters
Tak, Lee & Strain Cover Art
Jared Osborn Production
Special Thanks to David Gabriel
MacKenzie Cadenhead Editor
Cebulski & Paniccia Consulting Editors
Joe Quesada Chief
Dan Buckley Publisher

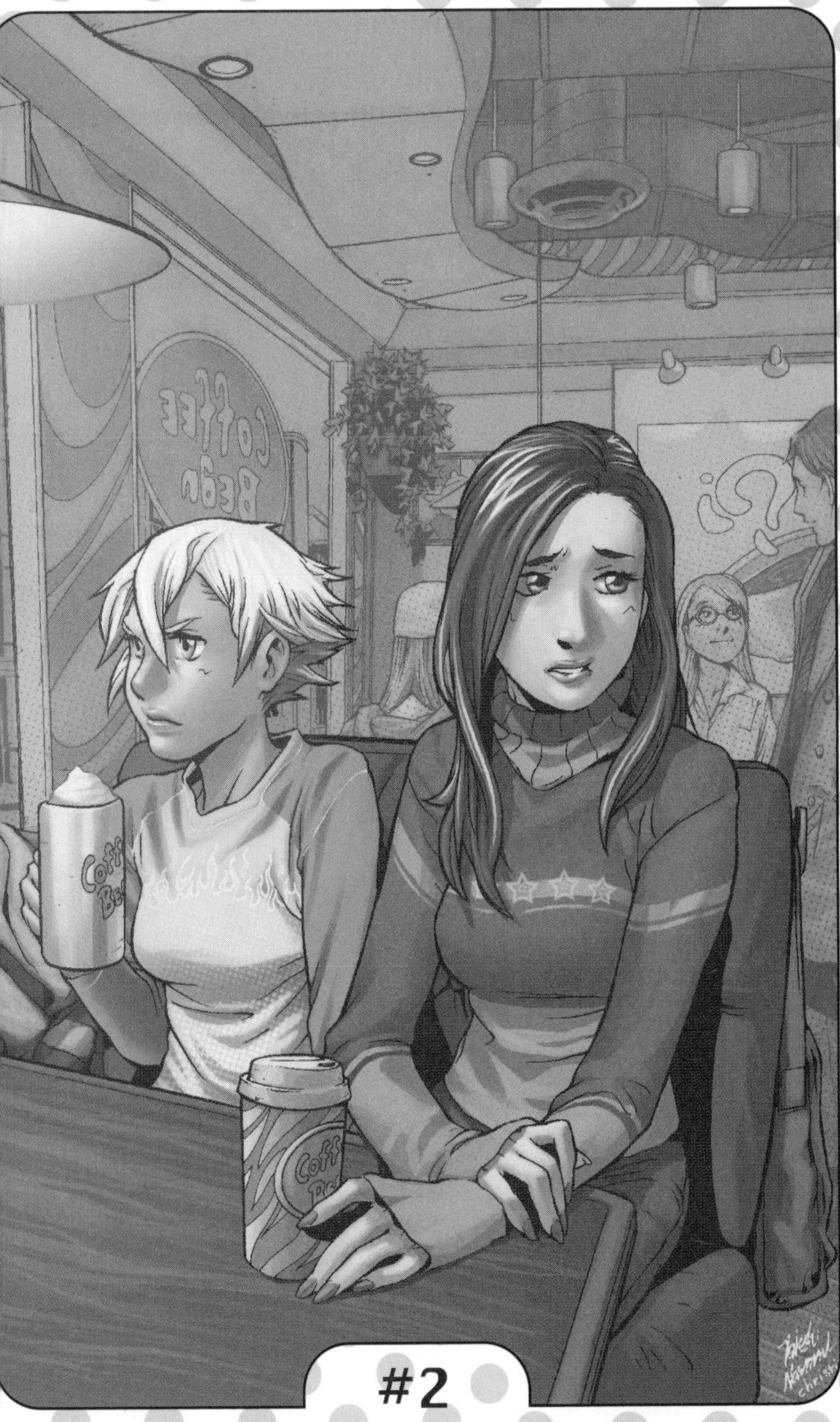

#2

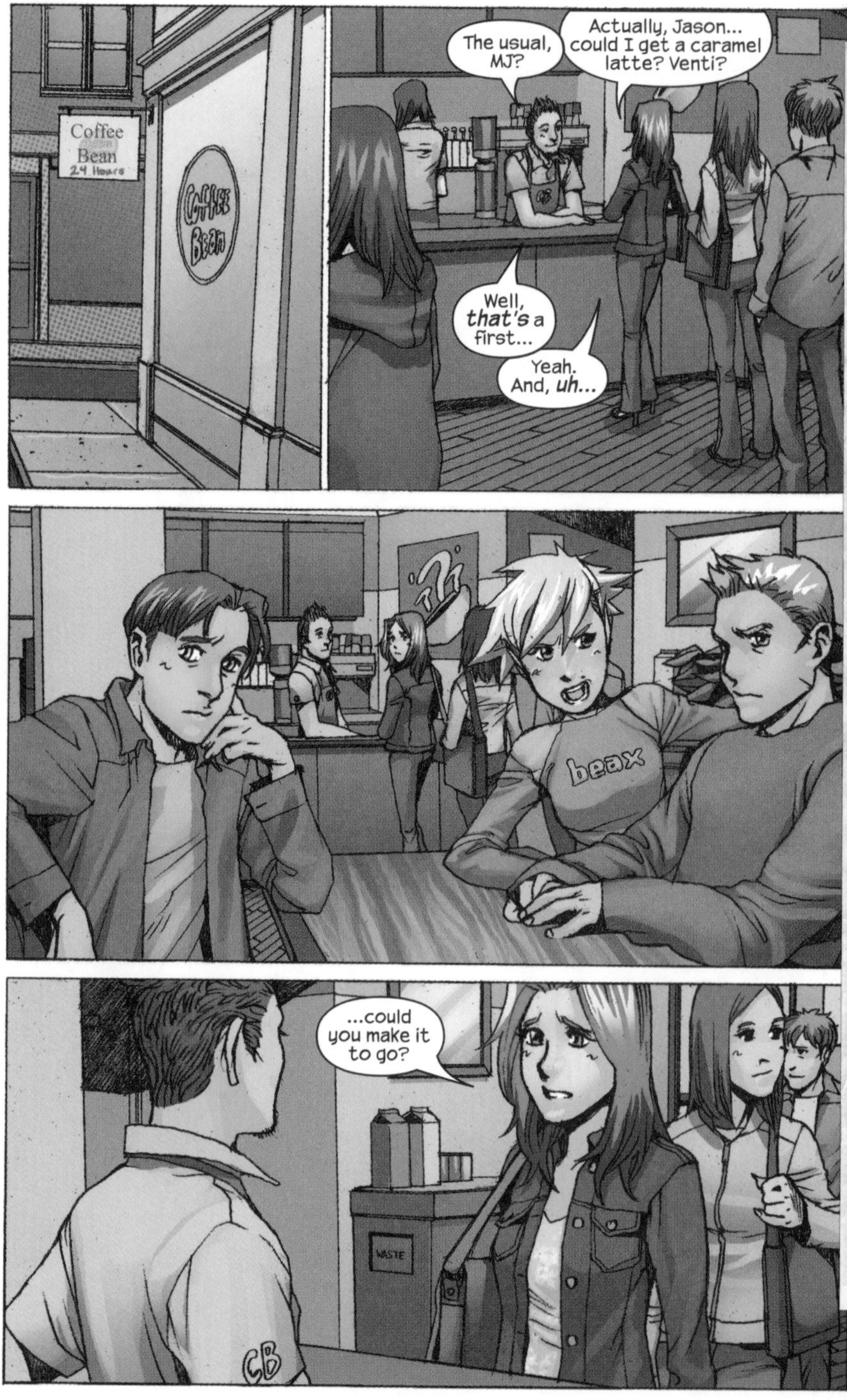
Coffee Bean
24 Hours
Coffee Bean
The usual, MJ?
Actually, Jason... could I get a caramel latte? Venti?
Well, that's a first...
Yeah. And, uh...
beax
...could you make it to go?
WASTE
CB

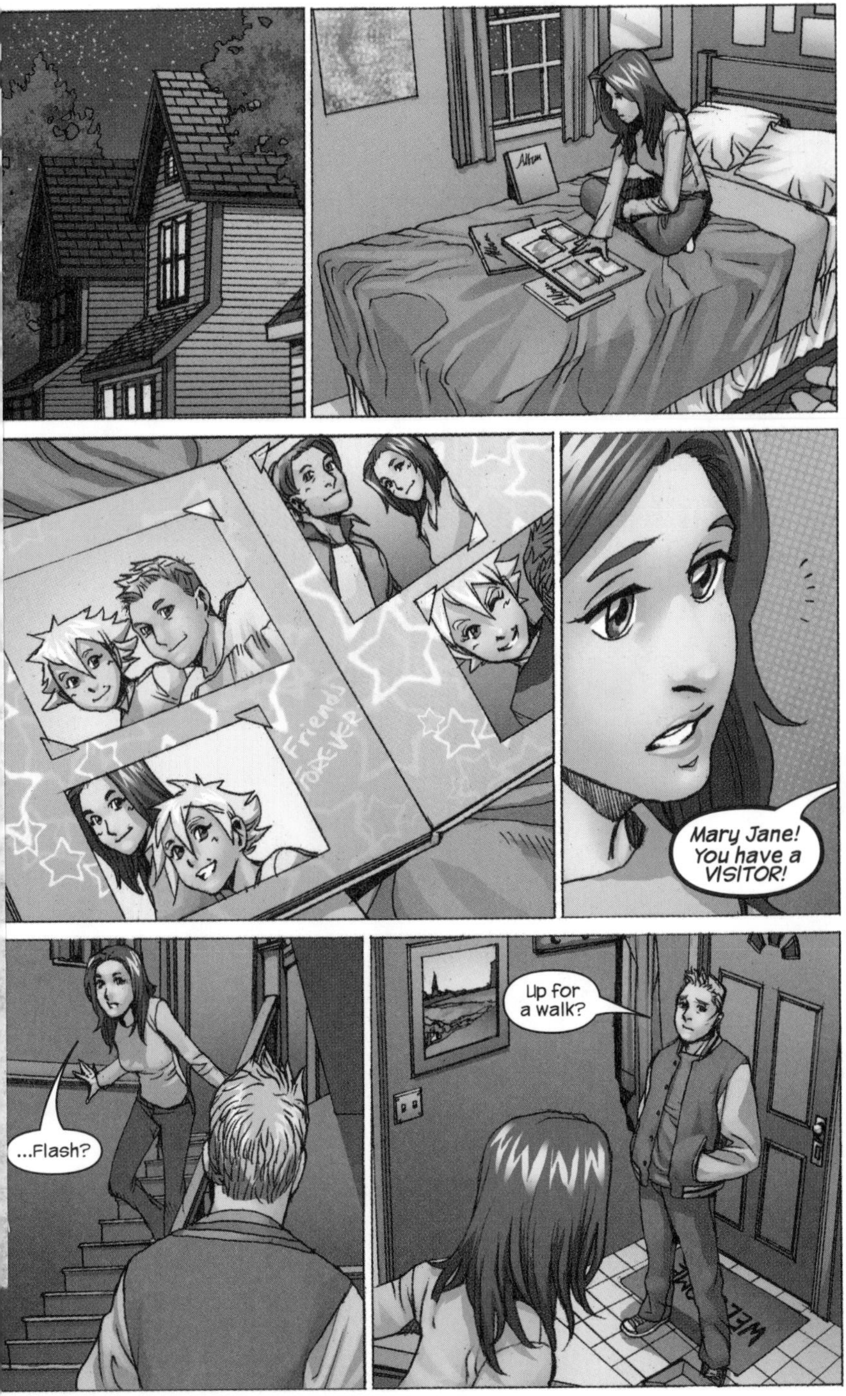
Album
Friends FOREVER
Mary Jane! You have a VISITOR!
...Flash?
Up for a walk?

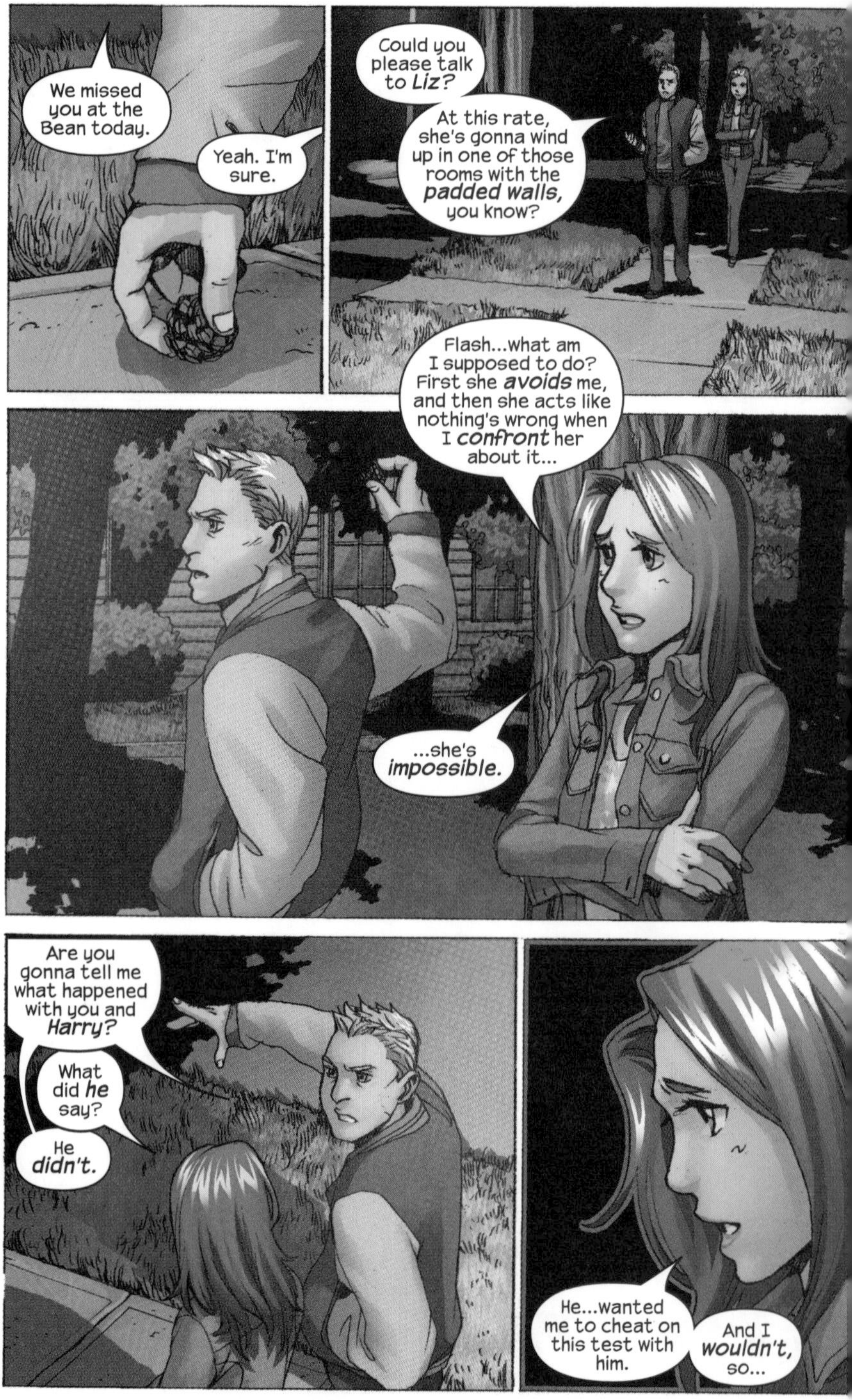
We missed you at the Bean today.
Yeah. I'm sure.
Could you please talk to Liz?
At this rate, she's gonna wind up in one of those rooms with the padded walls, you know?
Flash...what am I supposed to do? First she avoids me, and then she acts like nothing's wrong when I confront her about it...
...she's impossible.
Are you gonna tell me what happened with you and Harry?
What did he say?
He didn't.
He...wanted me to cheat on this test with him.
And I wouldn't, so...

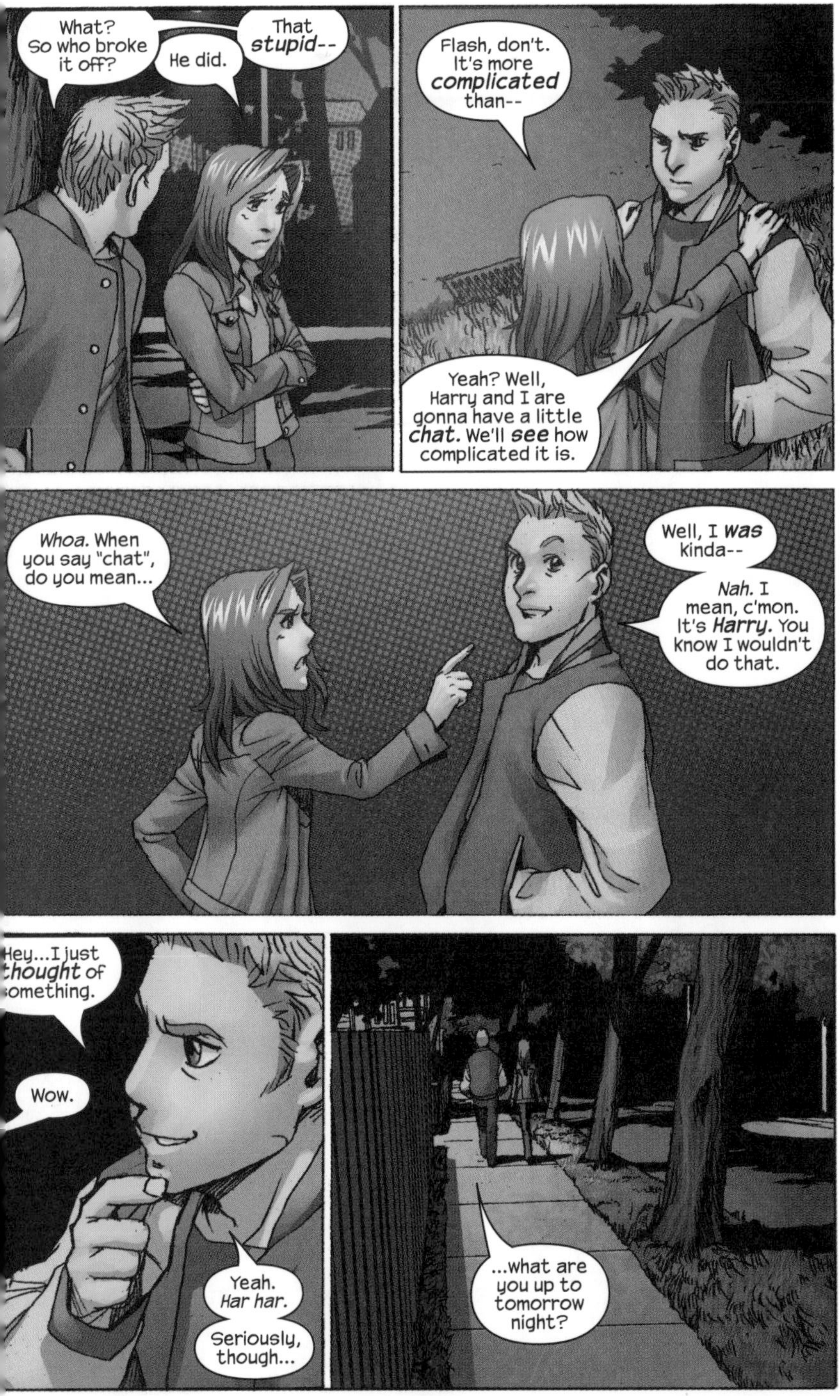
What? So who broke it off?
He did.
That stupid--
Flash, don't. It's more complicated than--
Yeah? Well, Harry and I are gonna have a little chat. We'll see how complicated it is.
Whoa. When you say "chat", do you mean...
Well, I was kinda--
Nah. I mean, c'mon. It's Harry. You know I wouldn't do that.
Hey...I just thought of something.
Wow.
Yeah. Har har.
Seriously, though...
...what are you up to tomorrow night?

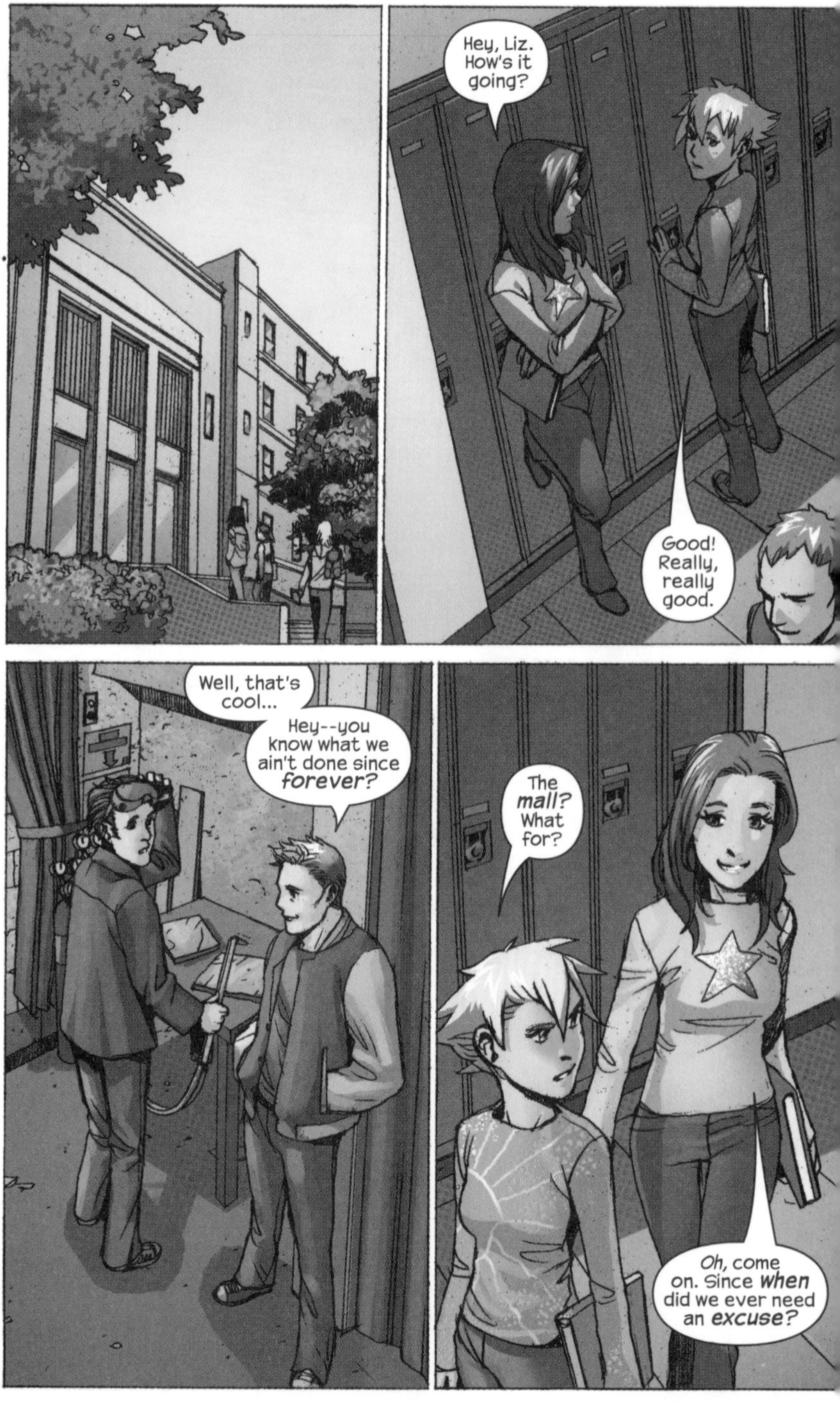
Hey, Liz. How's it going?
Good! Really, really good.
Well, that's cool...
Hey--you know what we ain't done since *forever?*
The *mall?* What for?
Oh, come on. Since ***when*** did we ever need an ***excuse?***

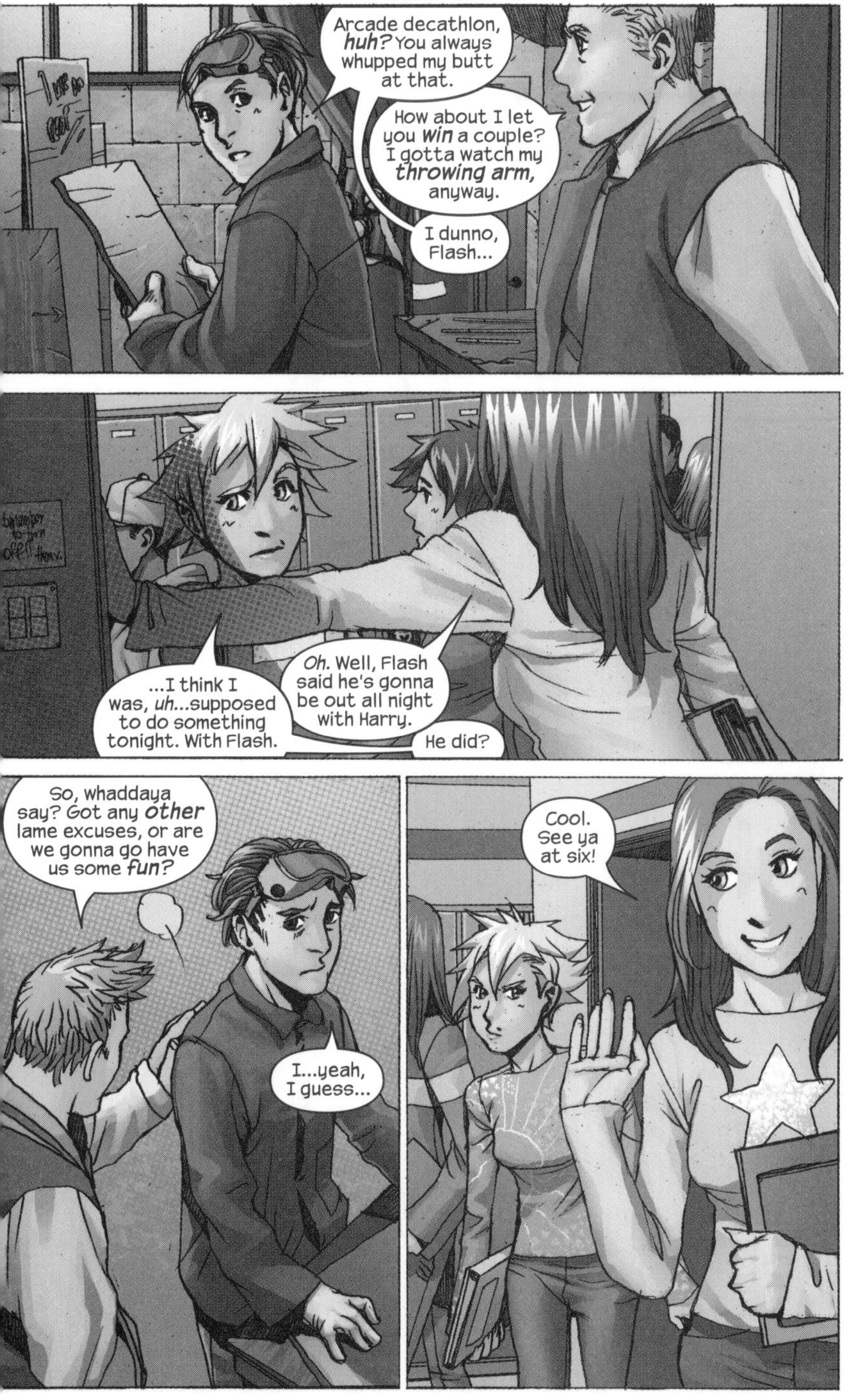
Arcade decathlon, *huh?* You always whupped my butt at that.
How about I let you *win* a couple? I gotta watch my *throwing arm,* anyway.
I dunno, Flash...
...I think I was, *uh*...supposed to do something tonight. With Flash.
Oh. Well, Flash said he's gonna be out all night with Harry.
He did?
So, whaddaya say? Got any *other* lame excuses, or are we gonna go have us some *fun?*
I...yeah, I guess...
Cool. See ya at six!

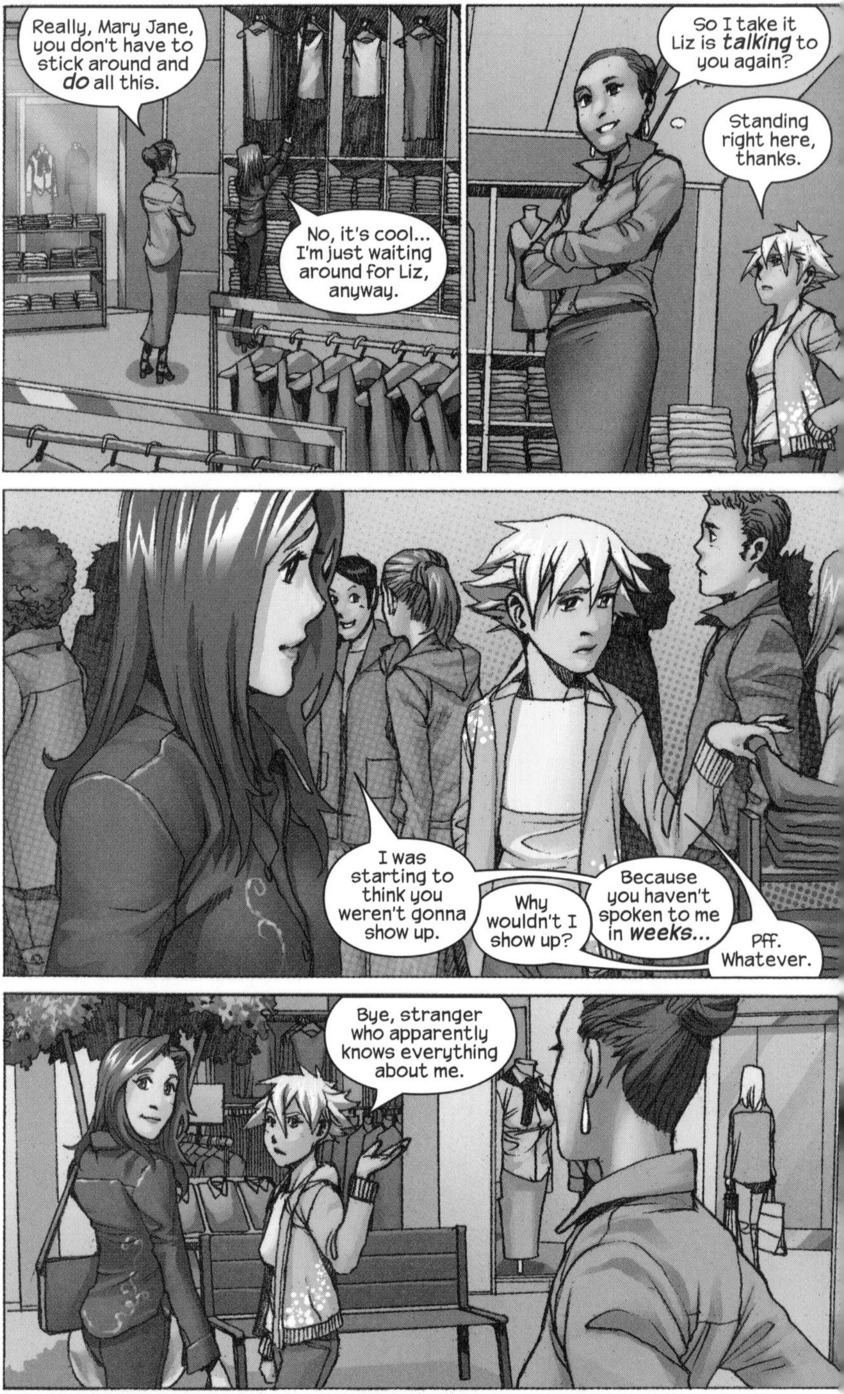

Really, Mary Jane, you don't have to stick around and *do* all this.
No, it's cool... I'm just waiting around for Liz, anyway.
So I take it Liz is *talking* to you again?
Standing right here, thanks.
I was starting to think you weren't gonna show up.
Why wouldn't I show up?
Because you haven't spoken to me in *weeks...*
Pff. Whatever.
Bye, stranger who apparently knows everything about me.

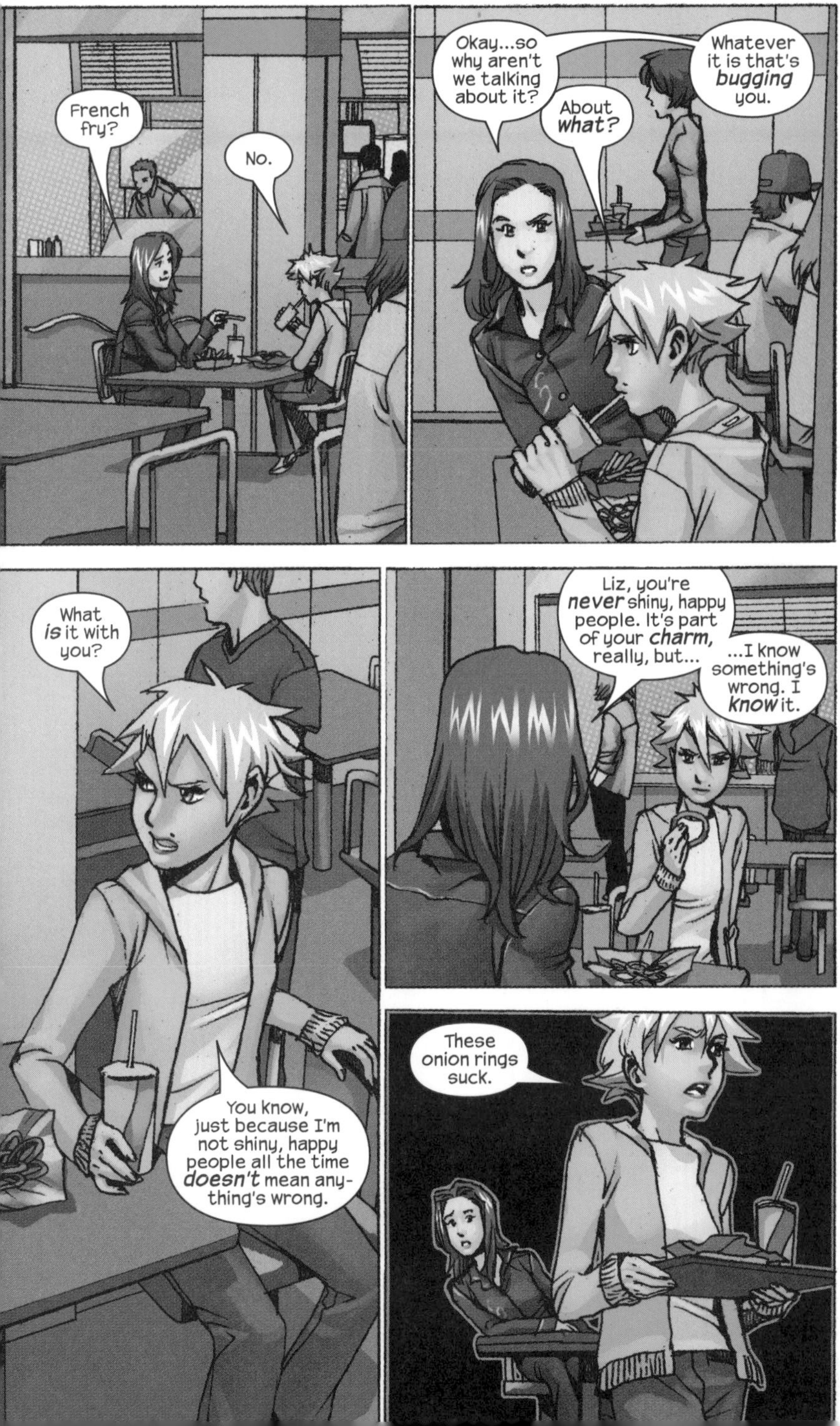

French fry?
No.
Okay...so why aren't we talking about it?
About *what?*
Whatever it is that's *bugging* you.
What *is* it with you?
You know, just because I'm not shiny, happy people all the time *doesn't* mean anything's wrong.
Liz, you're *never* shiny, happy people. It's part of your *charm,* really, but...
...I know something's wrong. I *know* it.
These onion rings suck.

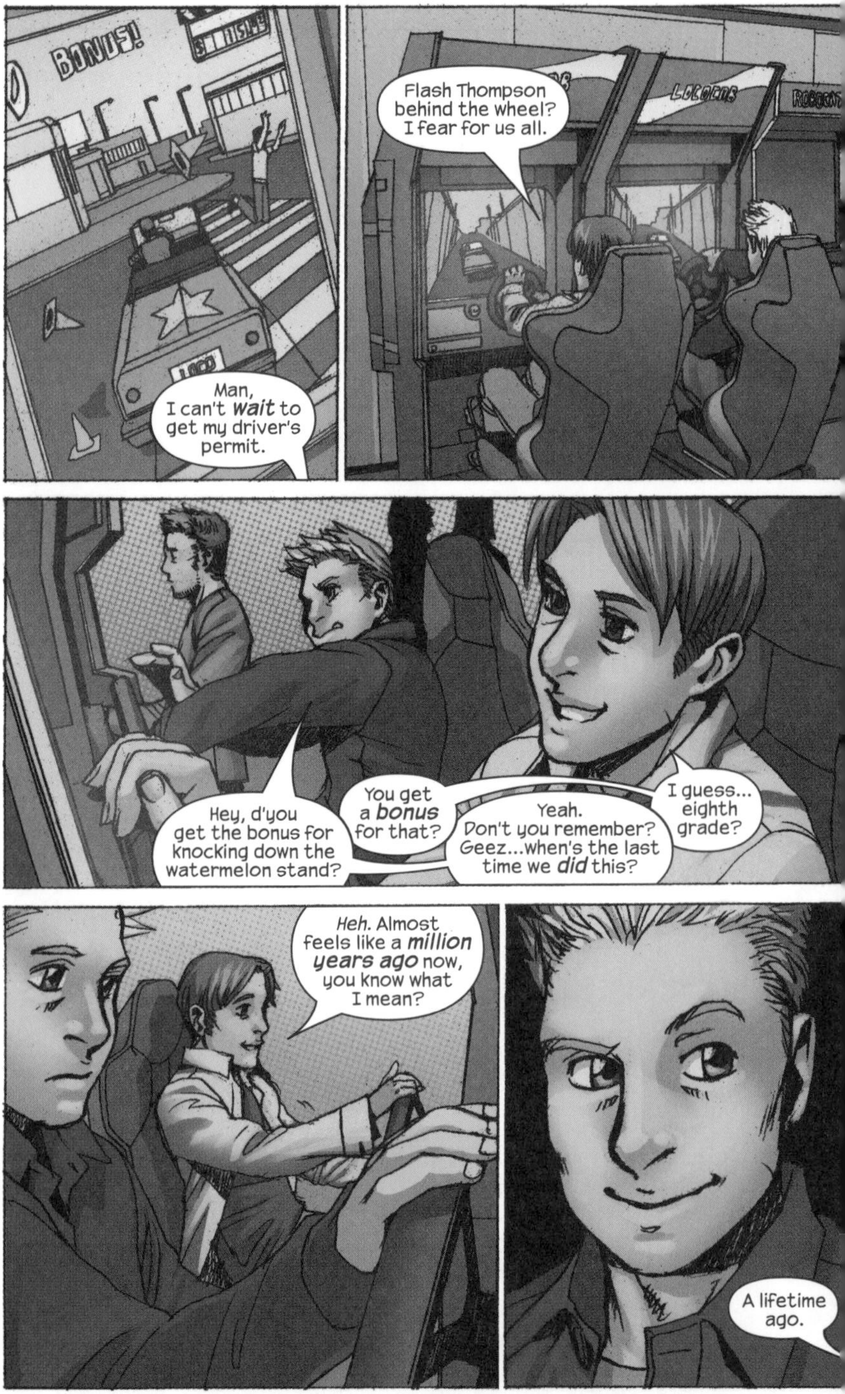
BONUS!
LOCO
Man, I can't *wait* to get my driver's permit.
Flash Thompson behind the wheel? I fear for us all.
Hey, d'you get the bonus for knocking down the watermelon stand?
You get a ***bonus*** for that?
Yeah. Don't you remember? Geez...when's the last time we ***did*** this?
I guess... eighth grade?
Heh. Almost feels like a ***million years ago*** now, you know what I mean?
A lifetime ago.

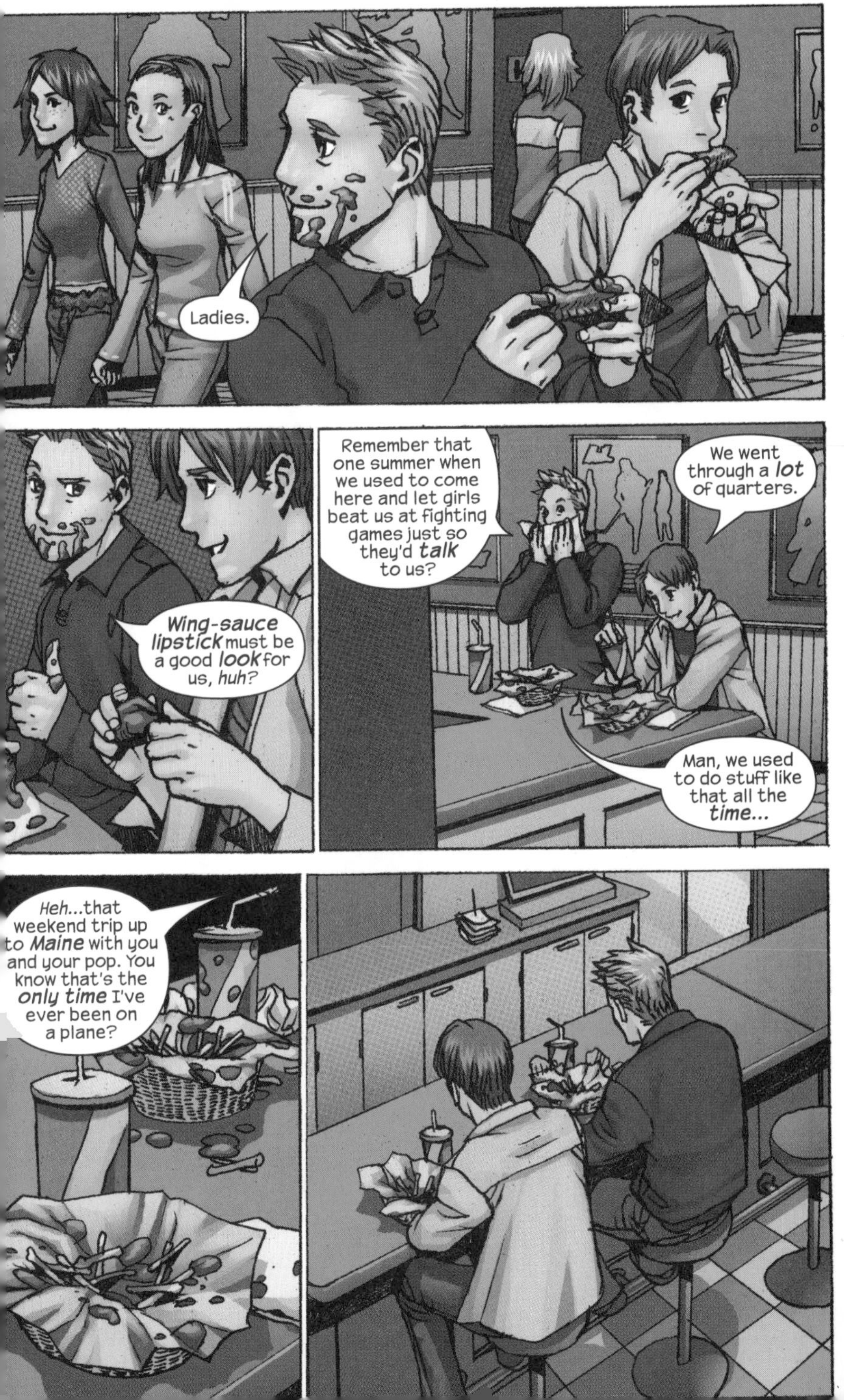
Ladies.
Wing-sauce lipstick must be a good look for us, huh?
Remember that one summer when we used to come here and let girls beat us at fighting games just so they'd talk to us?
We went through a lot of quarters.
Man, we used to do stuff like that all the time...
Heh...that weekend trip up to Maine with you and your pop. You know that's the only time I've ever been on a plane?

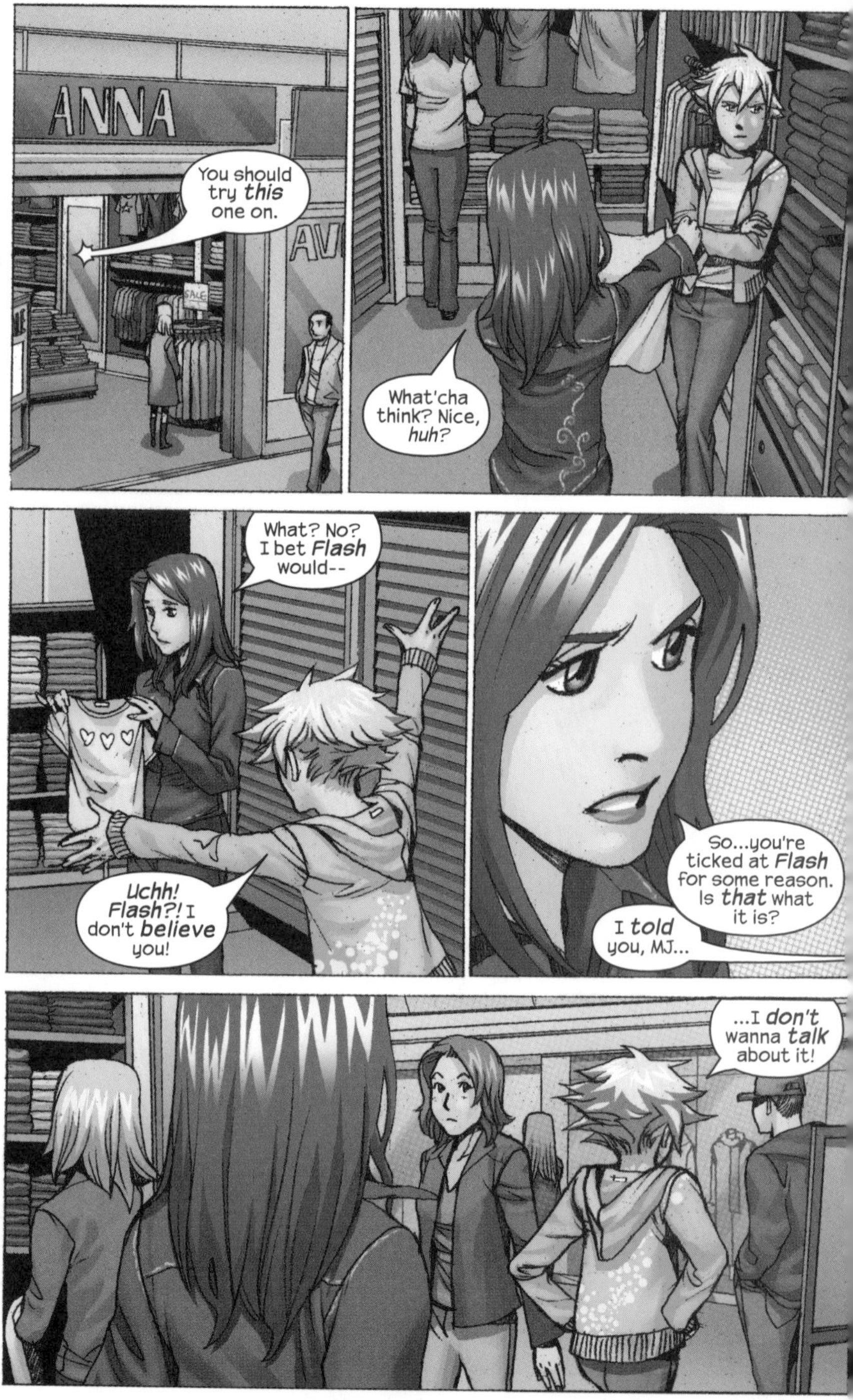
ANNA
You should try *this* one on.
What'cha think? Nice, *huh*?
What? No? I bet *Flash* would--
Uchh! *Flash?!* I don't *believe* you!
So...you're ticked at *Flash* for some reason. Is *that* what it is?
I *told* you, MJ...
...I *don't* wanna *talk* about it!

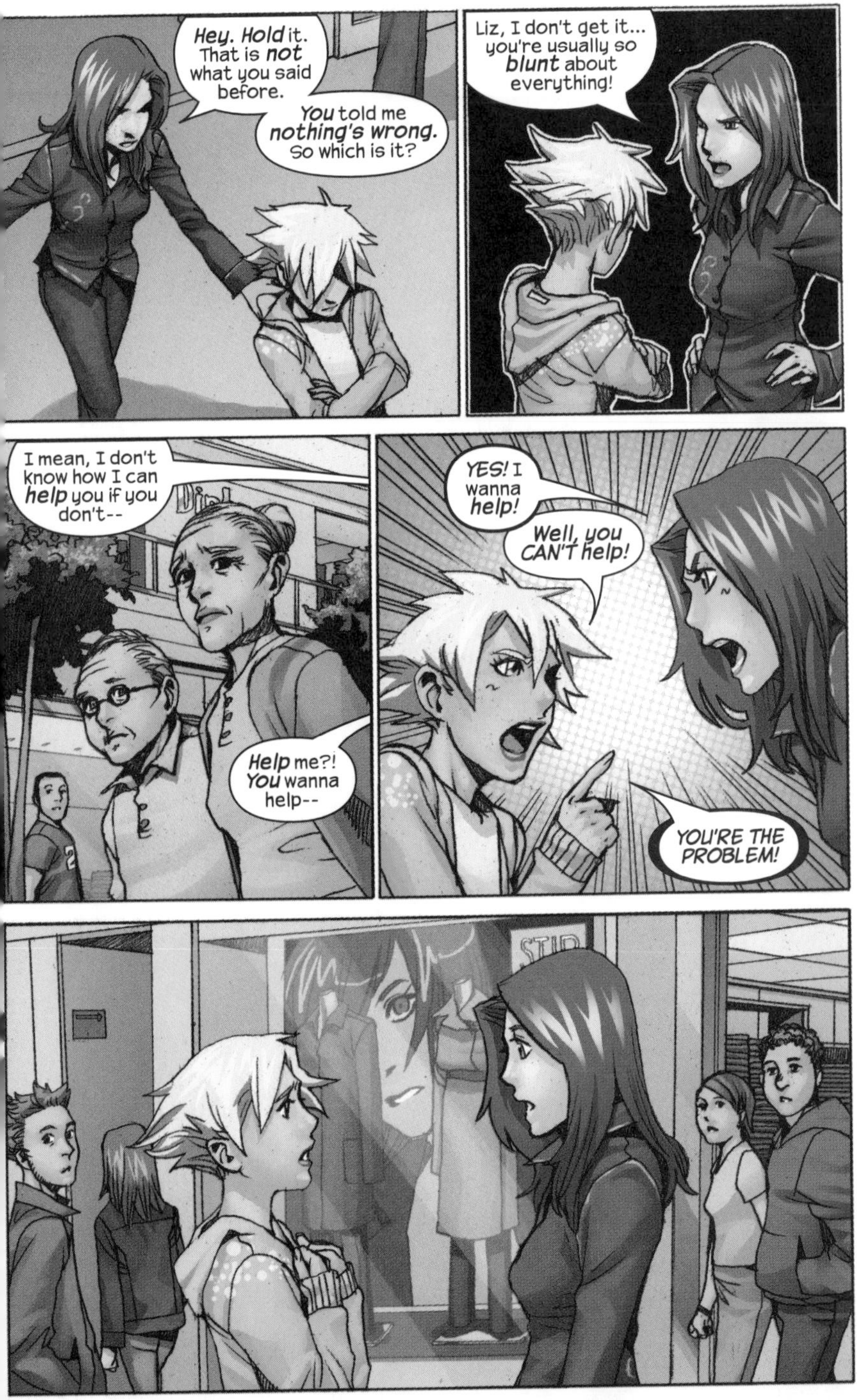

Hey. Hold it. That is not what you said before.
You told me nothing's wrong. So which is it?
Liz, I don't get it... you're usually so blunt about everything!
I mean, I don't know how I can help you if you don't--
Help me?! You wanna help--
YES! I wanna help!
Well, you CAN'T help!
YOU'RE THE PROBLEM!

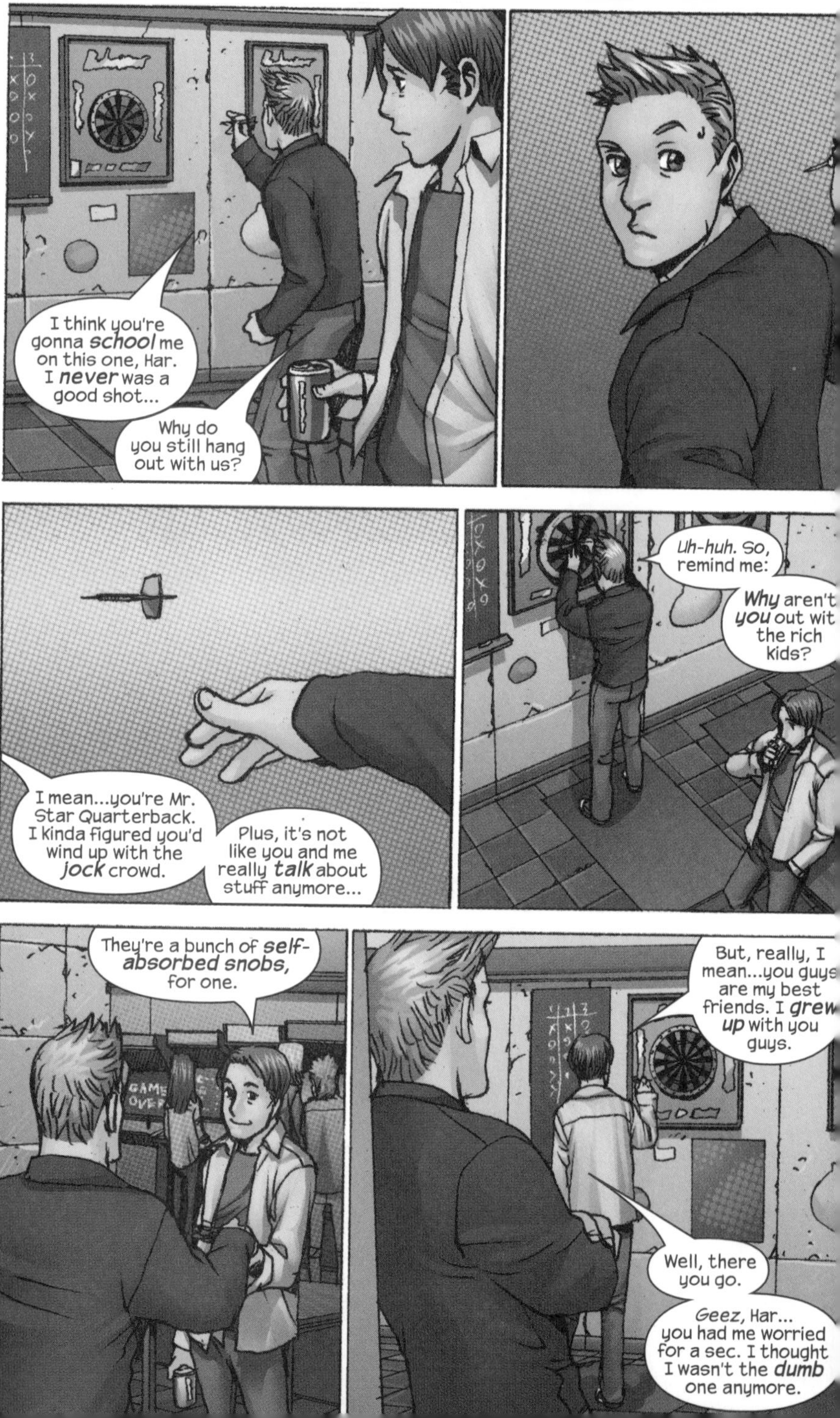

I think you're gonna *school* me on this one, Har. I *never* was a good shot...
Why do you still hang out with us?
Uh-huh. So, remind me:
Why aren't *you* out wit the rich kids?
I mean...you're Mr. Star Quarterback. I kinda figured you'd wind up with the *jock* crowd.
Plus, it's not like you and me really *talk* about stuff anymore...
They're a bunch of *self-absorbed snobs,* for one.
GAME OVER
But, really, I mean...you guys are my best friends. I *grew up* with you guys.
Well, there you go.
Geez, Har... you had me worried for a sec. I thought I wasn't the *dumb* one anymore.

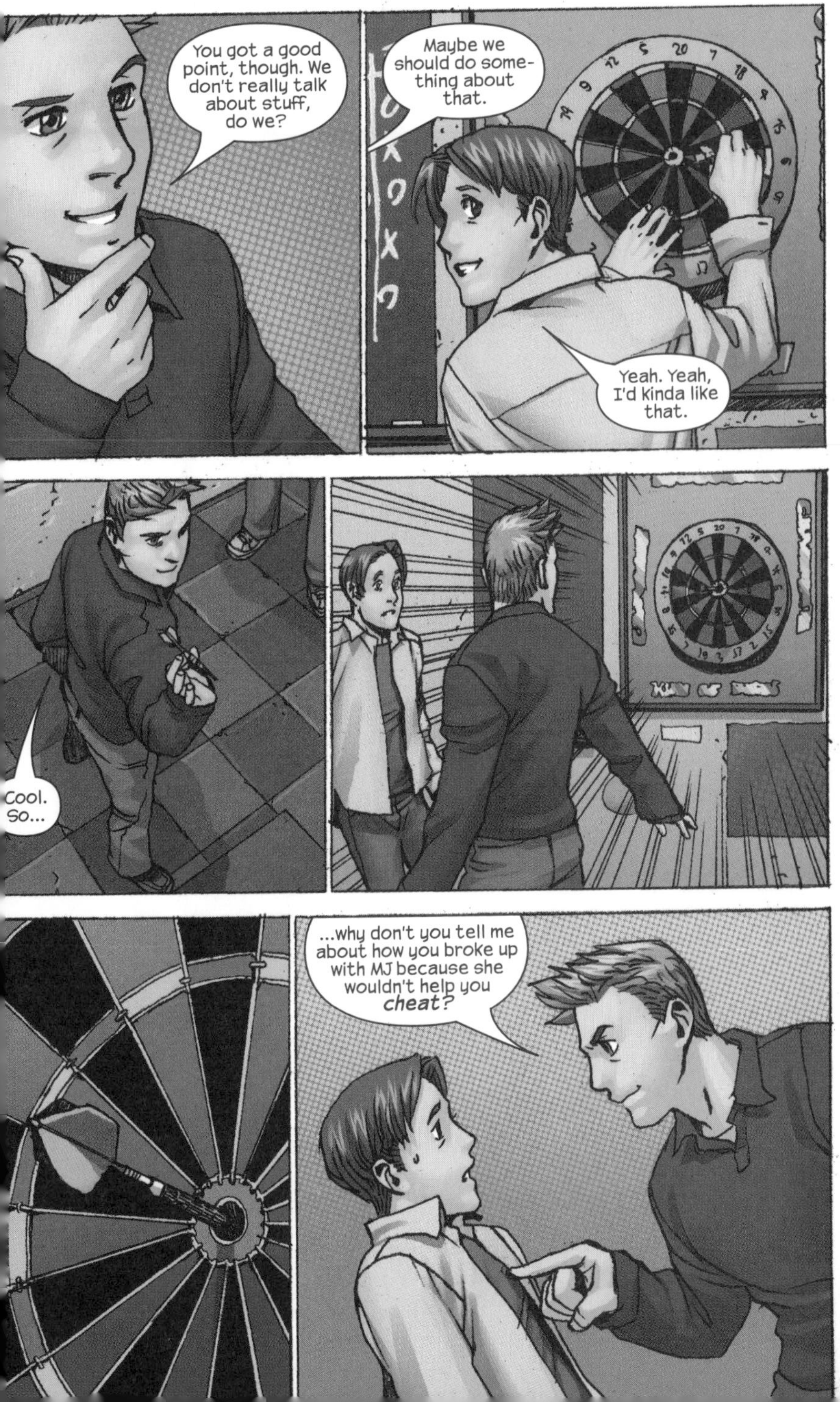

You got a good point, though. We don't really talk about stuff, do we?
Maybe we should do something about that.
Yeah. Yeah, I'd kinda like that.
Cool. So...
...why don't you tell me about how you broke up with MJ because she wouldn't help you *cheat?*

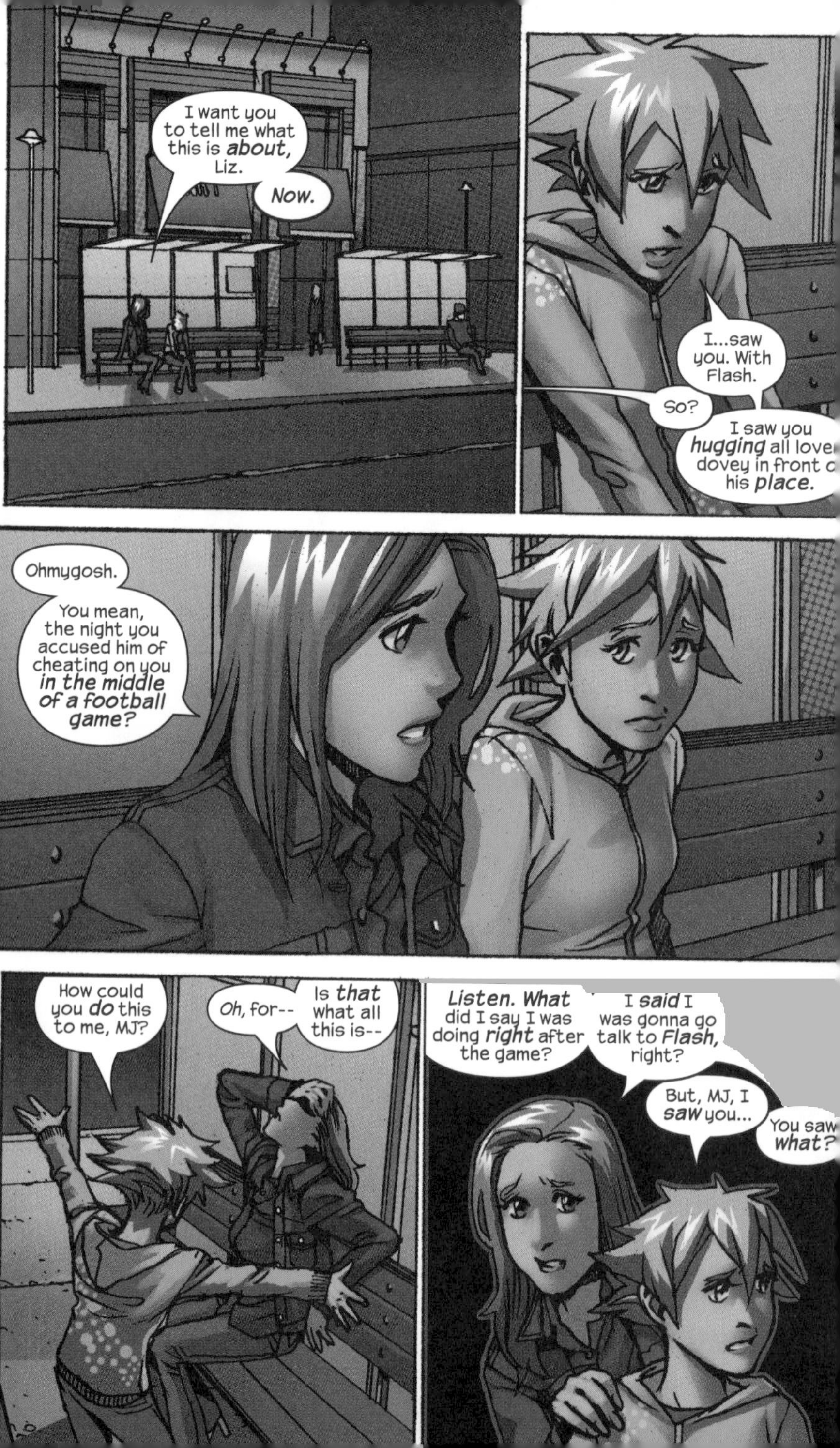
I want you to tell me what this is about, Liz.
Now.
I...saw you. With Flash.
So?
I saw you hugging all love dovey in front o his place.
Ohmygosh.
You mean, the night you accused him of cheating on you in the middle of a football game?
How could you do this to me, MJ?
Oh, for--
Is that what all this is--
Listen. What did I say I was doing right after the game?
I said I was gonna go talk to Flash, right?
But, MJ, I saw you...
You saw what?

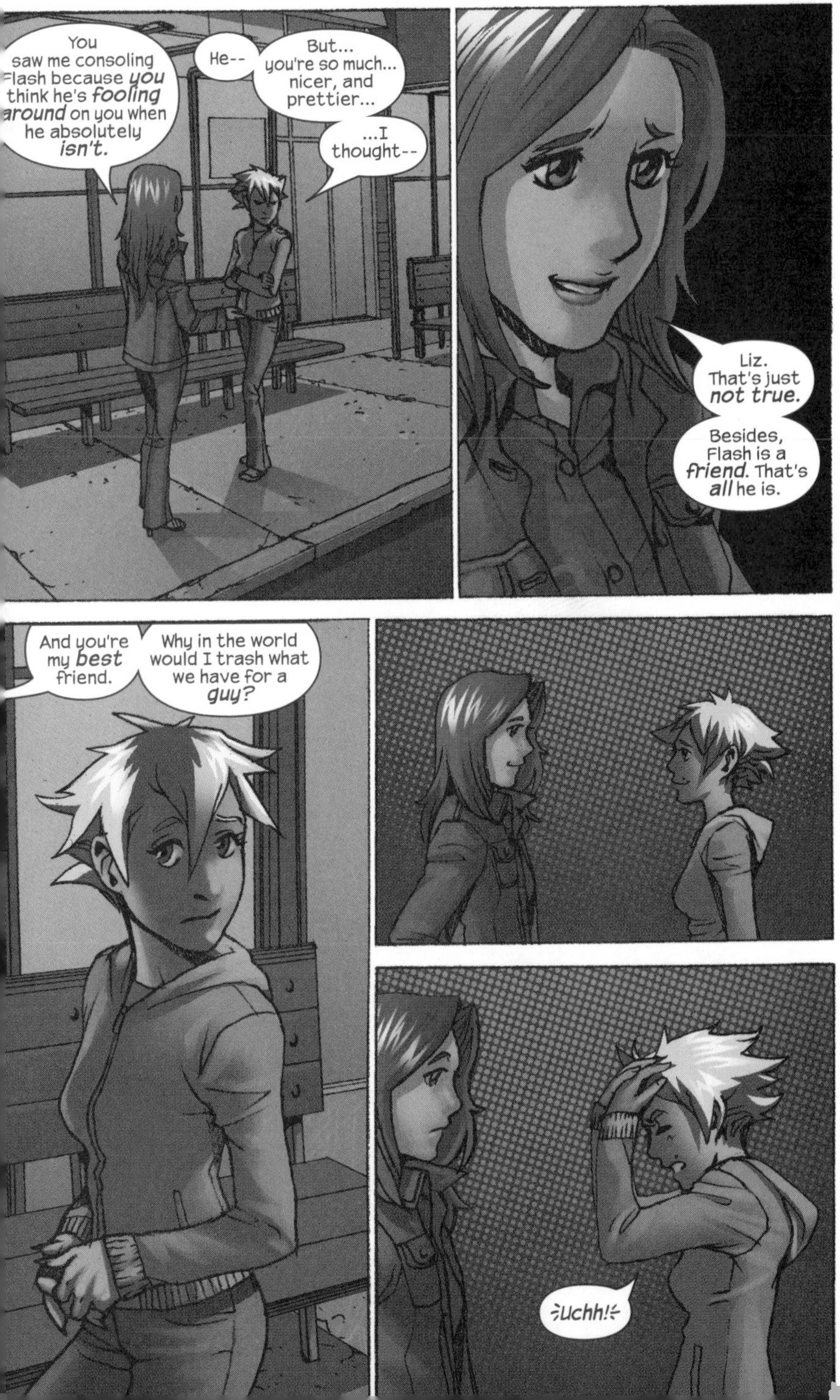
You saw me consoling Flash because *you* think he's *fooling around* on you when he absolutely *isn't.*
He--
But... you're so much... nicer, and prettier...
...I thought--
Liz. That's just *not true.*
Besides, Flash is a *friend.* That's *all* he is.
And you're my *best* friend.
Why in the world would I trash what we have for a *guy?*
UCHH!

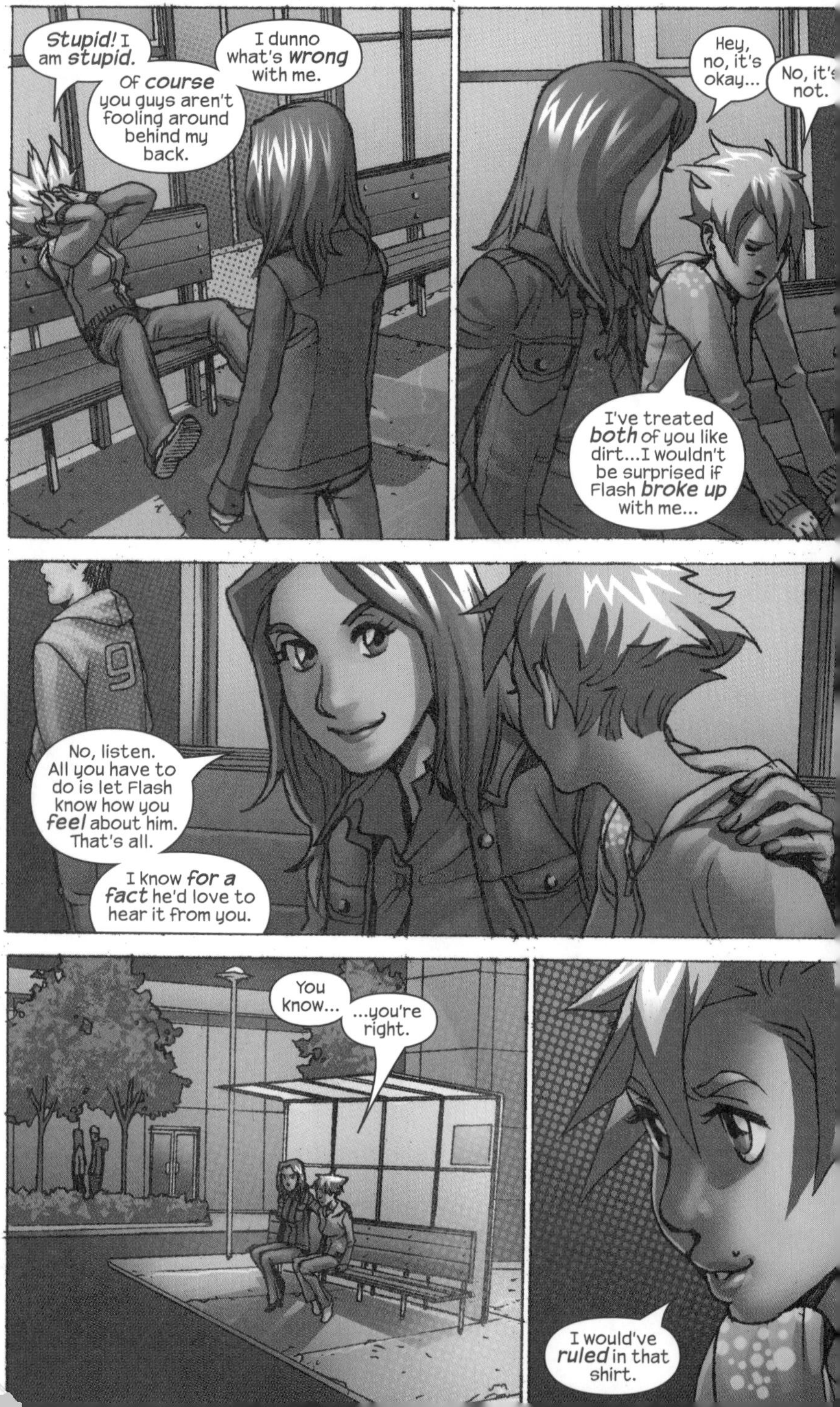

Stupid! I am stupid.
Of course you guys aren't fooling around behind my back.
I dunno what's wrong with me.
Hey, no, it's okay...
No, it's not.
I've treated both of you like dirt...I wouldn't be surprised if Flash broke up with me...
No, listen. All you have to do is let Flash know how you feel about him. That's all.
I know for a fact he'd love to hear it from you.
You know...
...you're right.
I would've ruled in that shirt.

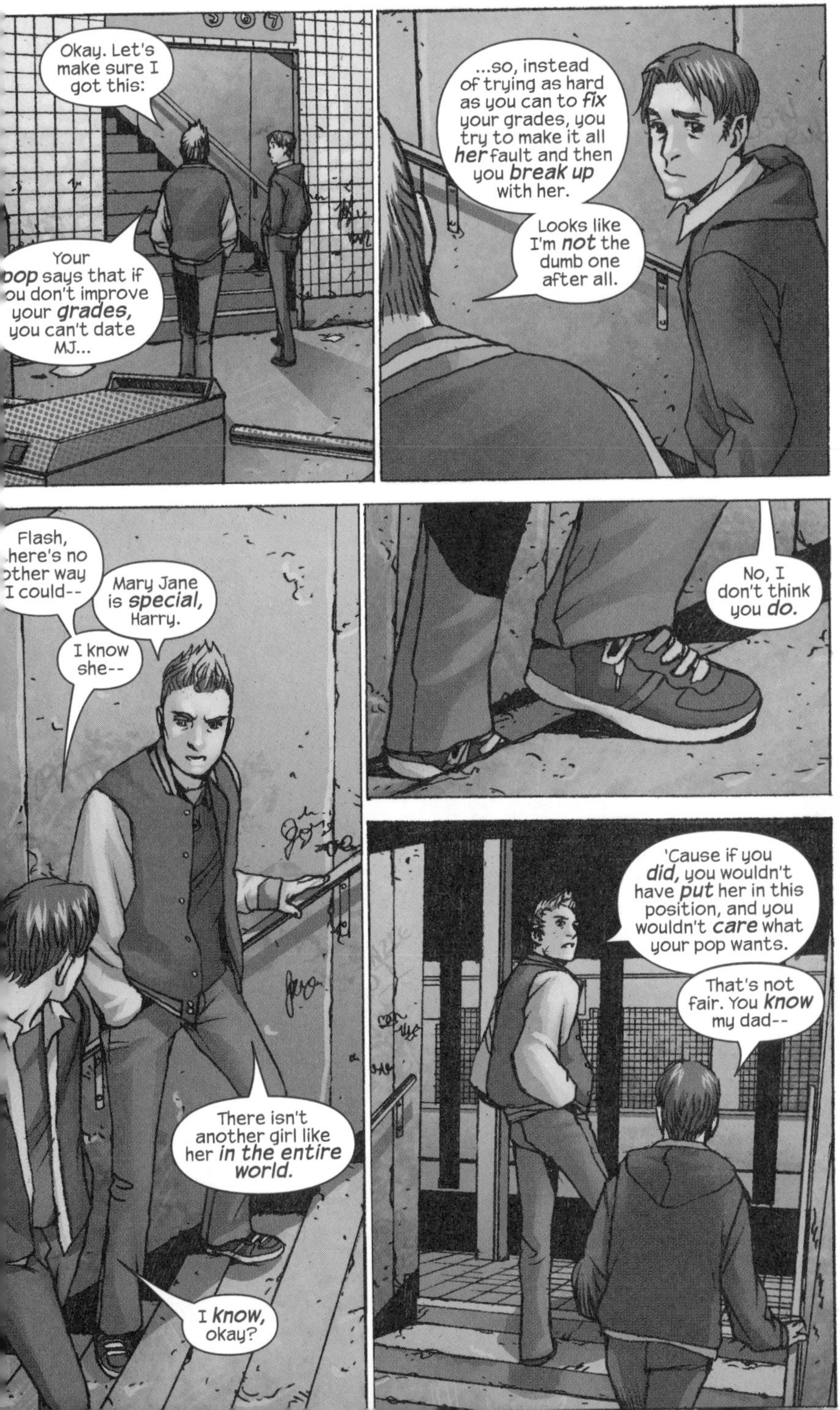

Okay. Let's make sure I got this:
Your pop says that if you don't improve your grades, you can't date MJ...
...so, instead of trying as hard as you can to fix your grades, you try to make it all her fault and then you break up with her.
Looks like I'm not the dumb one after all.
Flash, there's no other way I could--
Mary Jane is special, Harry.
I know she--
There isn't another girl like her in the entire world.
I know, okay?
No, I don't think you do.
'Cause if you did, you wouldn't have put her in this position, and you wouldn't care what your pop wants.
That's not fair. You know my dad--

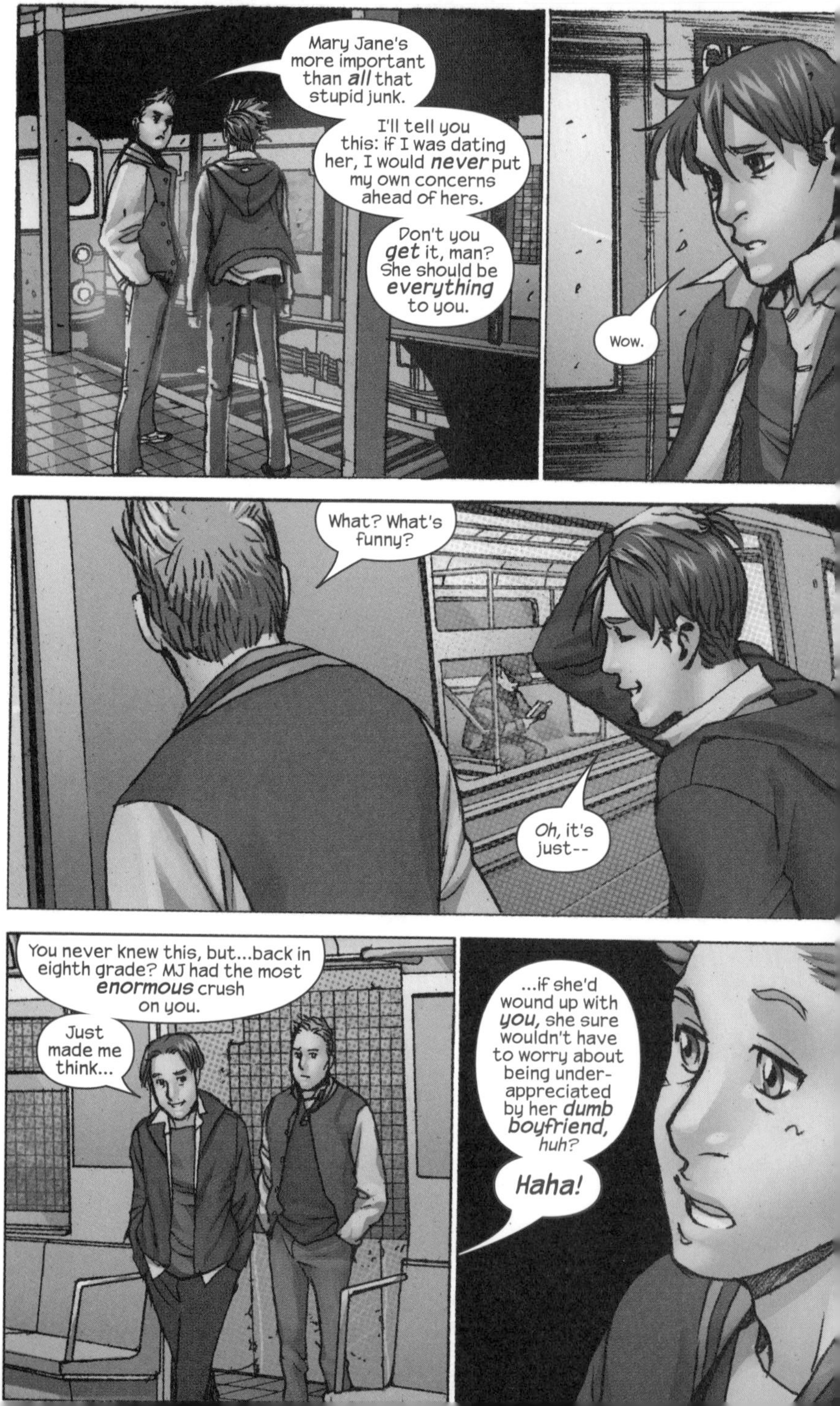
Mary Jane's more important than *all* that stupid junk.
I'll tell you this: if I was dating her, I would *never* put my own concerns ahead of hers.
Don't you *get* it, man? She should be *everything* to you.
Wow.
What? What's funny?
Oh, it's just--
You never knew this, but...back in eighth grade? MJ had the most *enormous* crush on you.
Just made me think...
...if she'd wound up with *you,* she sure wouldn't have to worry about being under-appreciated by her *dumb boyfriend,* huh?
Haha!

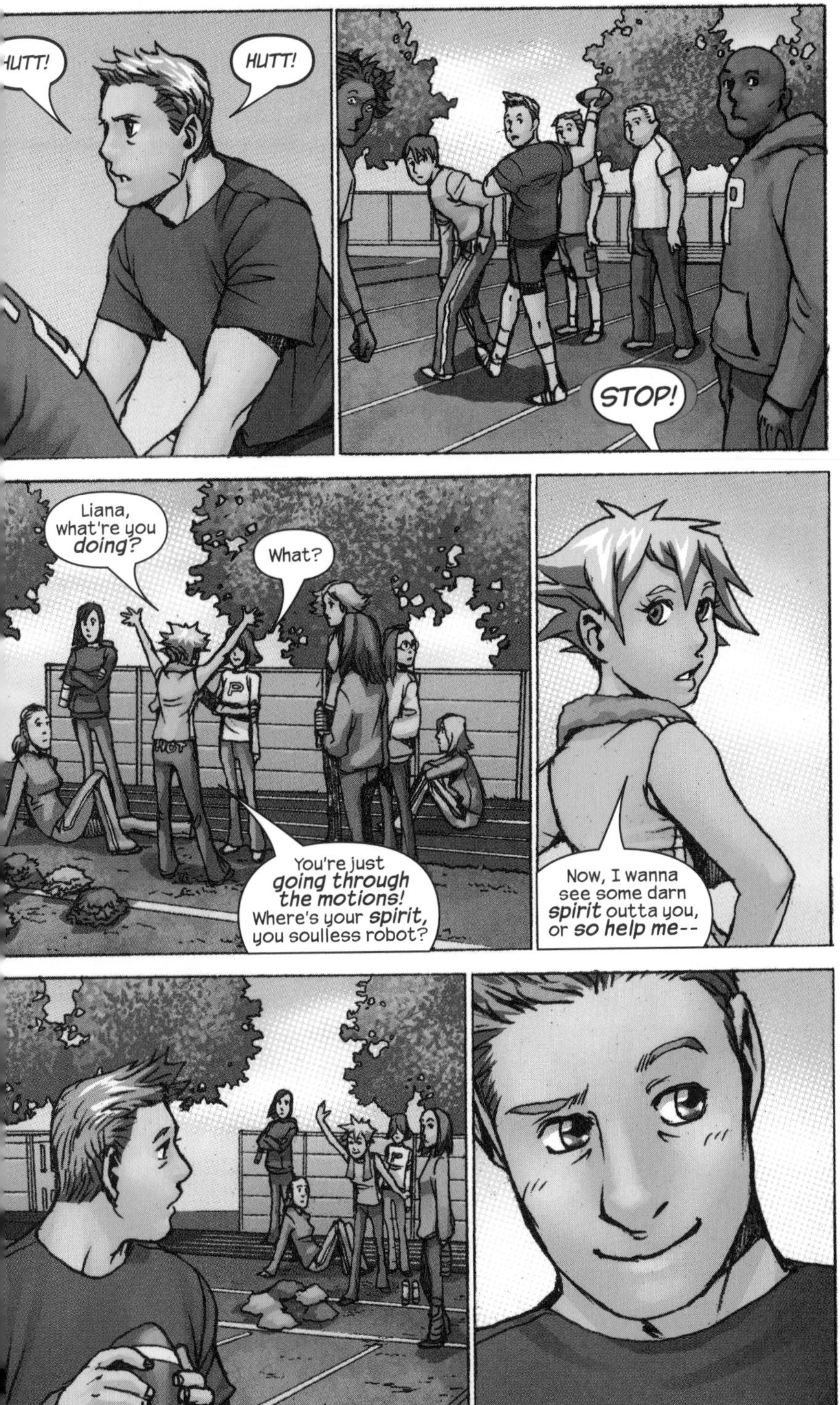
HUTT!
HUTT!
STOP!
Liana, what're you doing?
What?
You're just going through the motions! Where's your spirit, you soulless robot?
Now, I wanna see some darn spirit outta you, or so help me--

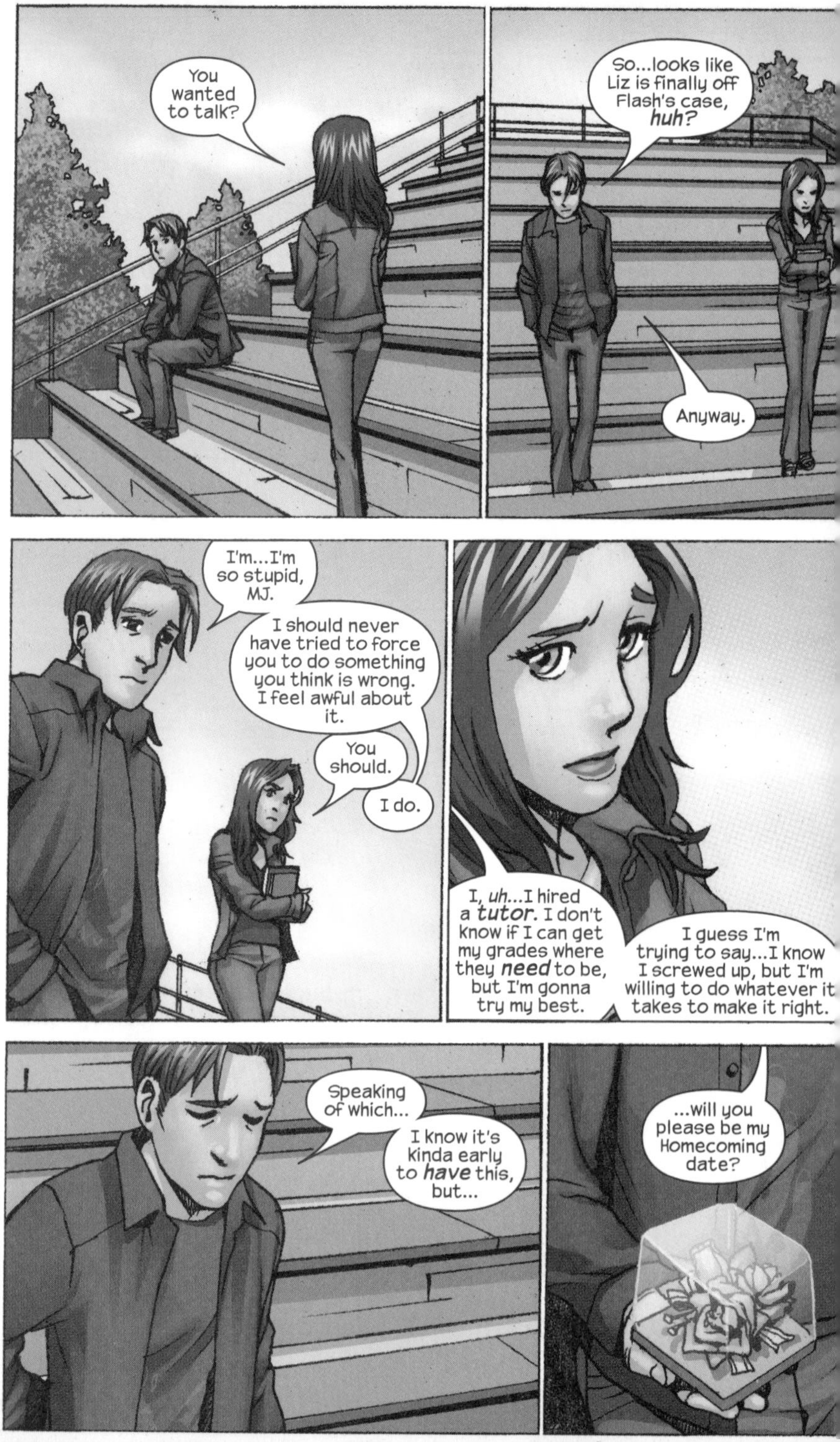
You wanted to talk?
So...looks like Liz is finally off Flash's case, *huh?*
Anyway.
I'm...I'm so stupid, MJ.
I should never have tried to force you to do something you think is wrong. I feel awful about it.
You should.
I do.
I, *uh*...I hired a *tutor.* I don't know if I can get my grades where they *need* to be, but I'm gonna try my best.
I guess I'm trying to say...I know I screwed up, but I'm willing to do whatever it takes to make it right.
Speaking of which...
I know it's kinda early to *have* this, but...
...will you please be my Homecoming date?

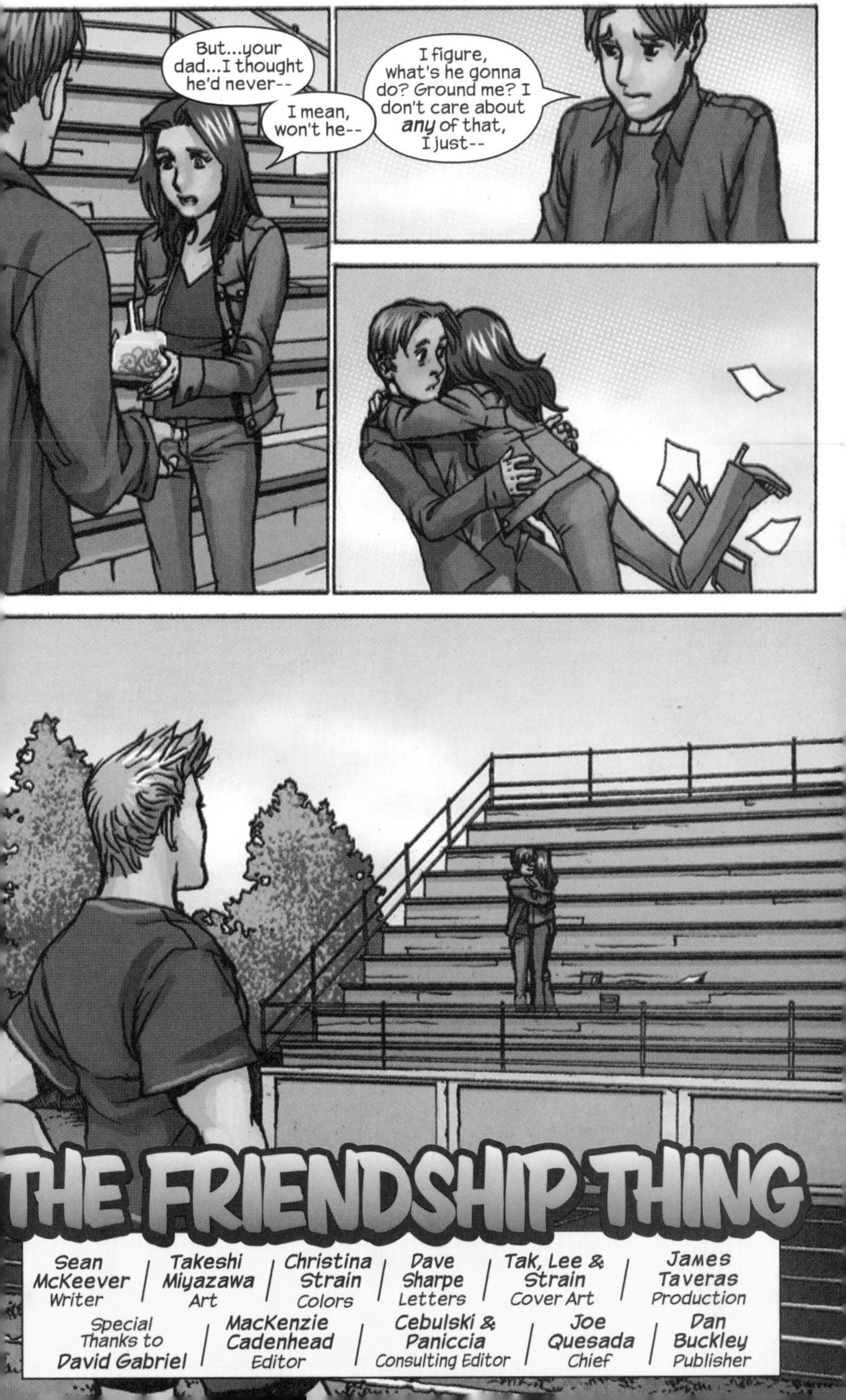

But...your dad...I thought he'd never--
I mean, won't he--
I figure, what's he gonna do? Ground me? I don't care about *any* of that, I just--
THE FRIENDSHIP THING
Sean McKeever Writer
Takeshi Miyazawa Art
Christina Strain Colors
Dave Sharpe Letters
Tak, Lee & Strain Cover Art
James Taveras Production
Special Thanks to David Gabriel
MacKenzie Cadenhead Editor
Cebulski & Paniccia Consulting Editor
Joe Quesada Chief
Dan Buckley Publisher

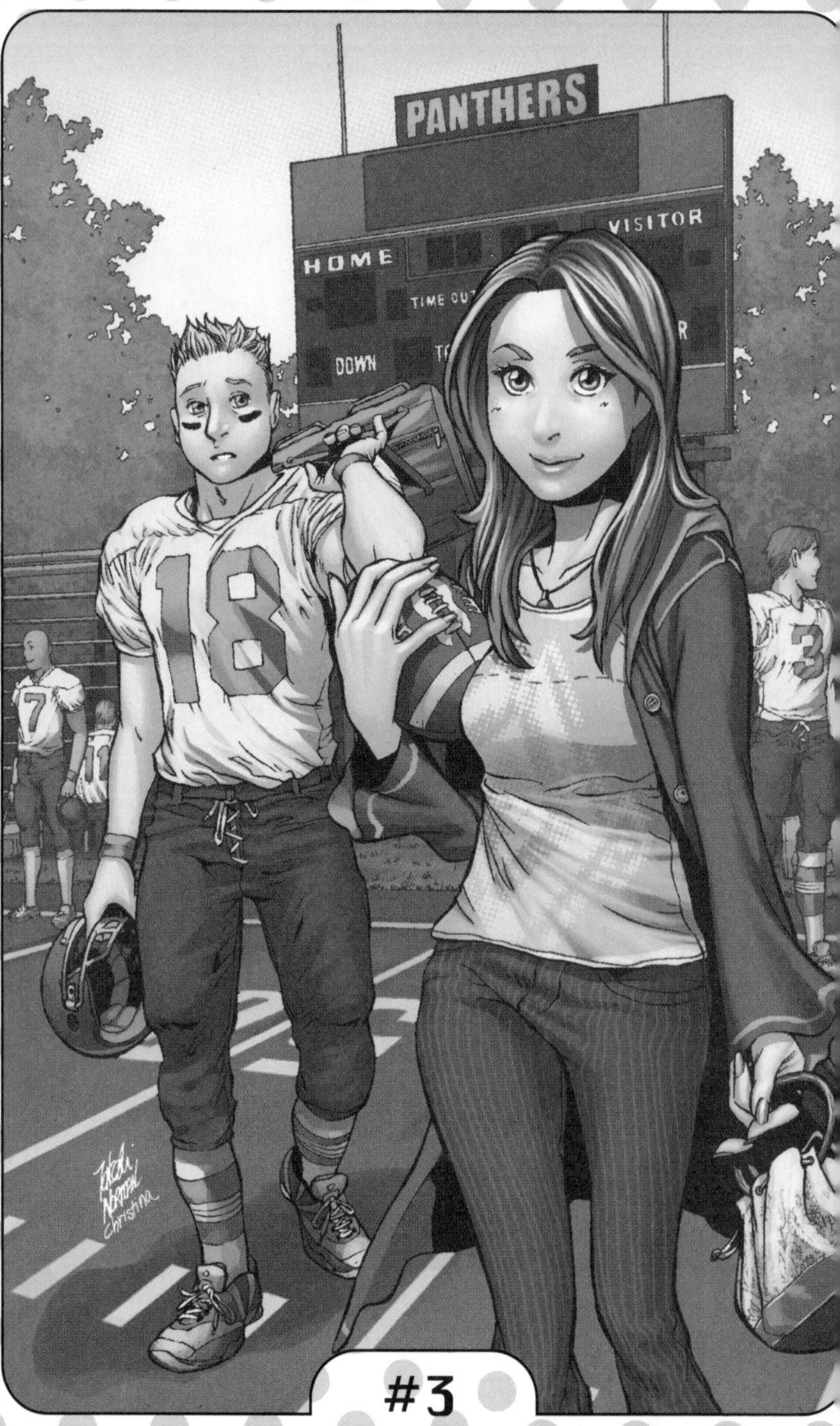
PANTHERS
VISITOR
HOME
TIME OUT
DOWN
18
7
3

#3

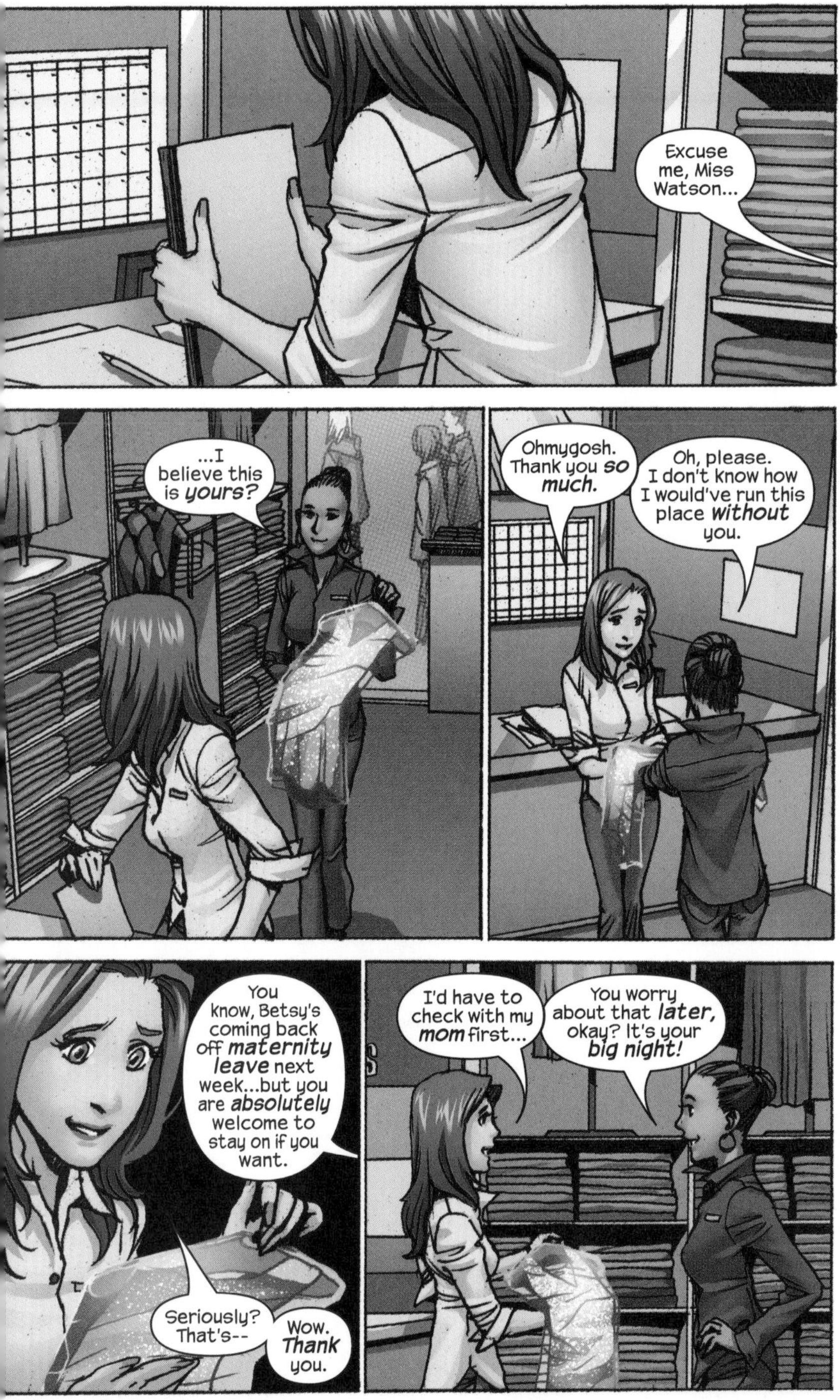
Excuse me, Miss Watson...
...I believe this is yours?
Ohmygosh. Thank you so much.
Oh, please. I don't know how I would've run this place without you.
You know, Betsy's coming back off maternity leave next week...but you are absolutely welcome to stay on if you want.
Seriously? That's--
Wow. Thank you.
I'd have to check with my mom first...
You worry about that later, okay? It's your big night!

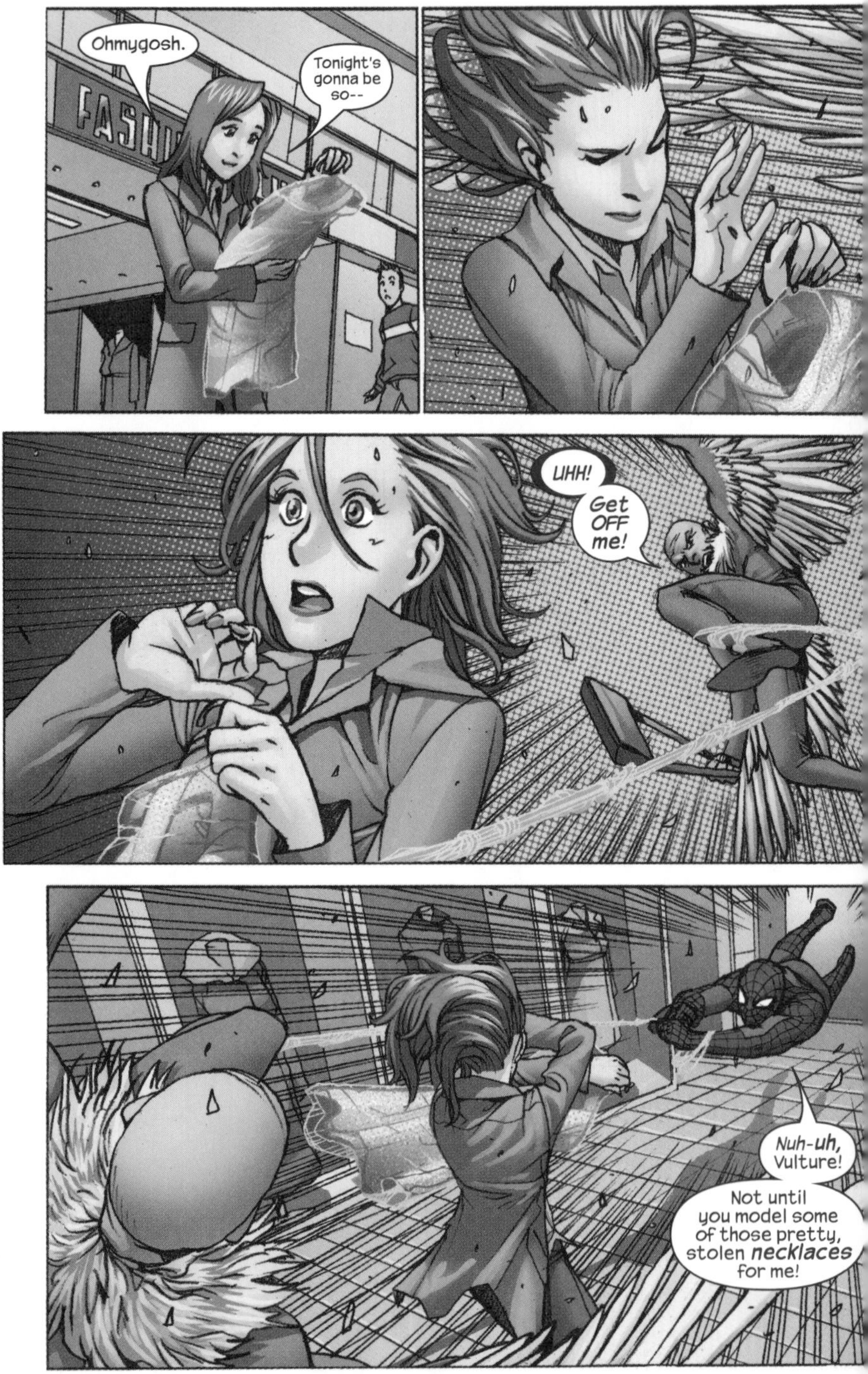
Ohmygosh.
Tonight's gonna be so--
UHH!
Get OFF me!
Nuh-uh, Vulture!
Not until you model some of those pretty, stolen necklaces for me!

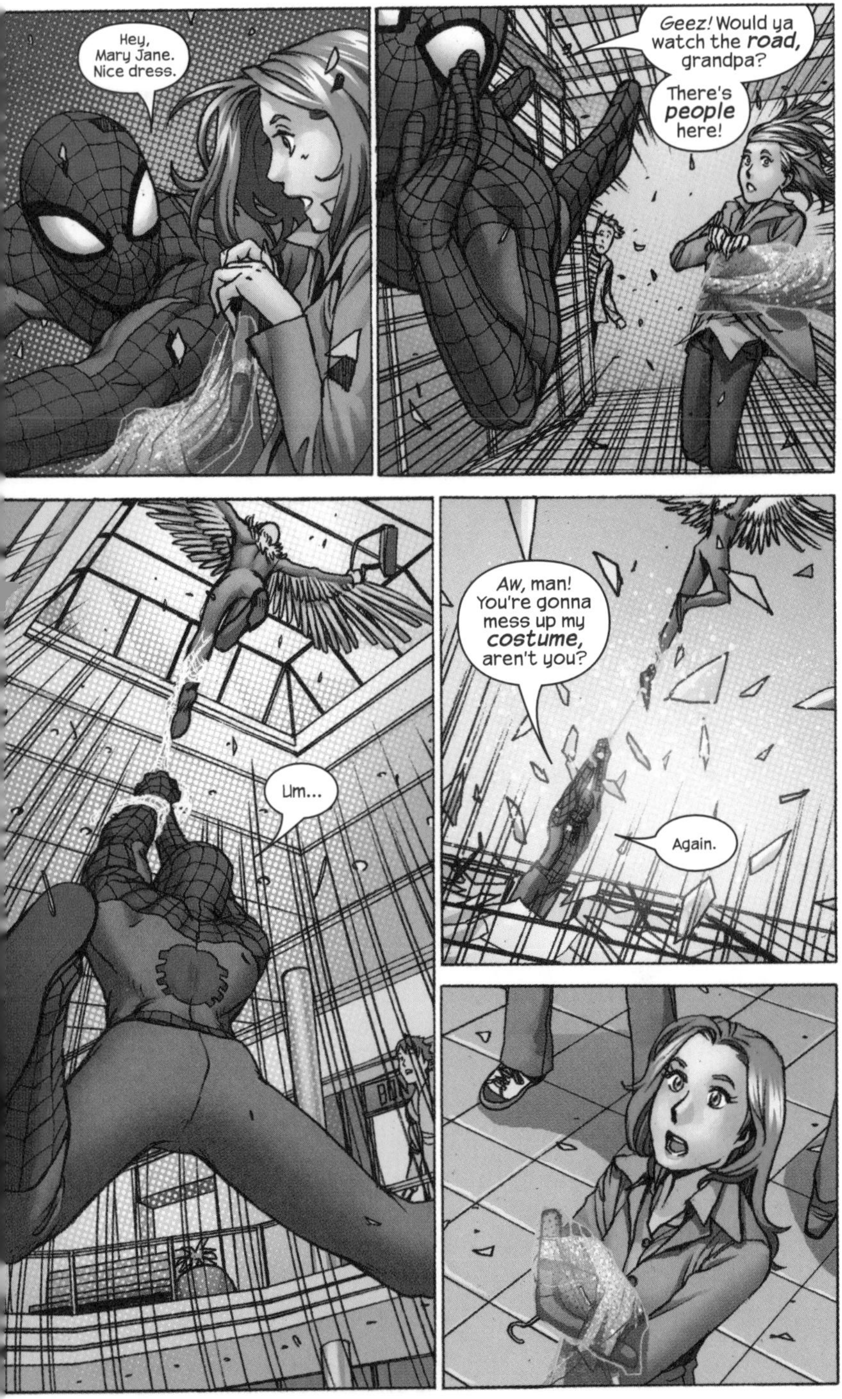
Hey, Mary Jane. Nice dress.
Geez! Would ya watch the road, grandpa?
There's people here!
Um...
Aw, man! You're gonna mess up my costume, aren't you?
Again.

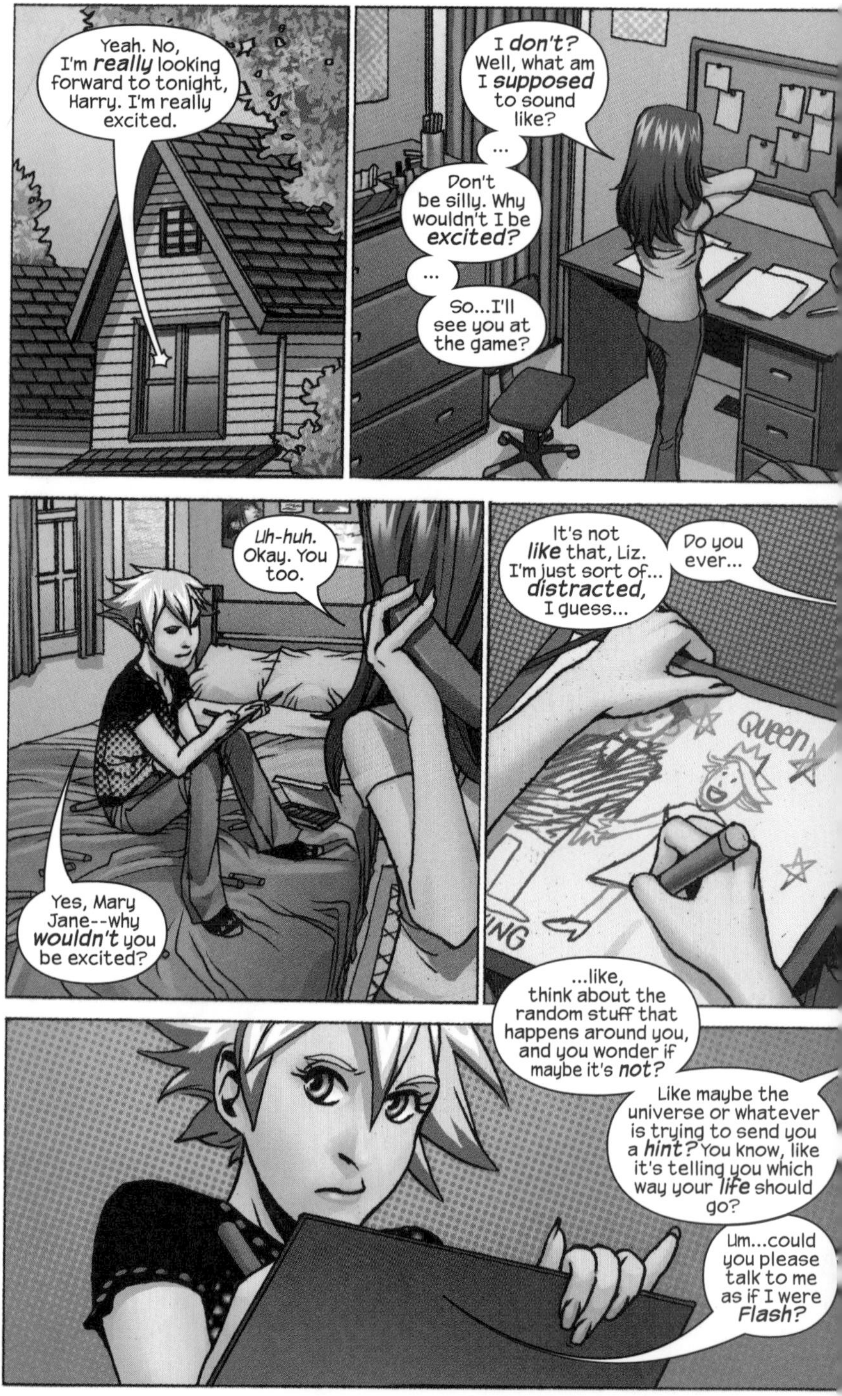

Yeah. No, I'm *really* looking forward to tonight, Harry. I'm really excited.
I *don't?* Well, what am I *supposed* to sound like?
...
Don't be silly. Why wouldn't I be *excited?*
...
So...I'll see you at the game?
Uh-huh. Okay. You too.
Yes, Mary Jane--why *wouldn't* you be excited?
It's not *like* that, Liz. I'm just sort of... *distracted,* I guess...
Do you ever...
QUEEN
ING
...like, think about the random stuff that happens around you, and you wonder if maybe it's *not?*
Like maybe the universe or whatever is trying to send you a *hint?* You know, like it's telling you which way your *life* should go?
Um...could you please talk to me as if I were *Flash?*

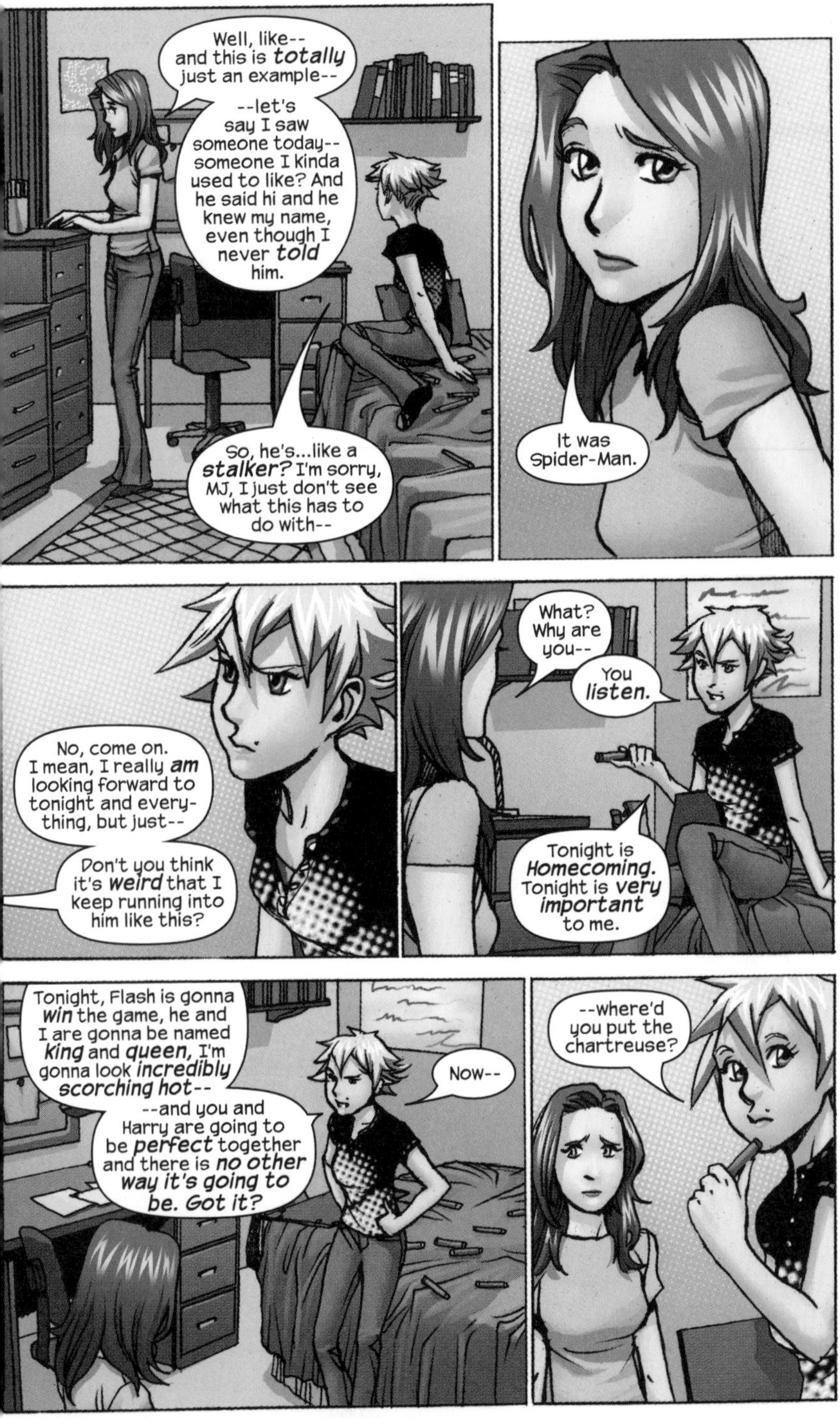
Well, like-- and this is totally just an example--
--let's say I saw someone today-- someone I kinda used to like? And he said hi and he knew my name, even though I never told him.
So, he's...like a stalker? I'm sorry, MJ, I just don't see what this has to do with--
It was Spider-Man.
No, come on. I mean, I really am looking forward to tonight and every-thing, but just--
Don't you think it's weird that I keep running into him like this?
What? Why are you--
You listen.
Tonight is Homecoming. Tonight is very important to me.
Tonight, Flash is gonna win the game, he and I are gonna be named king and queen, I'm gonna look incredibly scorching hot--
--and you and Harry are going to be perfect together and there is no other way it's going to be. Got it?
Now--
--where'd you put the chartreuse?

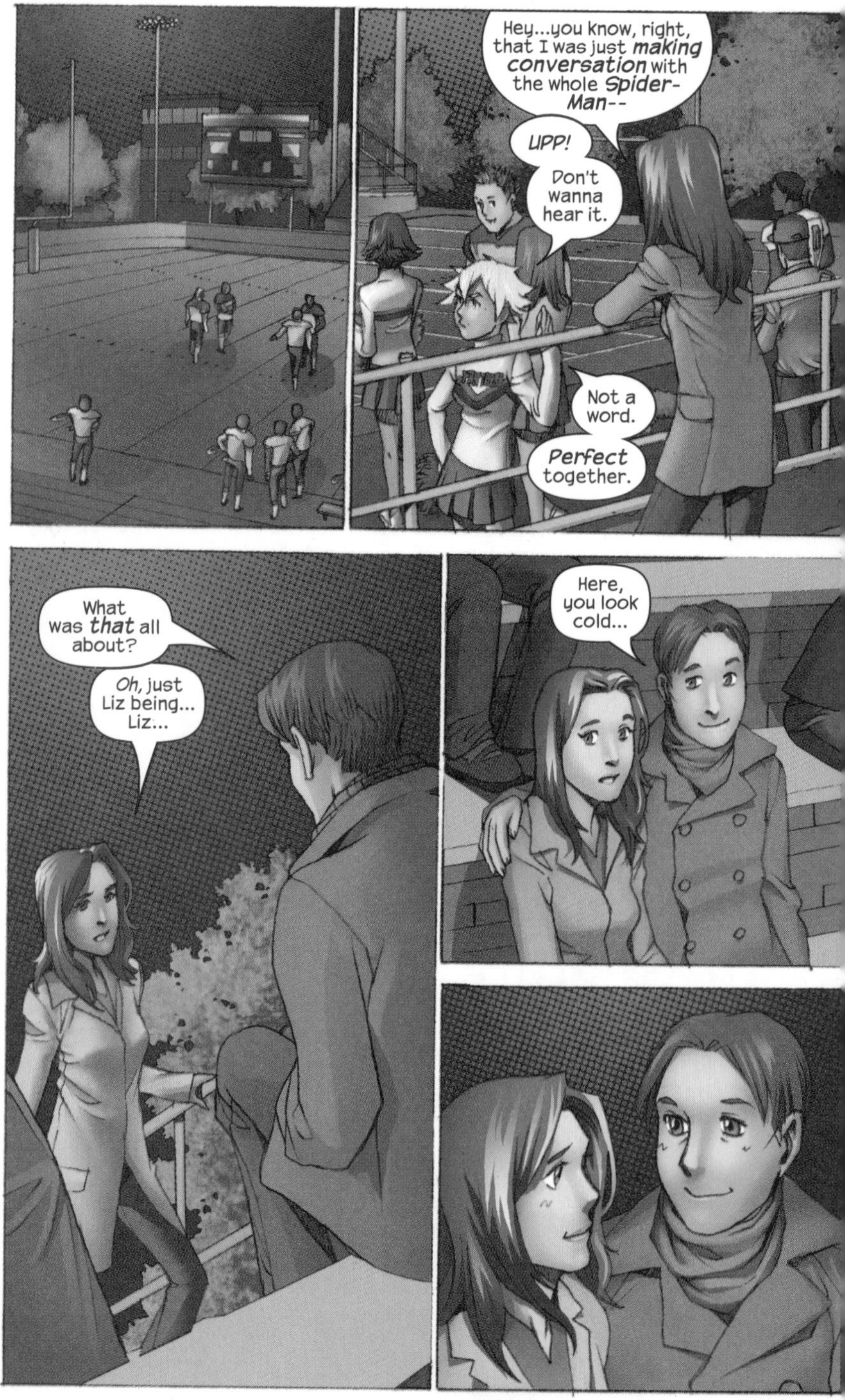

Hey...you know, right, that I was just *making conversation* with the whole *Spider-Man*--
UPP!
Don't wanna hear it.
Not a word.
Perfect together.
What was *that* all about?
Oh, just Liz being... Liz...
Here, you look cold...

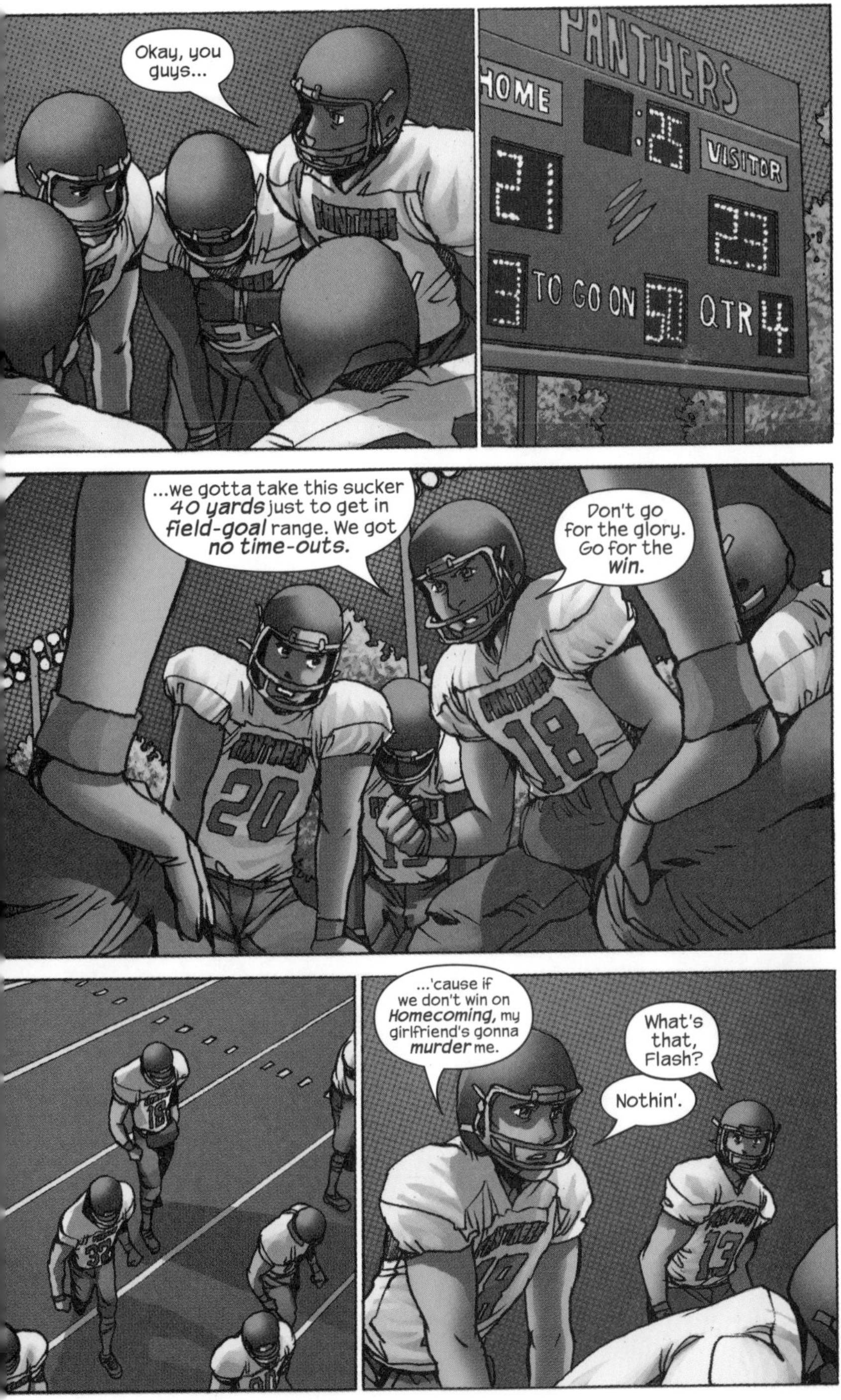
Okay, you guys...
PANTHERS
HOME
:25
VISITOR
21
23
3 TO GO ON 50 QTR 4
...we gotta take this sucker 40 yards just to get in field-goal range. We got no time-outs.
Don't go for the glory. Go for the win.
...'cause if we don't win on Homecoming, my girlfriend's gonna murder me.
What's that, Flash?
Nothin'.

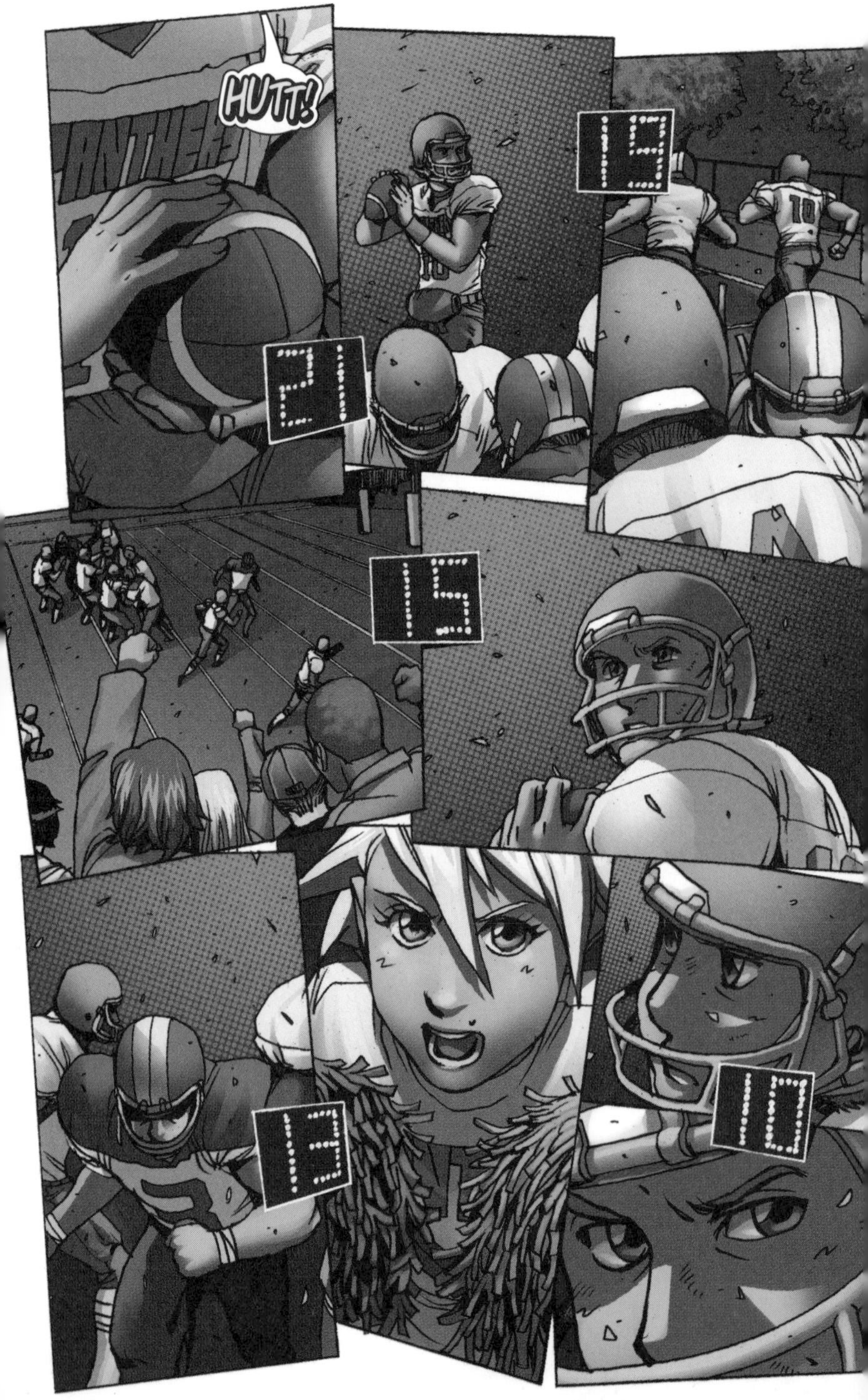

HUTT!
21
19
15
13
10

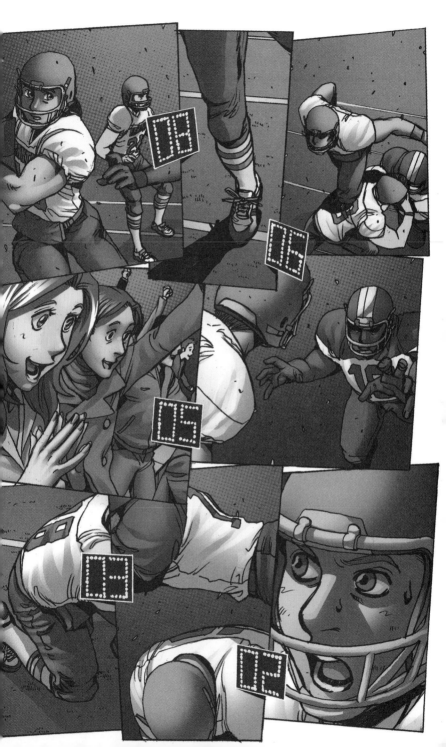

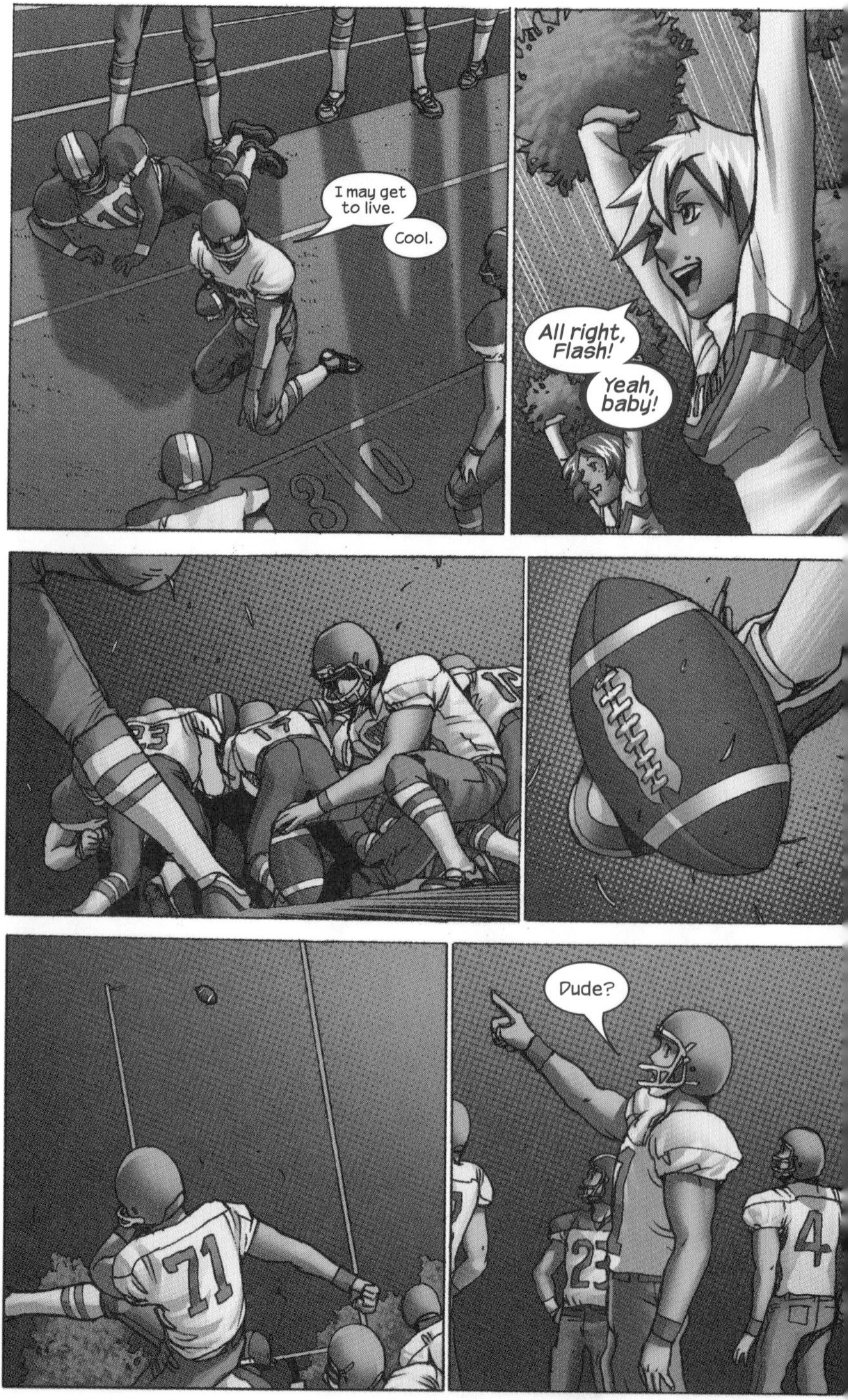
I may get to live.
Cool.
All right, Flash!
Yeah, baby!
Dude?

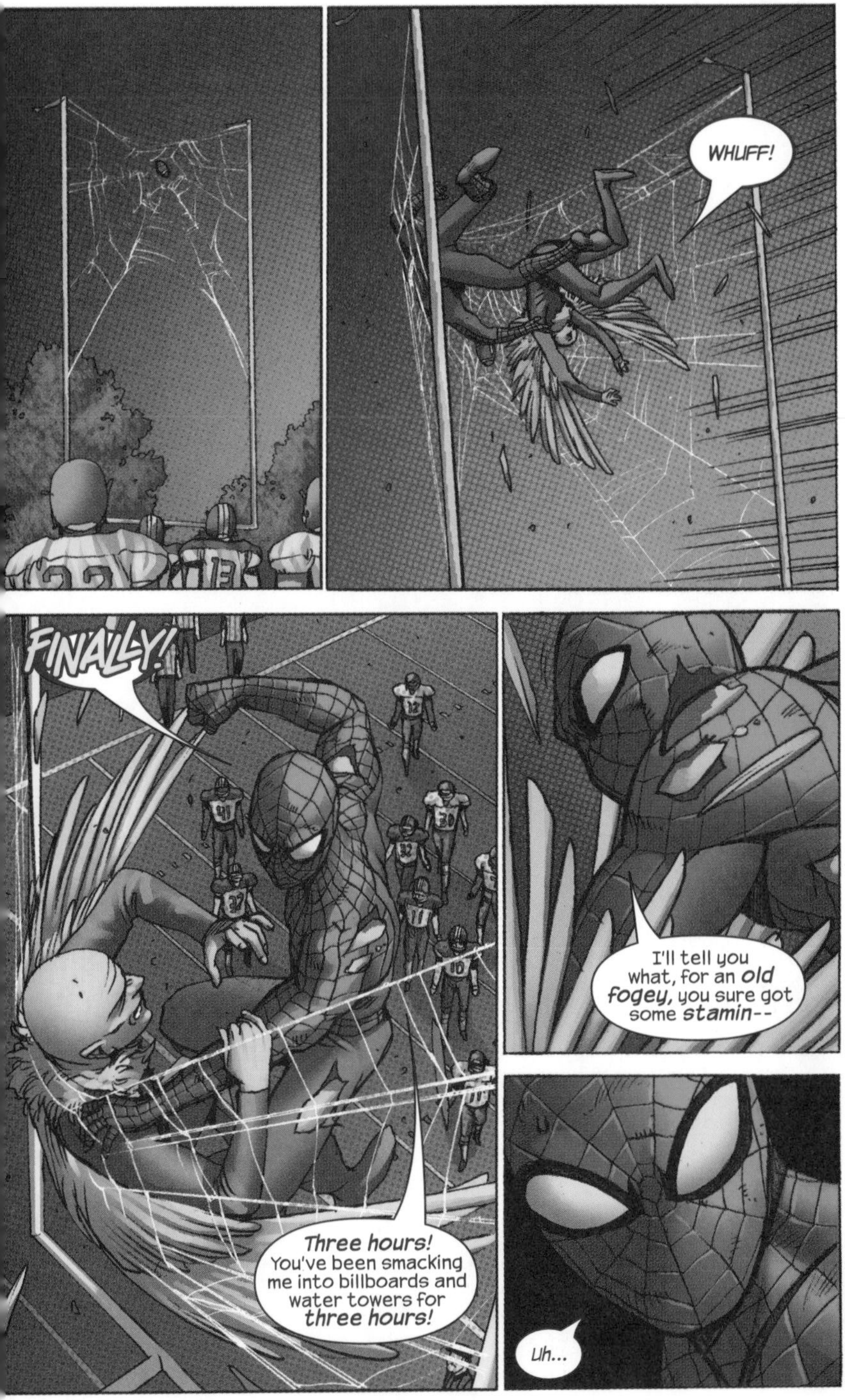
WHUFF!
FINALLY!
Three hours! You've been smacking me into billboards and water towers for three hours!
I'll tell you what, for an old fogey, you sure got some stamin--
Uh...

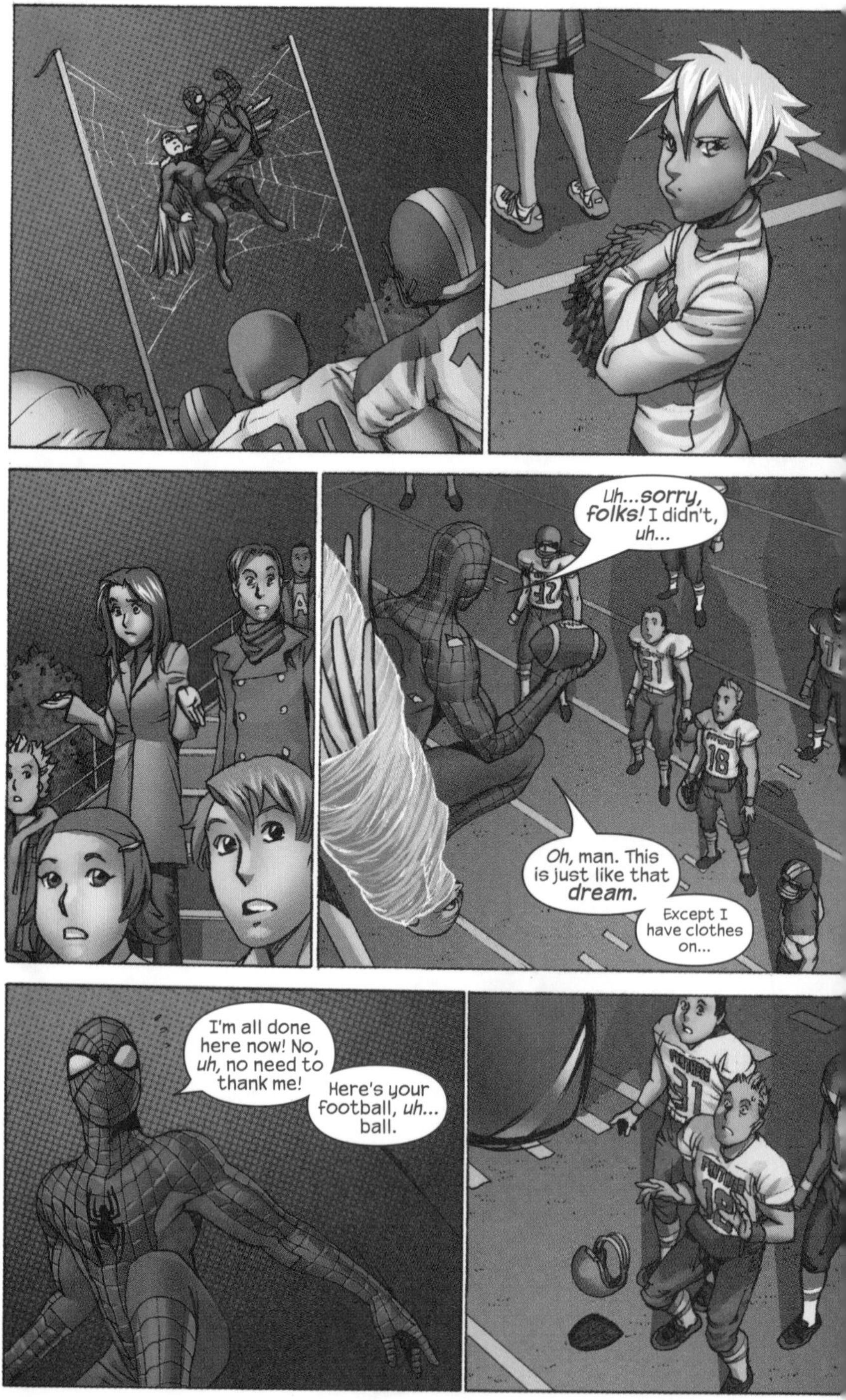
Uh...sorry, folks! I didn't, uh...
Oh, man. This is just like that dream.
Except I have clothes on...
I'm all done here now! No, uh, no need to thank me!
Here's your football, uh... ball.

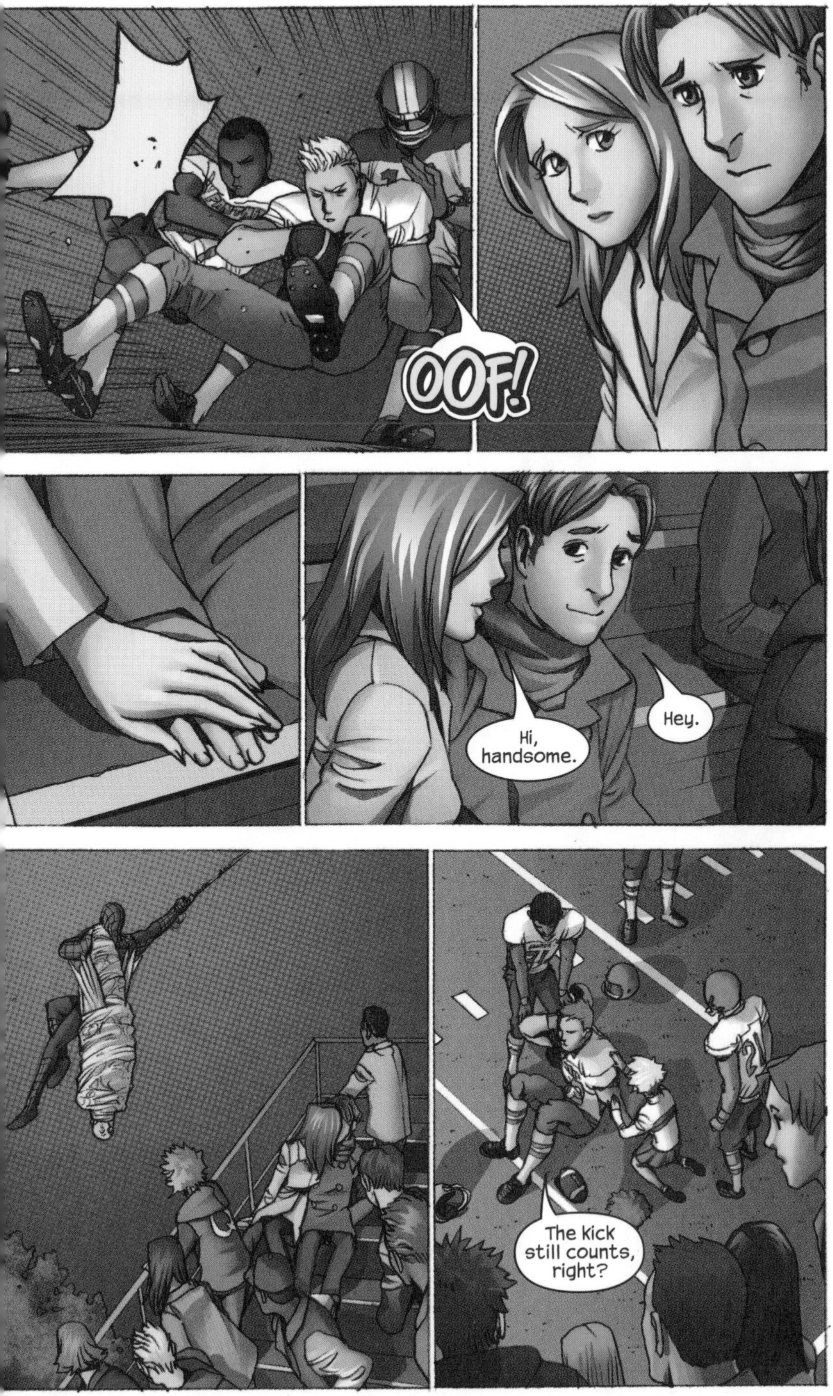
OOF!
Hi, handsome.
Hey.
The kick still counts, right?

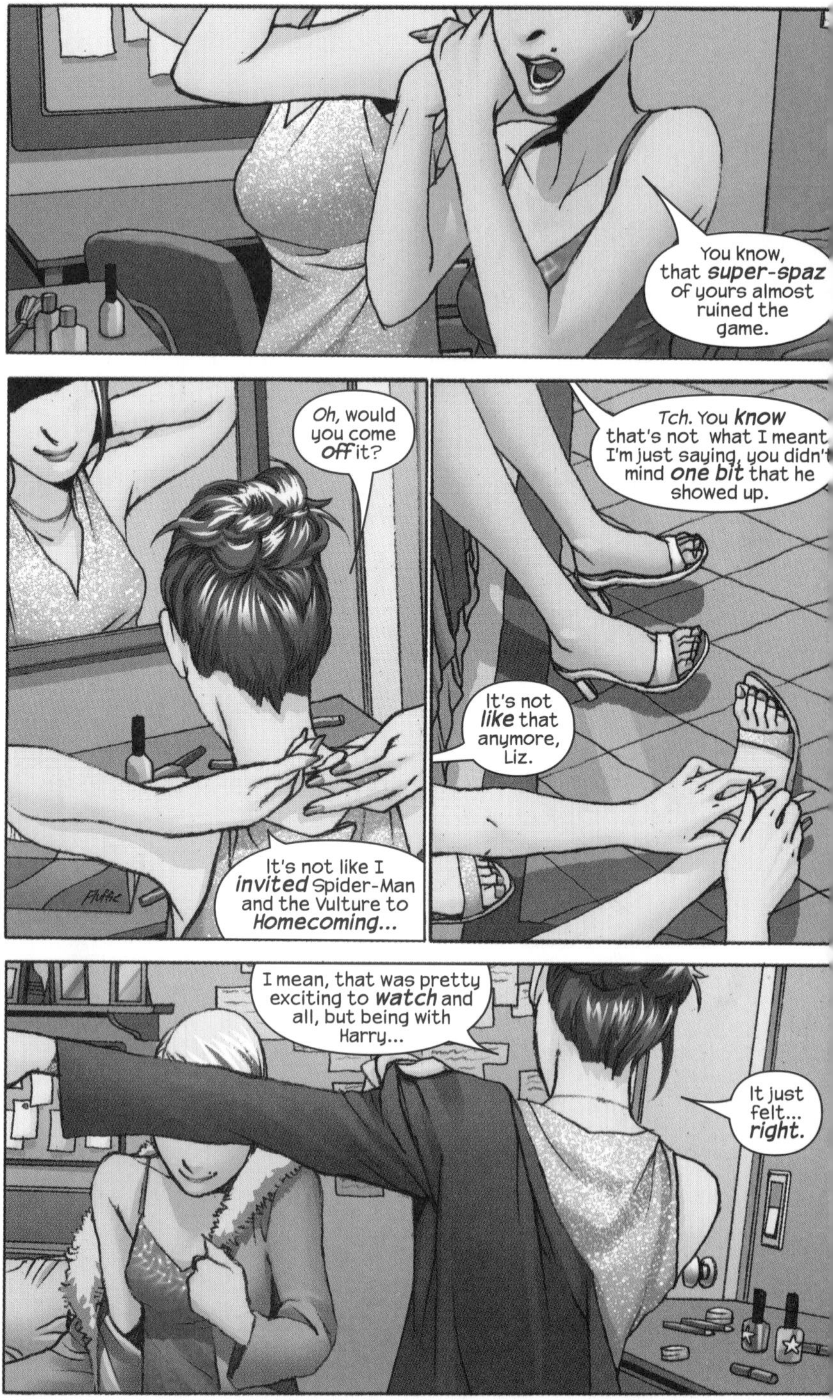

You know, that *super-spaz* of yours almost ruined the game.
Oh, would you come *off* it?
Tch. You **know** that's not what I meant. I'm just saying, you didn't mind ***one bit*** that he showed up.
It's not ***like*** that anymore, Liz.
It's not like I ***invited*** Spider-Man and the Vulture to ***Homecoming...***
I mean, that was pretty exciting to ***watch*** and all, but being with Harry...
It just felt... ***right.***

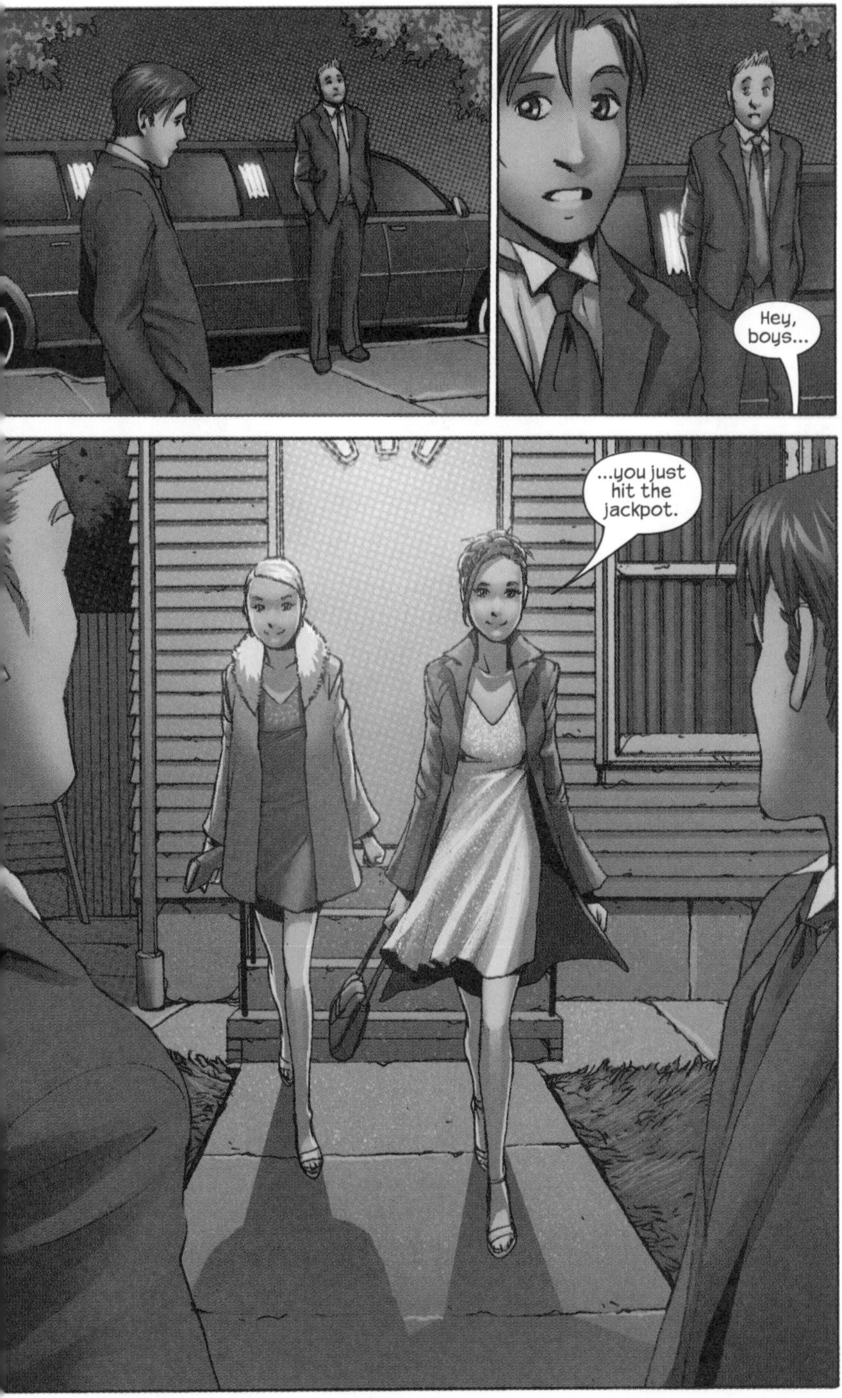
Hey, boys...
...you just hit the jackpot.

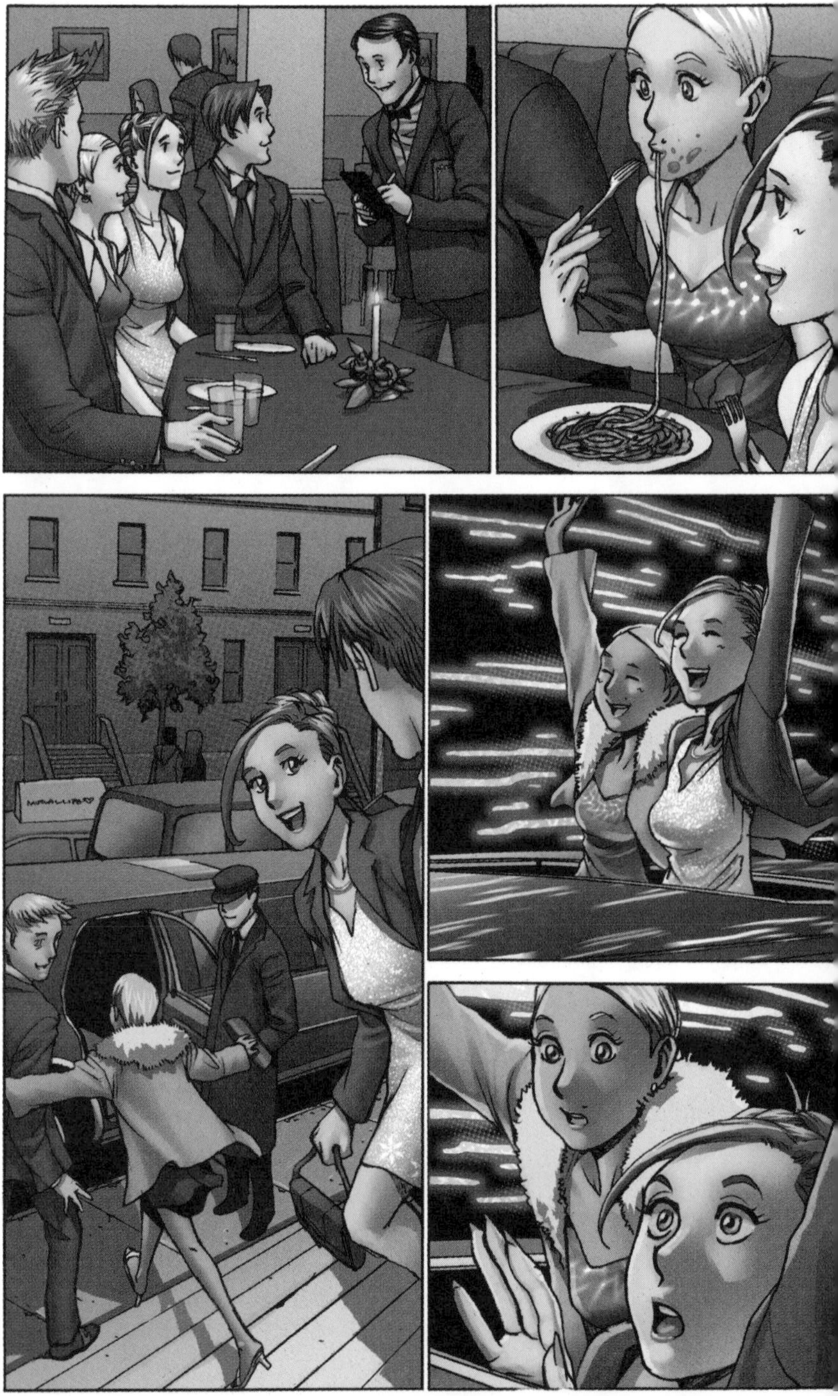

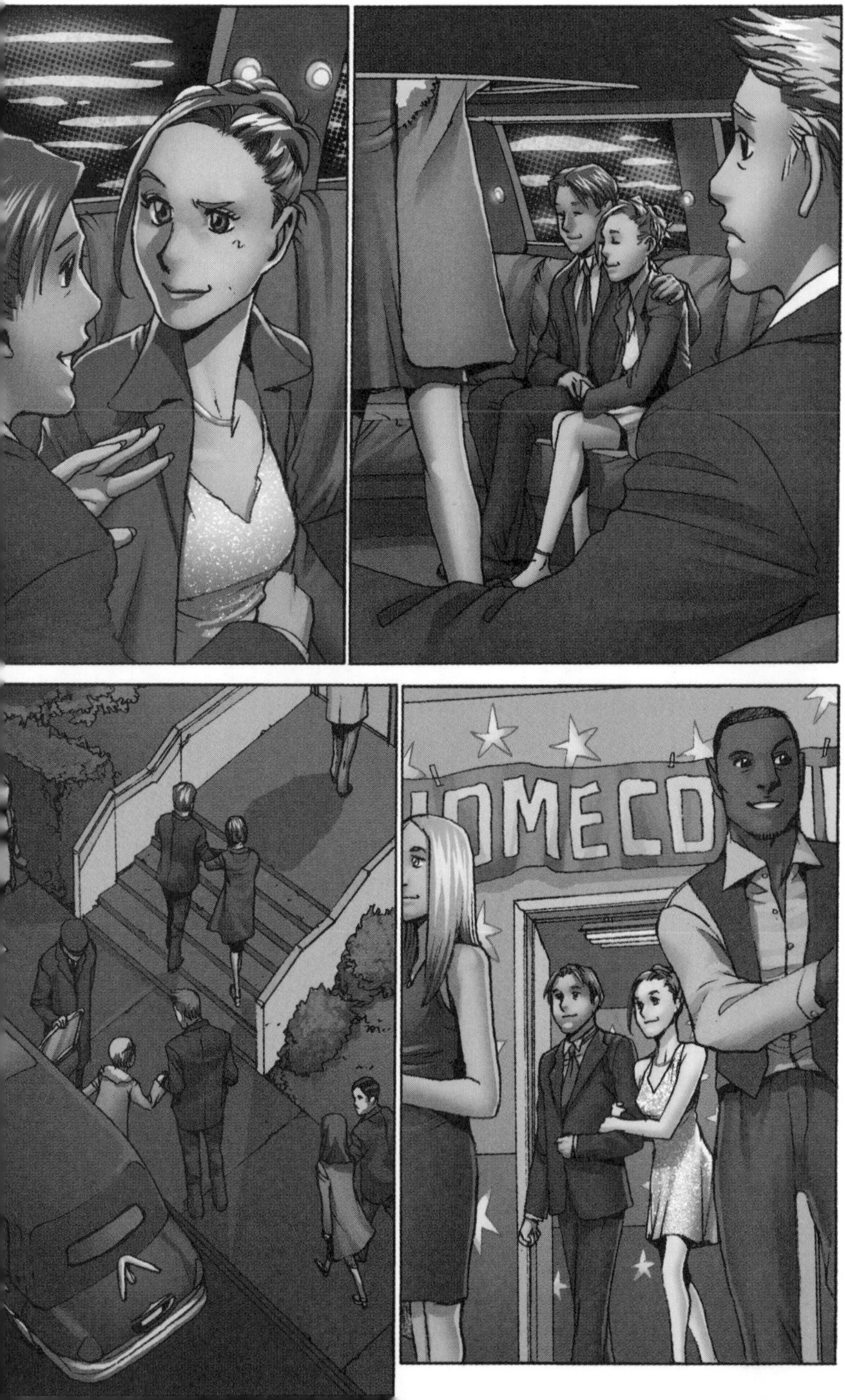

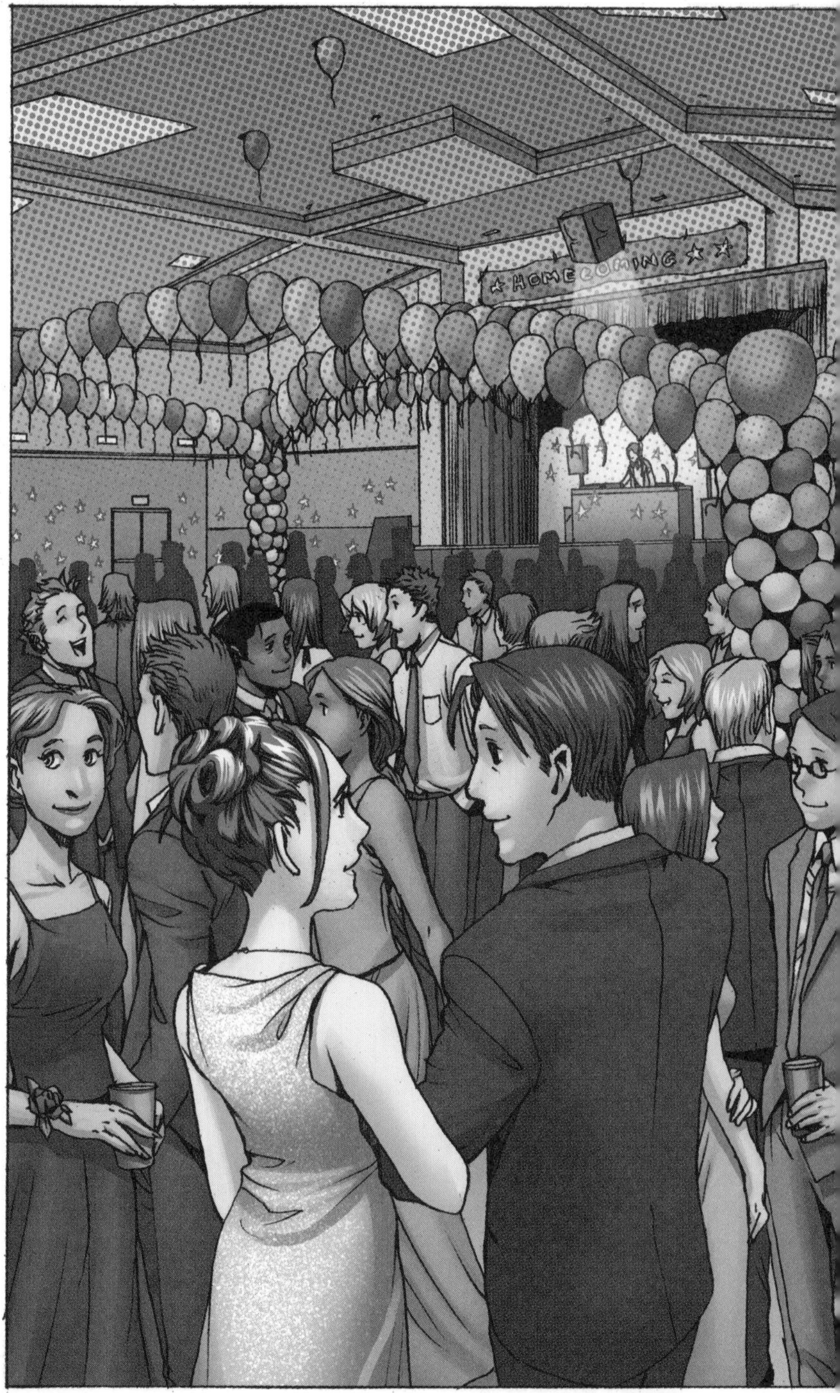

HOMECOMING

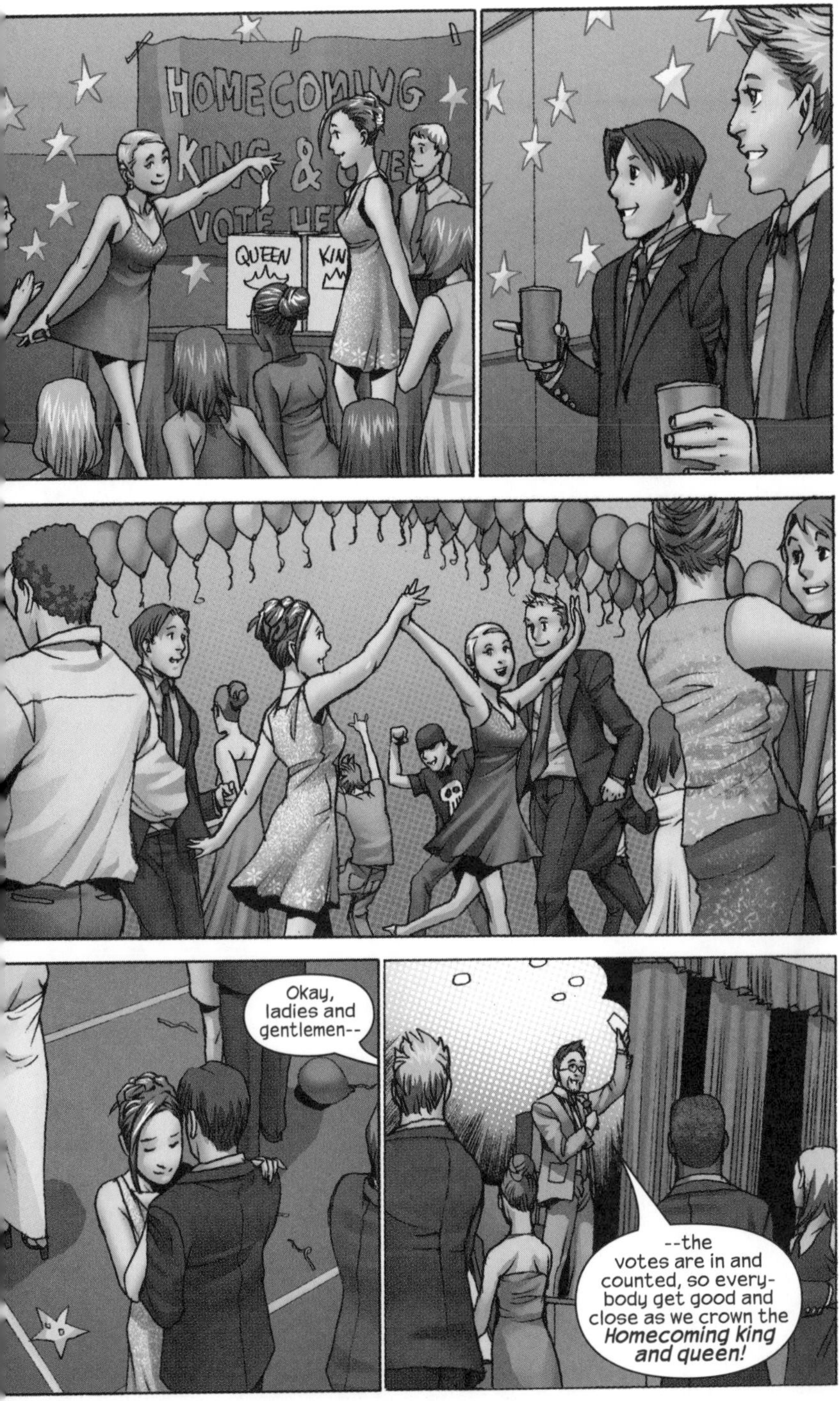
HOMECOMING
KING & QUEEN
VOTE HERE
QUEEN
KING
Okay, ladies and gentlemen--
--the votes are in and counted, so every-body get good and close as we crown the *Homecoming king and queen!*

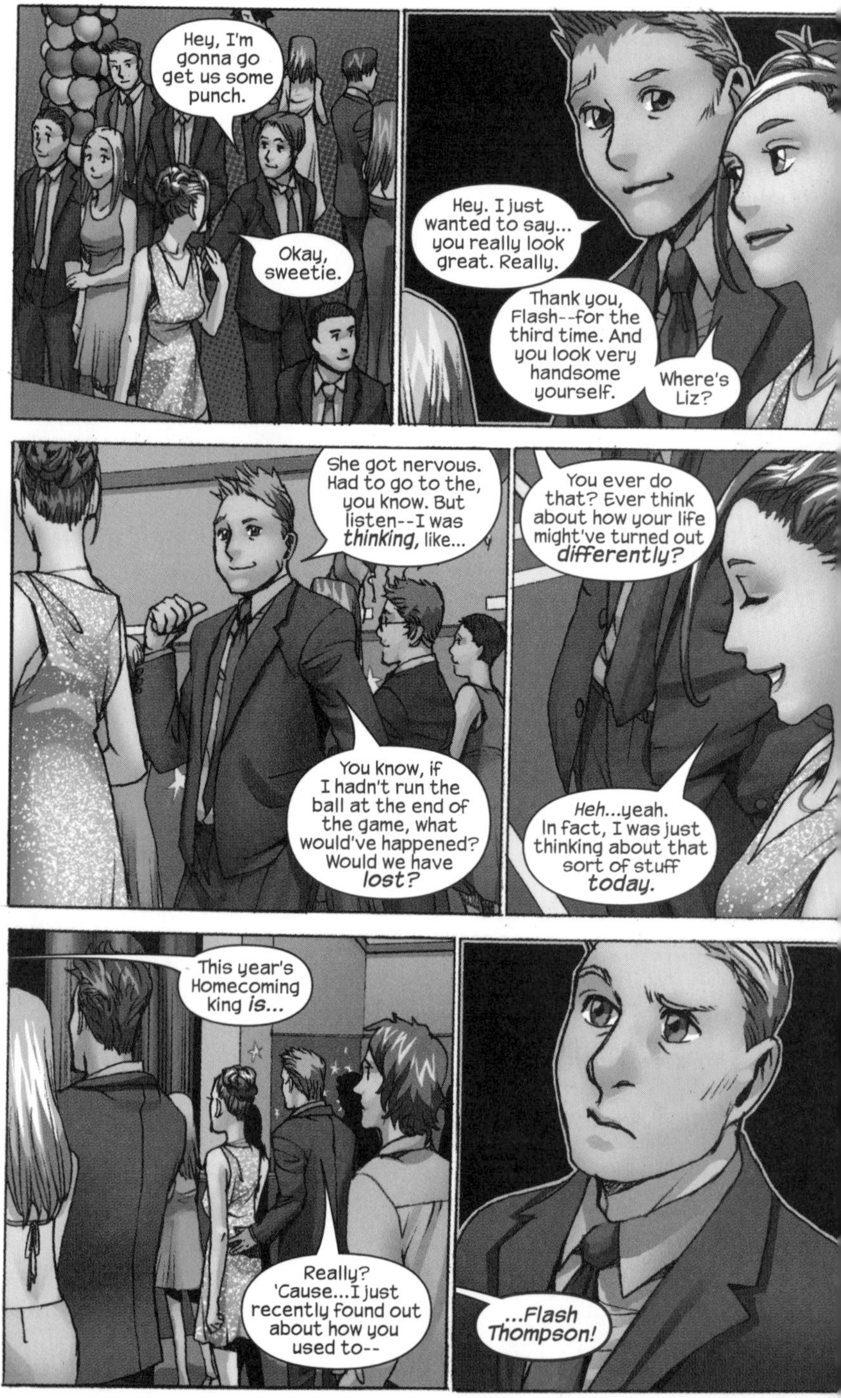
Hey, I'm gonna go get us some punch.
Okay, sweetie.
Hey. I just wanted to say... you really look great. Really.
Thank you, Flash--for the third time. And you look very handsome yourself.
Where's Liz?
She got nervous. Had to go to the, you know. But listen--I was thinking, like...
You know, if I hadn't run the ball at the end of the game, what would've happened? Would we have lost?
You ever do that? Ever think about how your life might've turned out differently?
Heh...yeah. In fact, I was just thinking about that sort of stuff today.
This year's Homecoming king is...
Really? 'Cause...I just recently found out about how you used to--
...Flash Thompson!

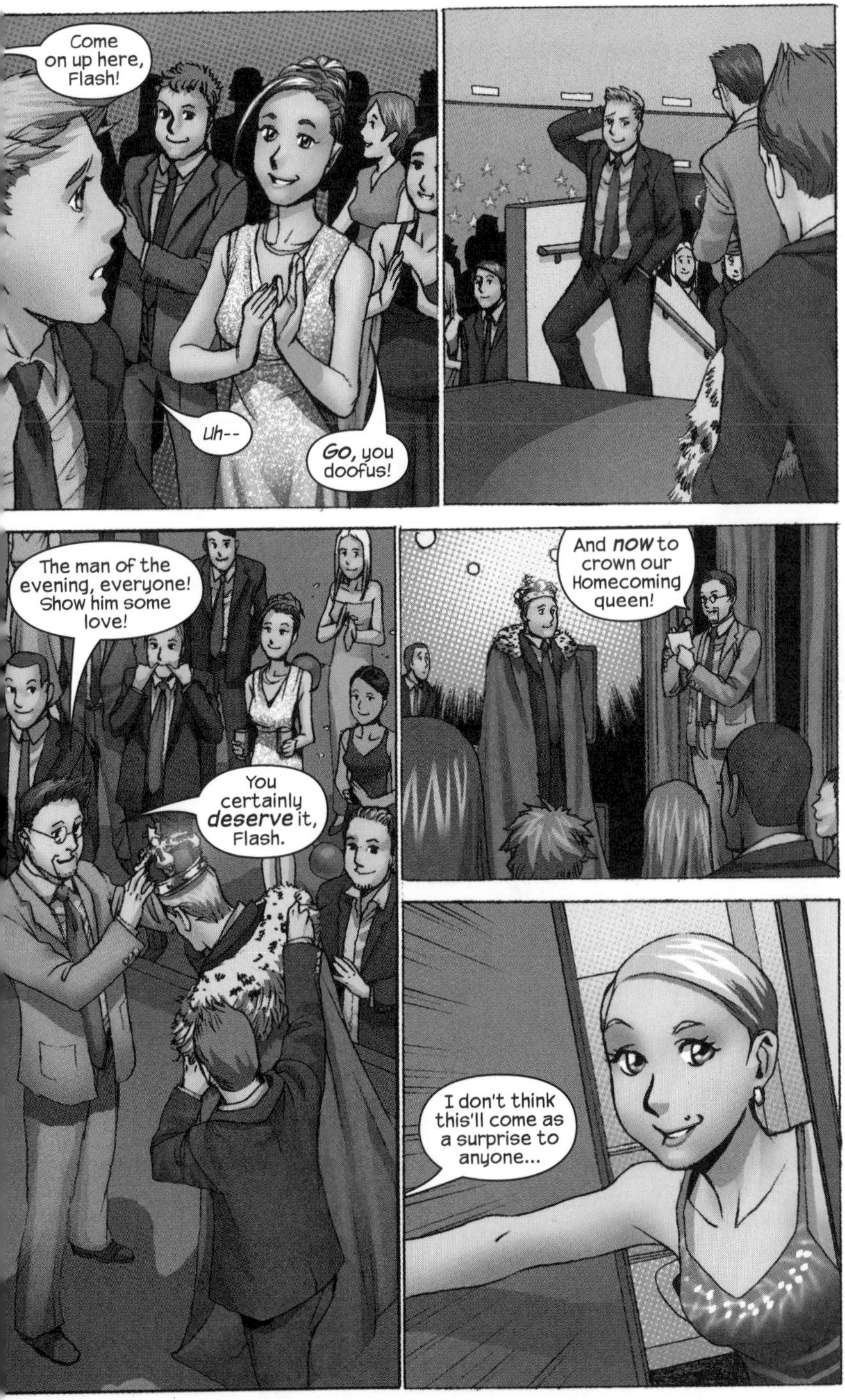
Come on up here, Flash!
Uh--
Go, you doofus!
The man of the evening, everyone! Show him some love!
You certainly deserve it, Flash.
And now to crown our Homecoming queen!
I don't think this'll come as a surprise to anyone...

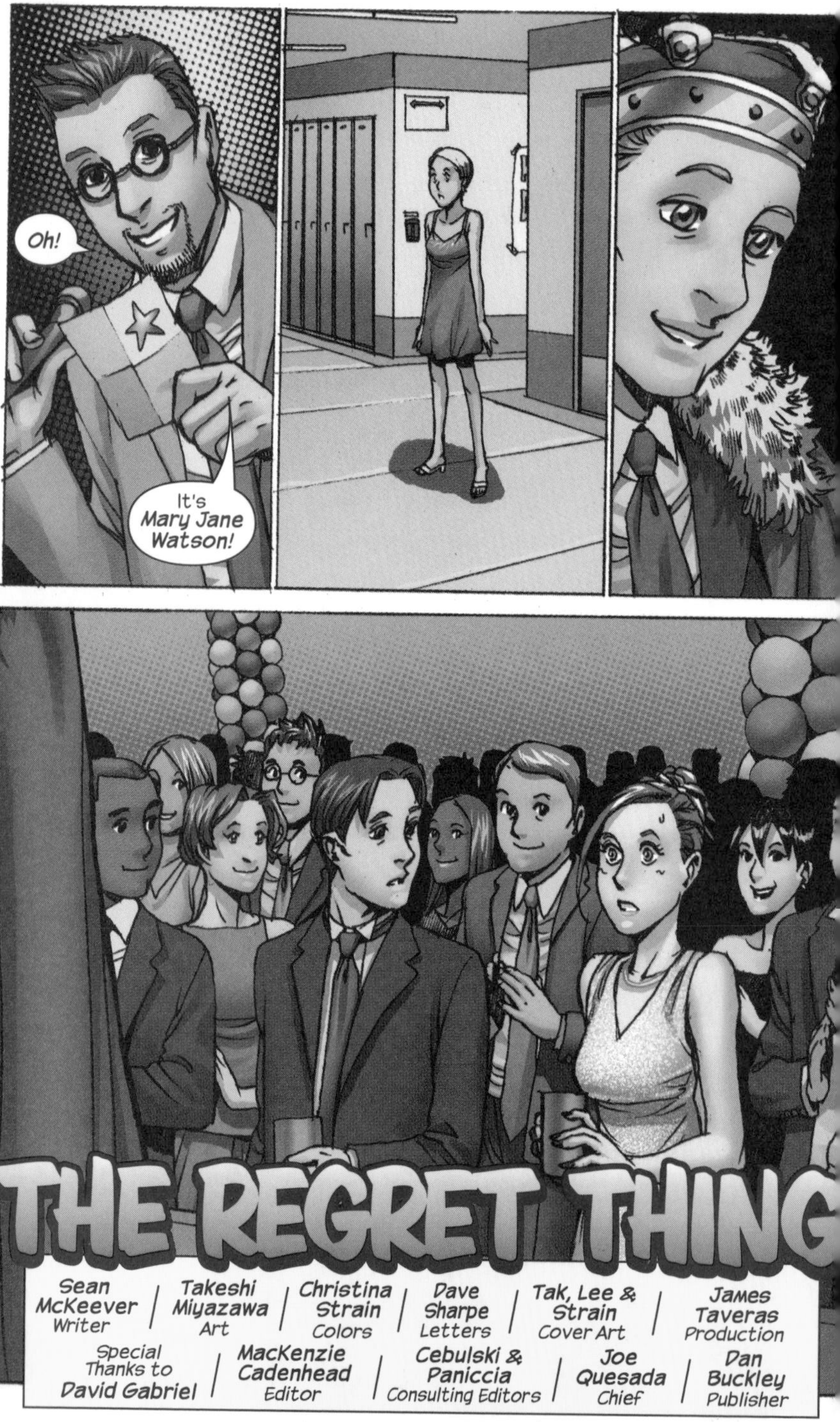

Oh!
It's Mary Jane Watson!
THE REGRET THING
Sean McKeever Writer
Takeshi Miyazawa Art
Christina Strain Colors
Dave Sharpe Letters
Tak, Lee & Strain Cover Art
James Taveras Production
Special Thanks to David Gabriel
MacKenzie Cadenhead Editor
Cebulski & Paniccia Consulting Editors
Joe Quesada Chief
Dan Buckley Publisher

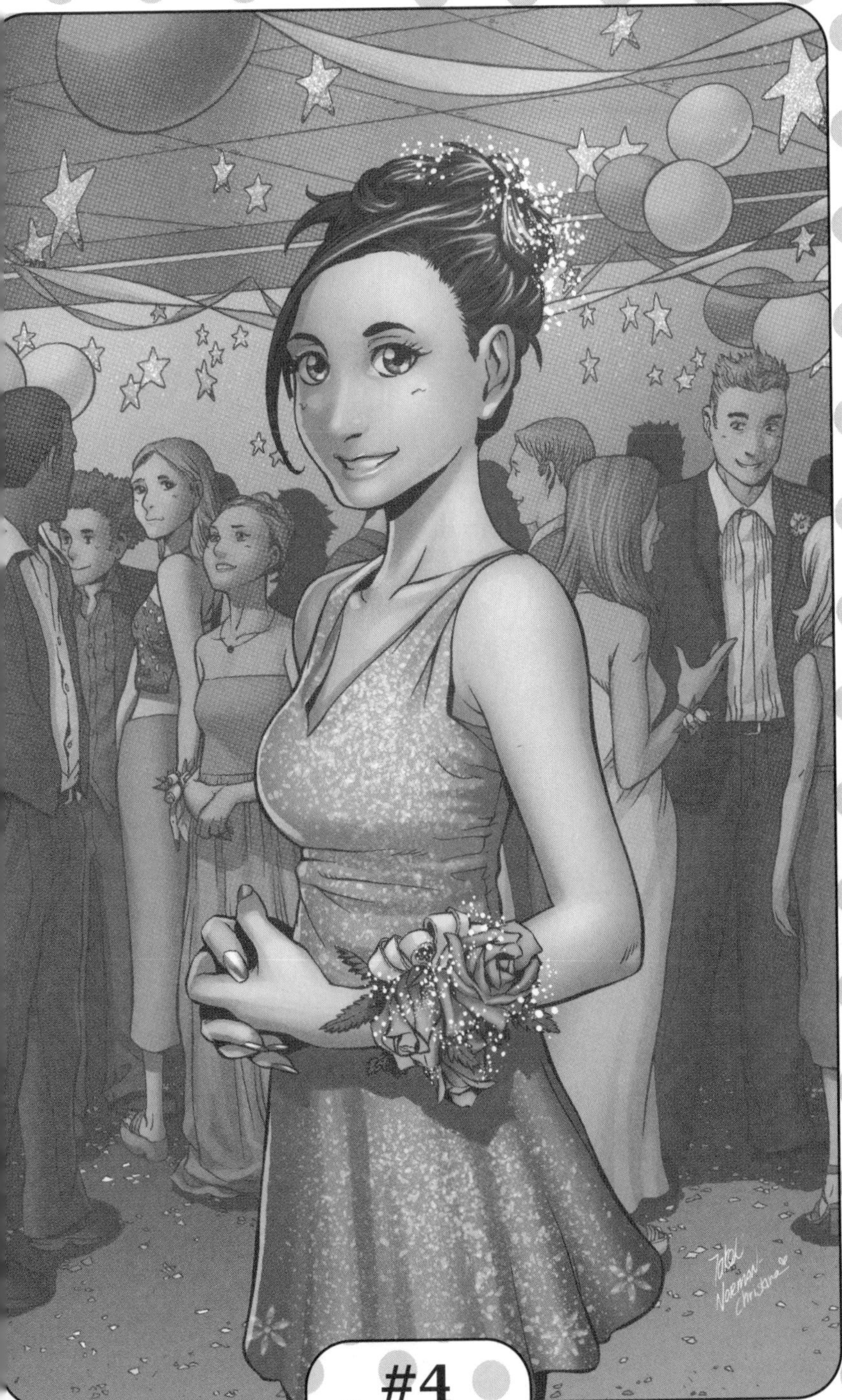

#4

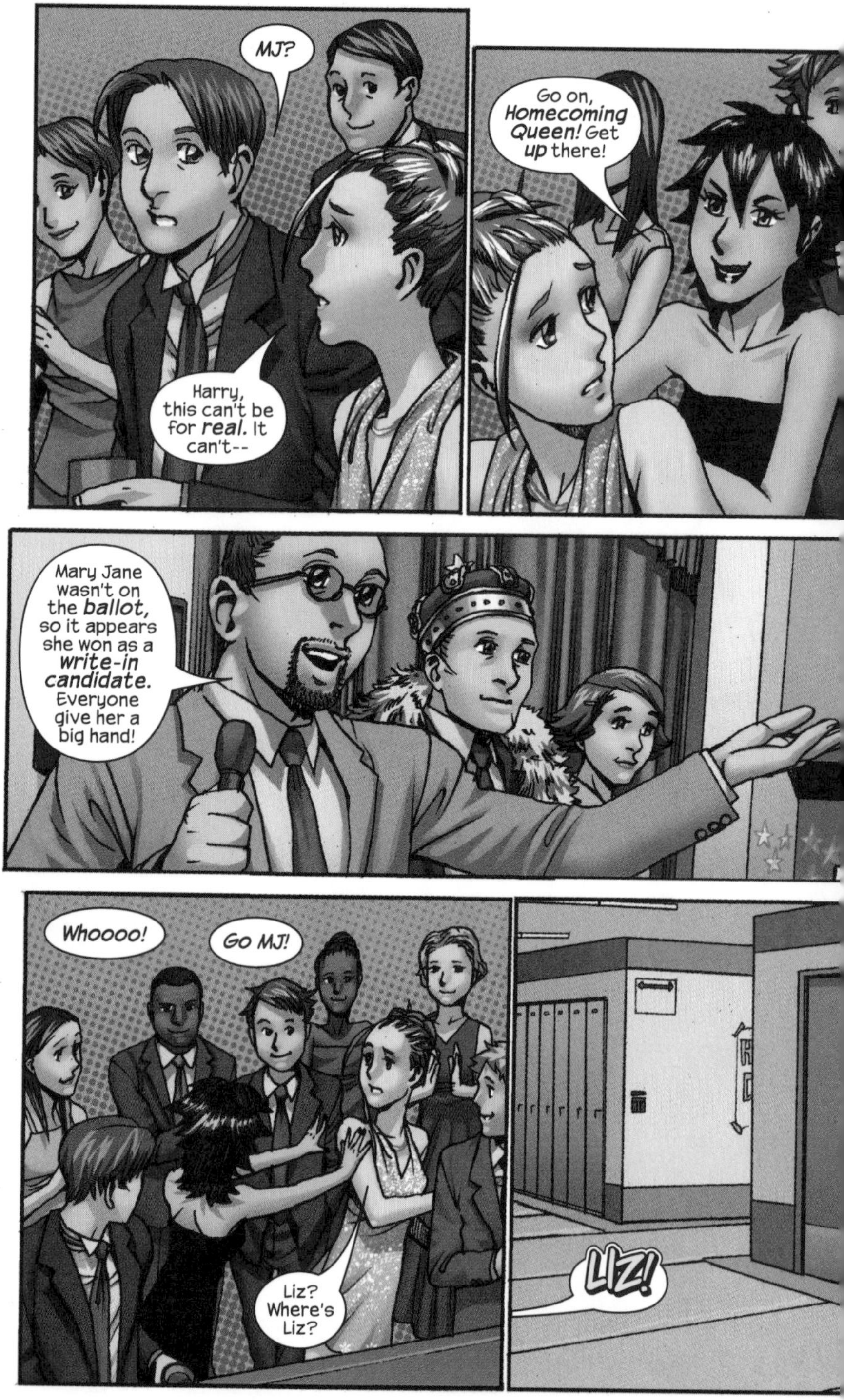
MJ?
Harry, this can't be for real. It can't--
Go on, Homecoming Queen! Get up there!
Mary Jane wasn't on the ballot, so it appears she won as a write-in candidate. Everyone give her a big hand!
Whoooo!
Go MJ!
Liz? Where's Liz?
LIZ!

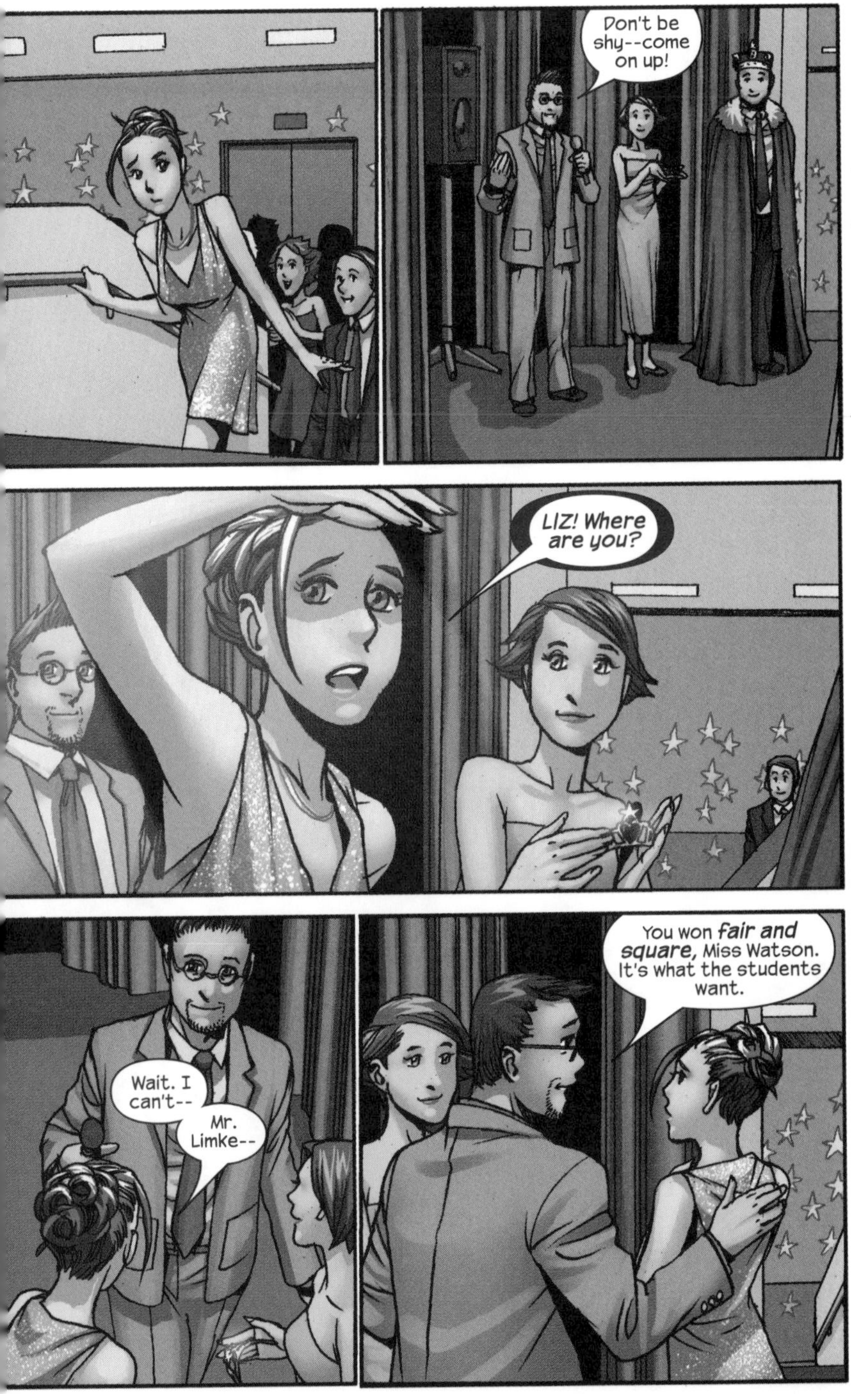
Don't be shy--come on up!
LIZ! Where are you?
Wait. I can't--
Mr. Limke--
You won fair and square, Miss Watson. It's what the students want.

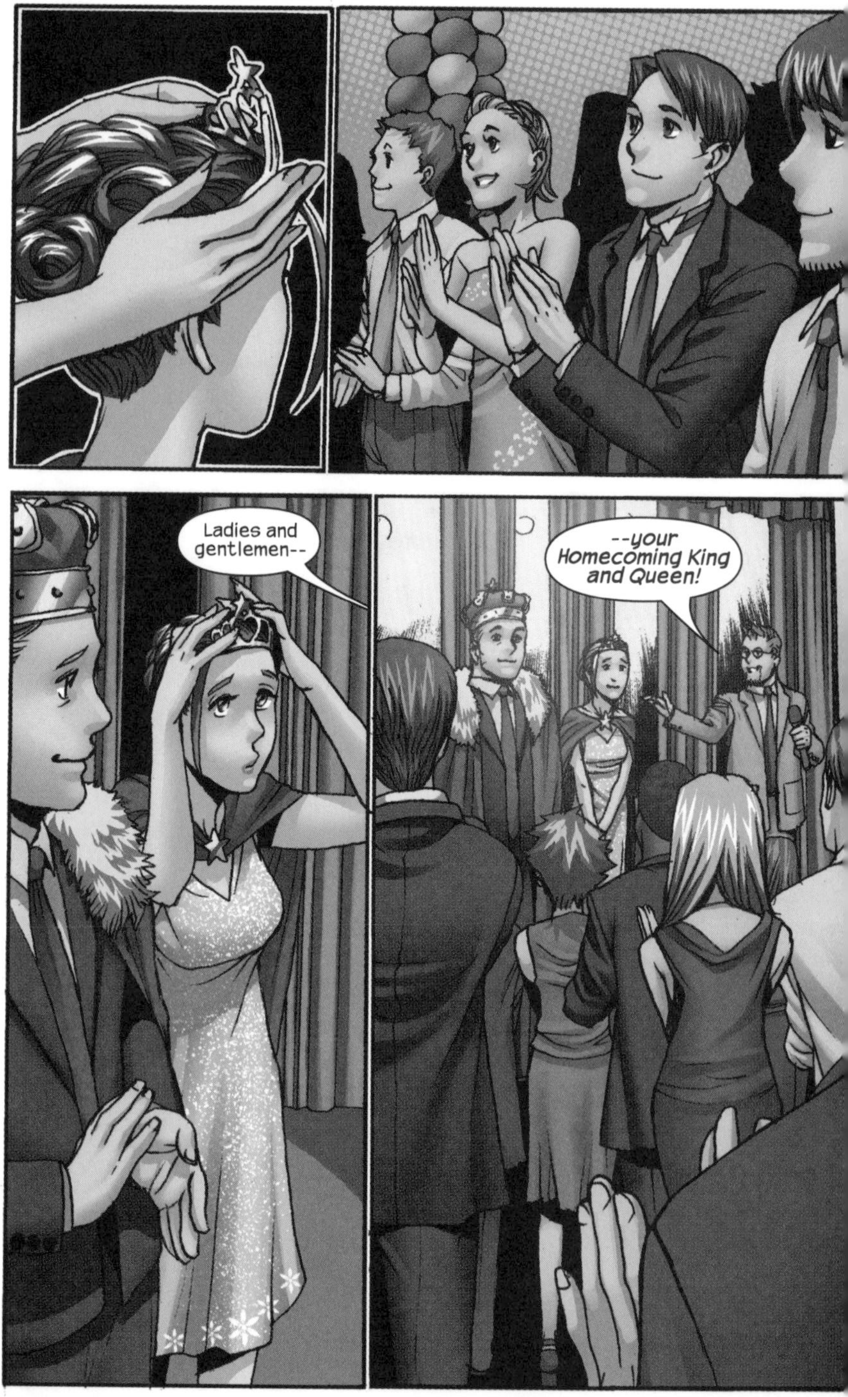
Ladies and gentlemen--
--your Homecoming King and Queen!

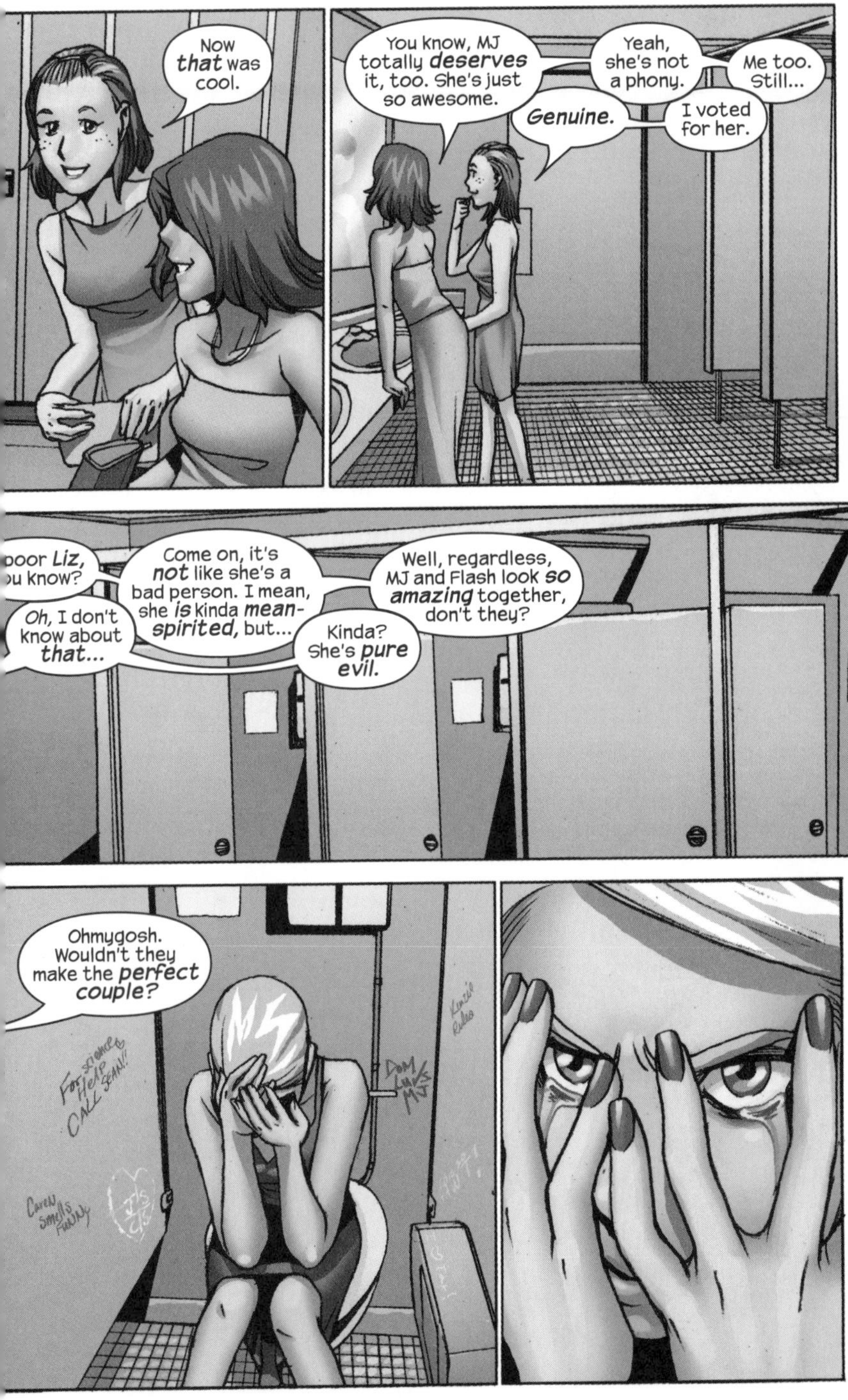
Now that was cool.
You know, MJ totally deserves it, too. She's just so awesome.
Yeah, she's not a phony.
Me too. Still...
Genuine.
I voted for her.
poor Liz, u know?
Come on, it's not like she's a bad person. I mean, she is kinda mean-spirited, but...
Oh, I don't know about that...
Kinda? She's pure evil.
Well, regardless, MJ and Flash look so amazing together, don't they?
Ohmygosh. Wouldn't they make the perfect couple?

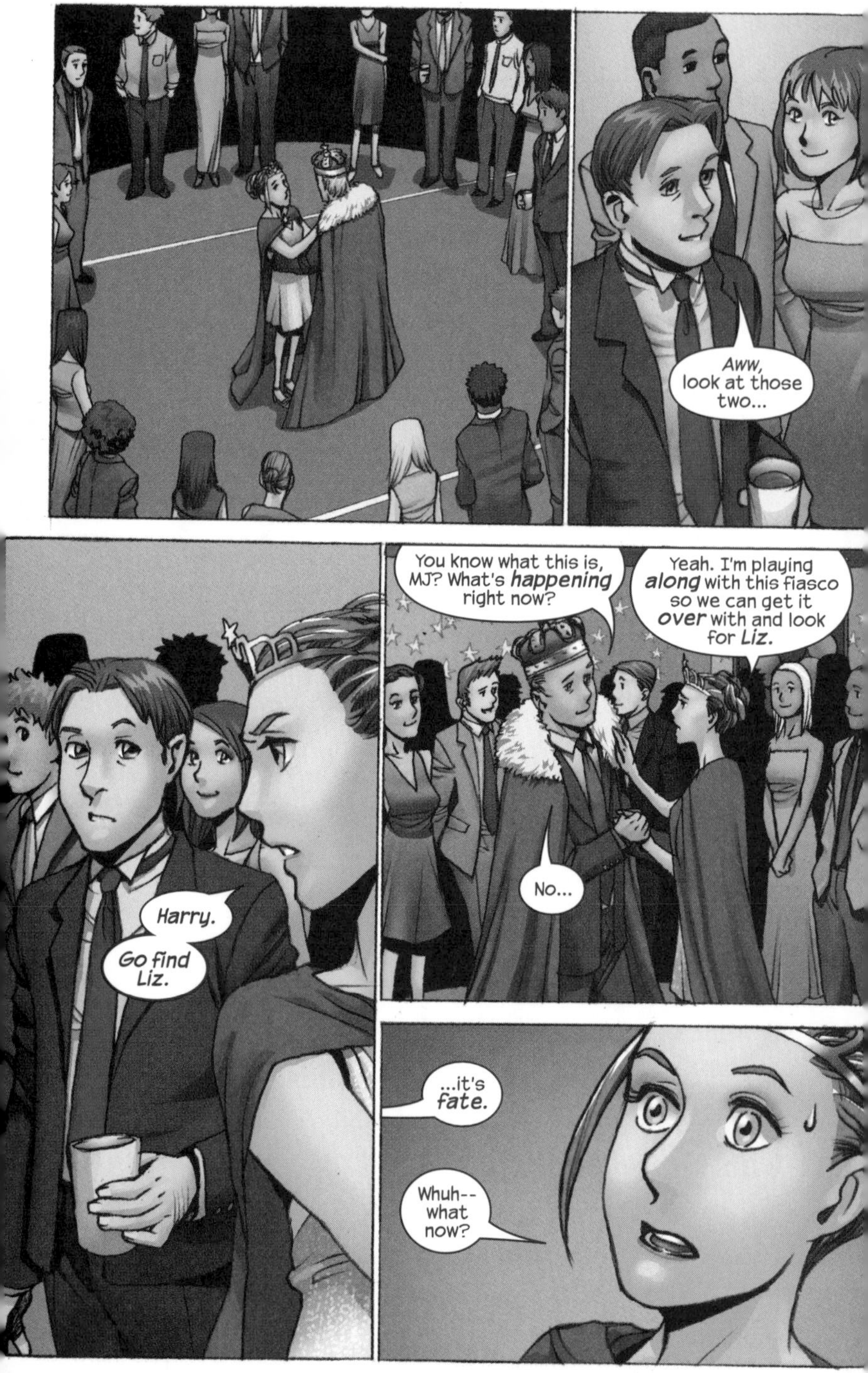
Aww, look at those two...
Harry.
Go find Liz.
You know what this is, MJ? What's happening right now?
Yeah. I'm playing along with this fiasco so we can get it over with and look for Liz.
No...
...it's fate.
Whuh-- what now?

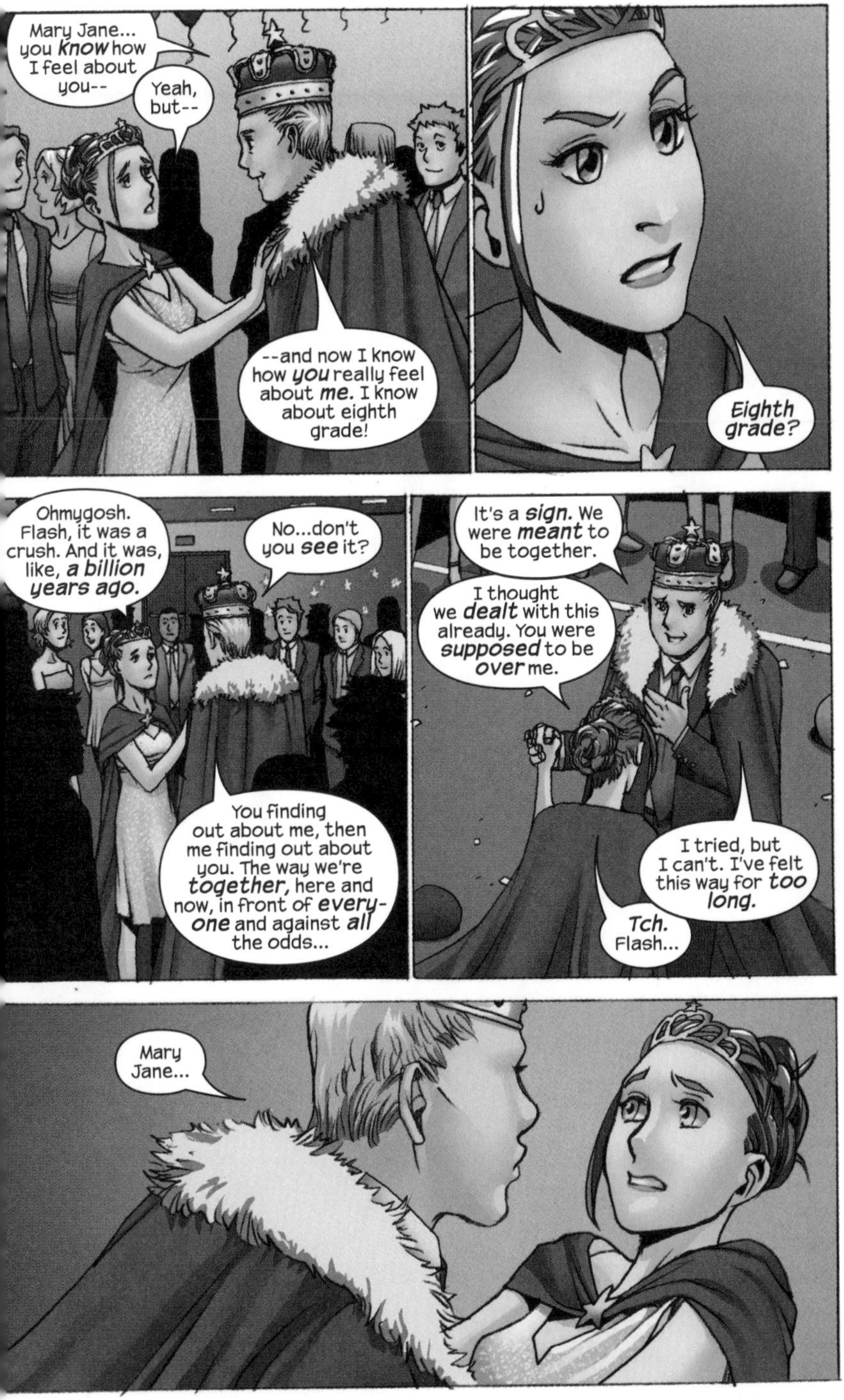
Mary Jane... you *know* how I feel about you--
Yeah, but--
--and now I know how *you* really feel about *me.* I know about eighth grade!
Eighth grade?
Ohmygosh. Flash, it was a crush. And it was, like, ***a billion years ago.***
No...don't you *see* it?
You finding out about me, then me finding out about you. The way we're *together,* here and now, in front of *every-one* and against *all* the odds...
It's a *sign.* We were *meant* to be together.
I thought we *dealt* with this already. You were *supposed* to be *over* me.
I tried, but I can't. I've felt this way for ***too long.***
Tch. Flash...
Mary Jane...

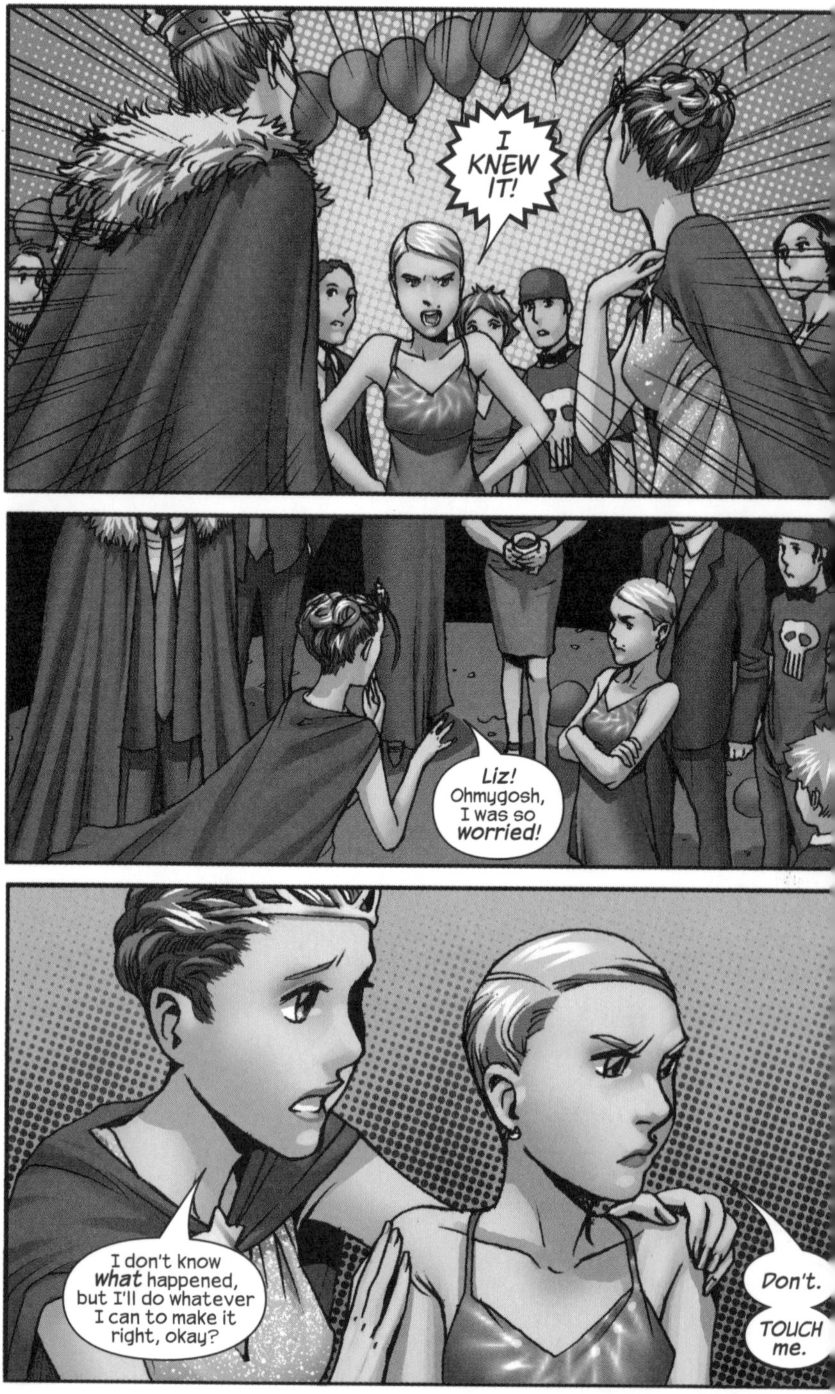

I KNEW IT!
Liz! Ohmygosh, I was so worried!
I don't know what happened, but I'll do whatever I can to make it right, okay?
Don't.
TOUCH me.

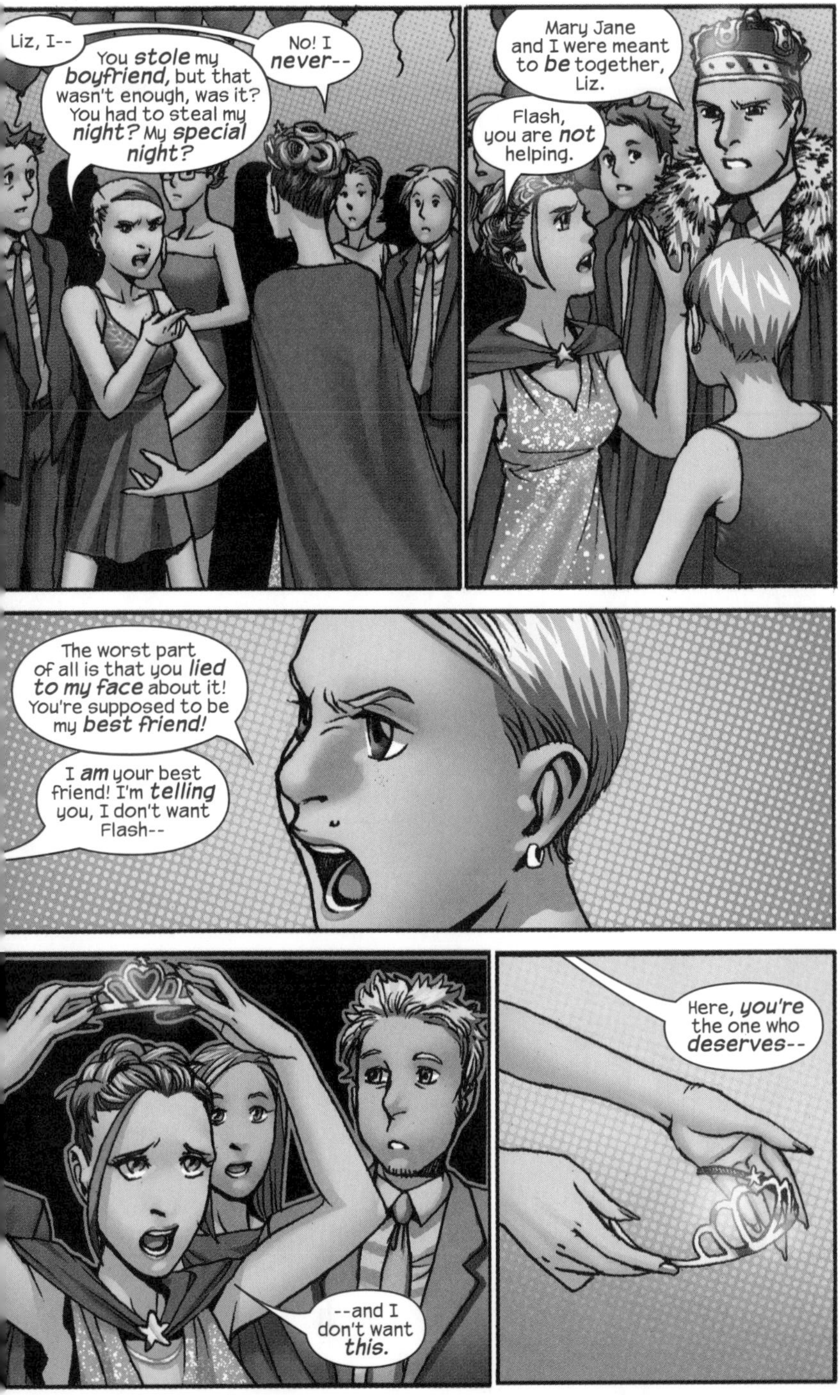
Liz, I--
You stole my boyfriend, but that wasn't enough, was it? You had to steal my night? My special night?
No! I never--
Mary Jane and I were meant to be together, Liz.
Flash, you are not helping.
The worst part of all is that you lied to my face about it! You're supposed to be my best friend!
I am your best friend! I'm telling you, I don't want Flash--
--and I don't want this.
Here, you're the one who deserves--

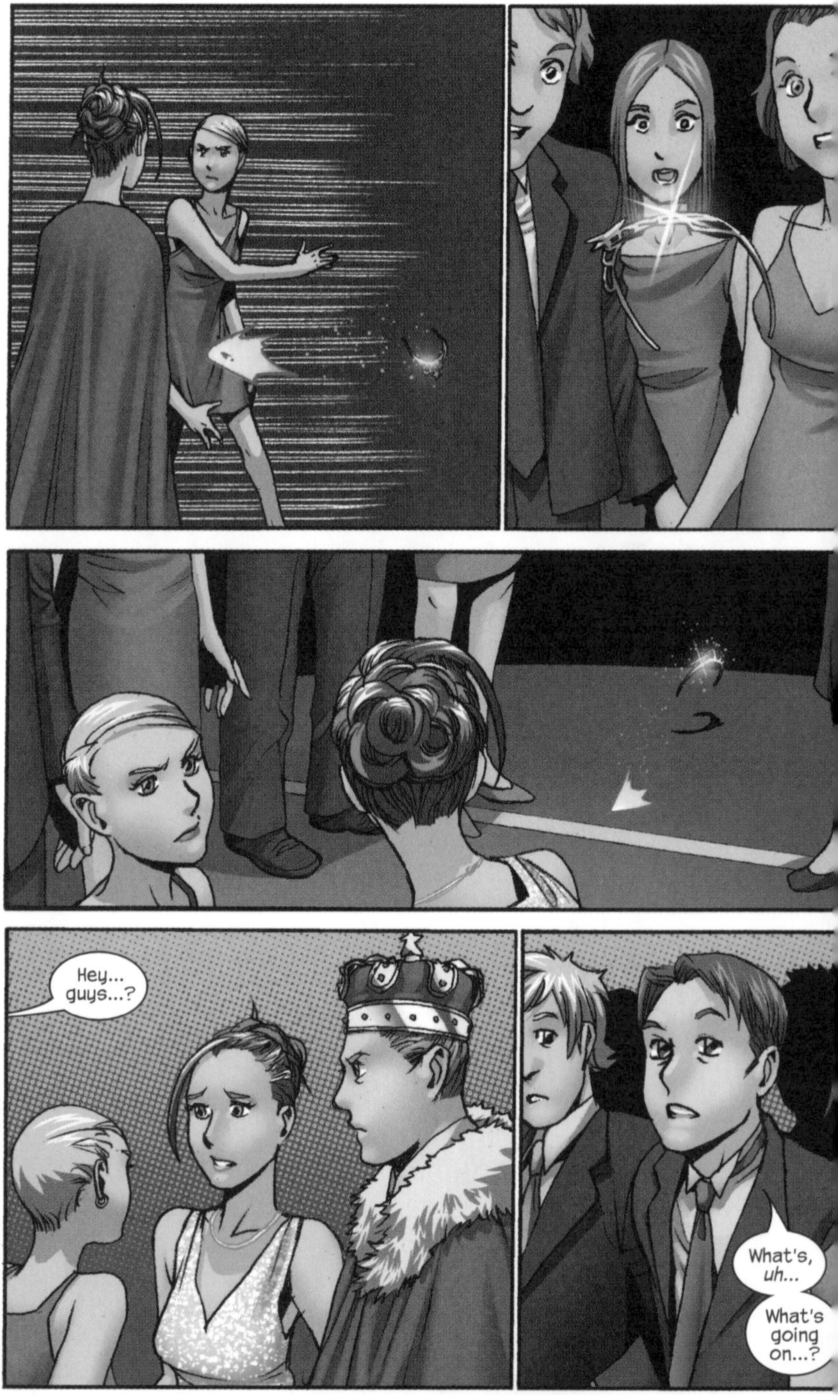
Hey... guys...?
What's, uh...
What's going on...?

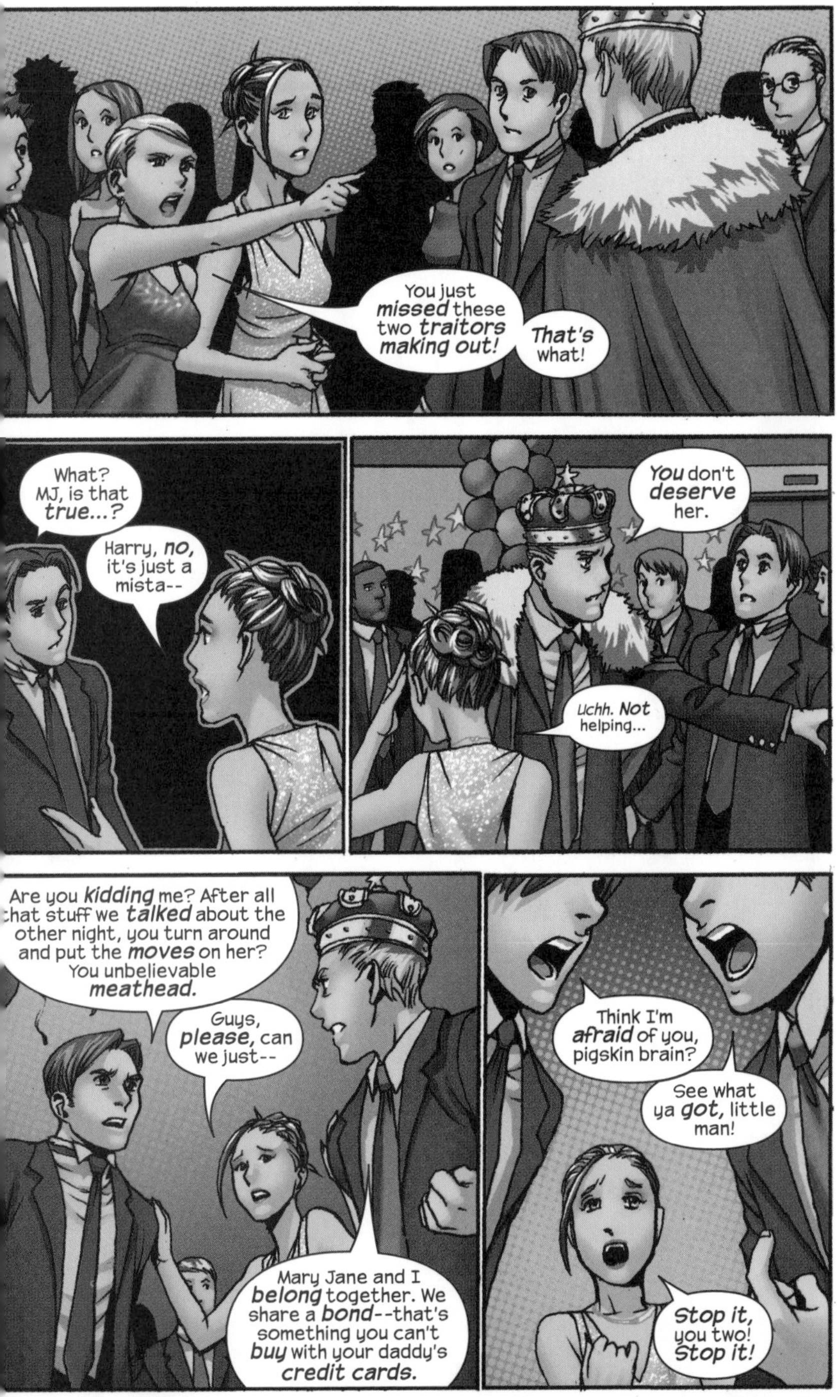
You just missed these two traitors making out!
That's what!
What? MJ, is that true...?
Harry, no, it's just a mista--
You don't deserve her.
Uchh. Not helping...
Are you kidding me? After all that stuff we talked about the other night, you turn around and put the moves on her? You unbelievable meathead.
Guys, please, can we just--
Mary Jane and I belong together. We share a bond--that's something you can't buy with your daddy's credit cards.
Think I'm afraid of you, pigskin brain?
See what ya got, little man!
Stop it, you two! Stop it!

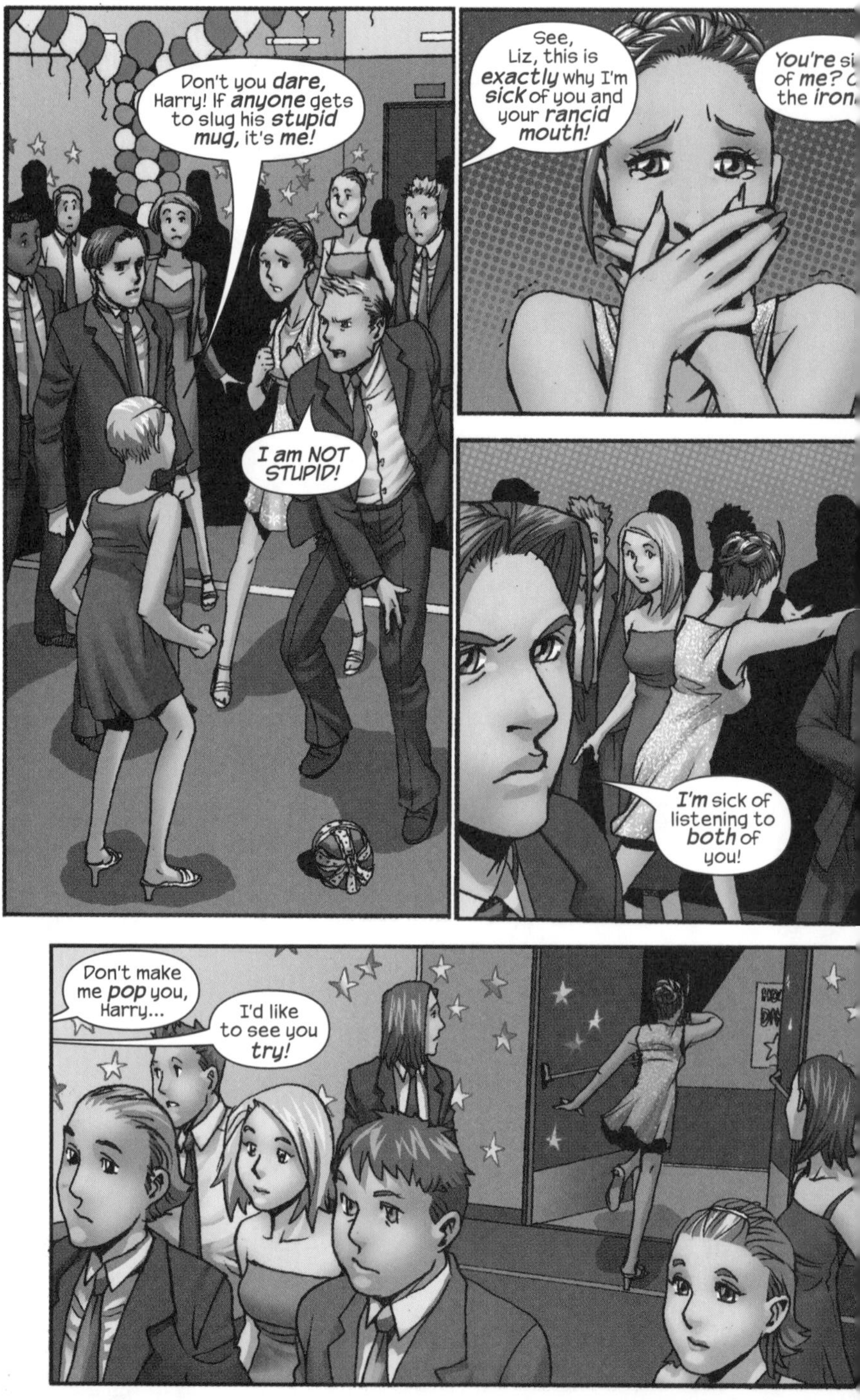

Don't you **dare,** Harry! If **anyone** gets to slug his **stupid mug,** it's **me!**
I am NOT STUPID!
See, Liz, this is **exactly** why I'm **sick** of you and your **rancid mouth!**
You're si
of *me?*
the *iron*
I'm sick of listening to ***both*** of you!
Don't make me **pop** you, Harry...
I'd like to see you *try!*

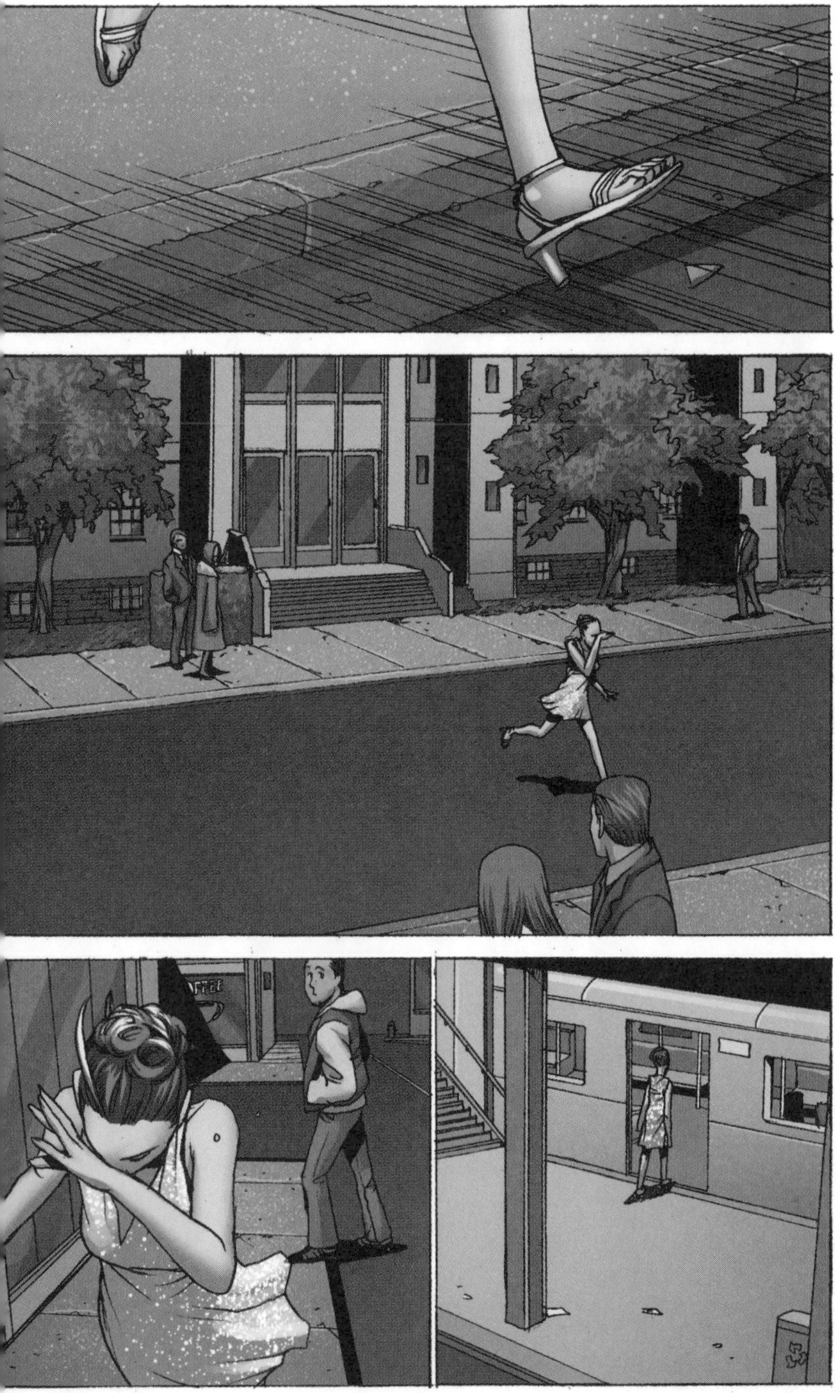

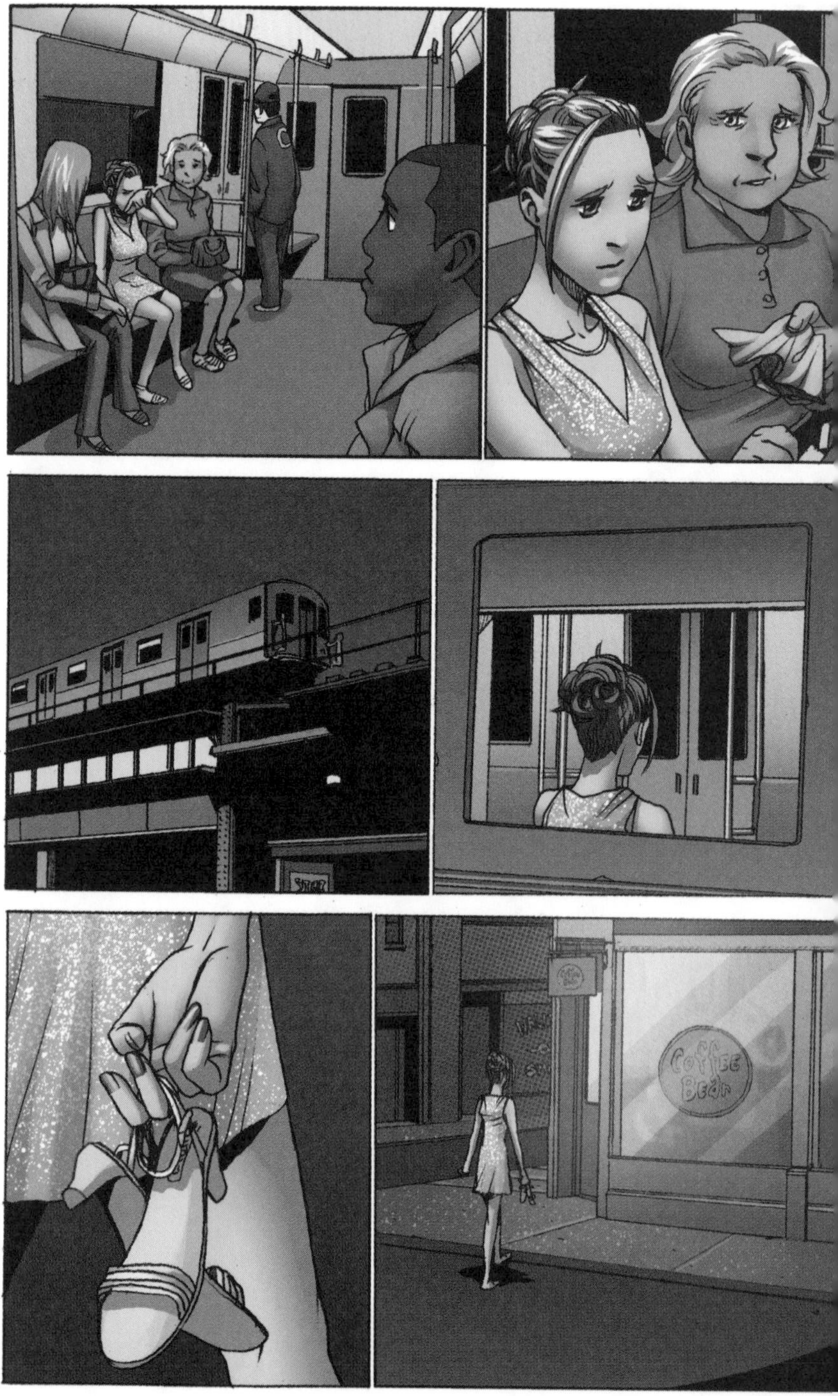
Coffee Bean

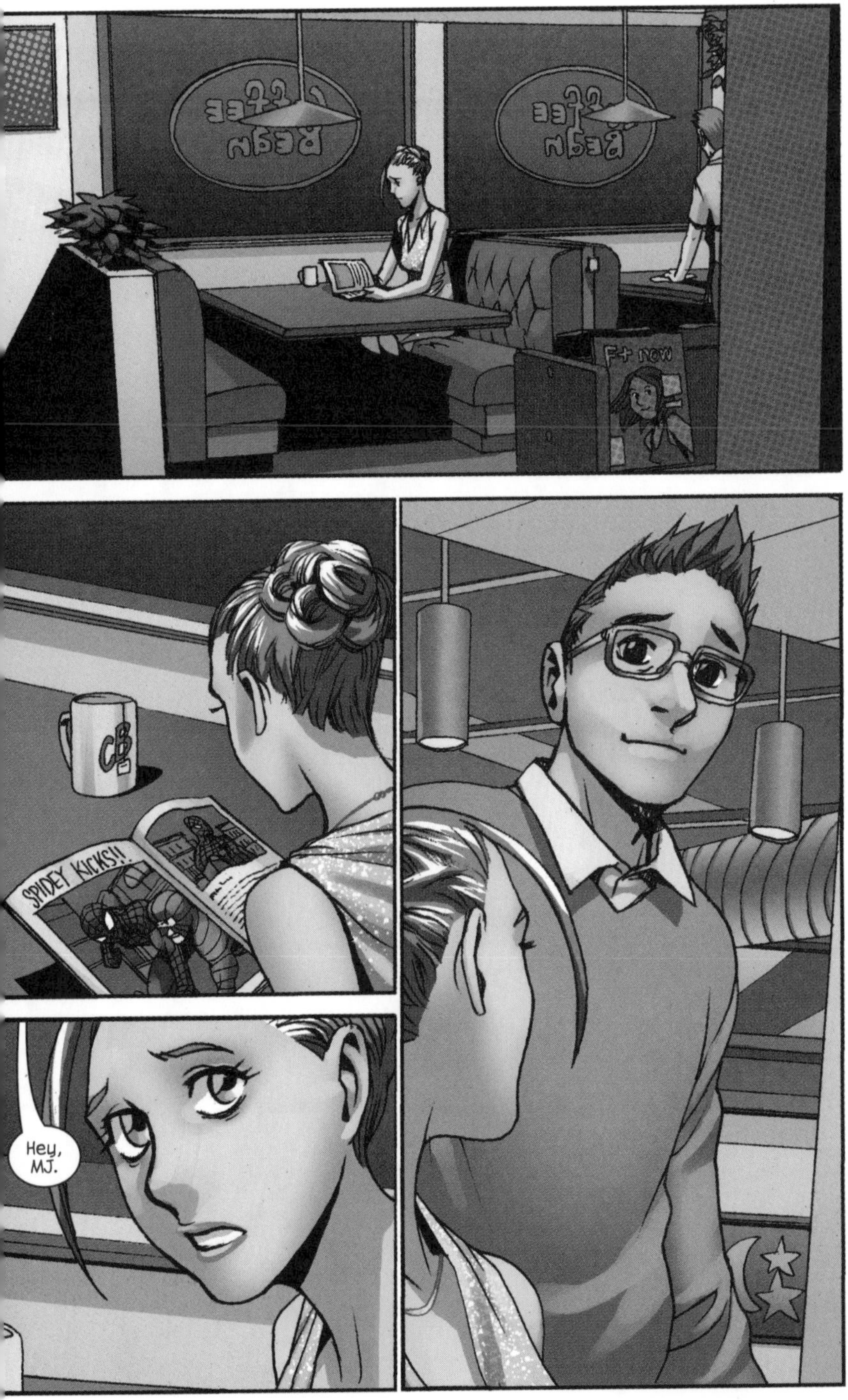

SPIDEY KICKS!!
Hey, MJ.

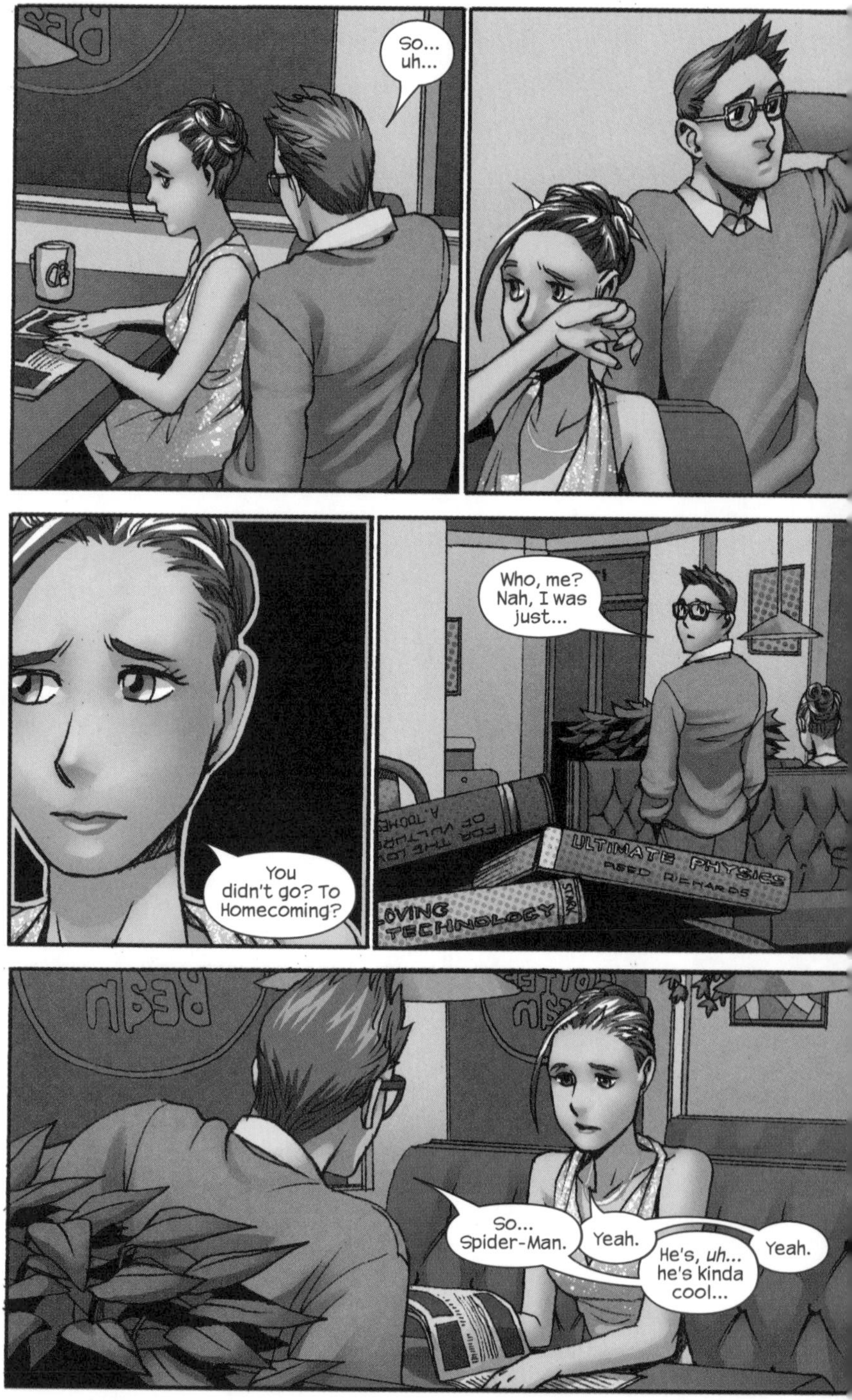
So... uh...
Who, me? Nah, I was just...
You didn't go? To Homecoming?
ULTIMATE PHYSICS
REED RICHARDS
LOVING TECHNOLOGY
STARK
So... Spider-Man.
Yeah.
He's, *uh*... he's kinda cool...
Yeah.

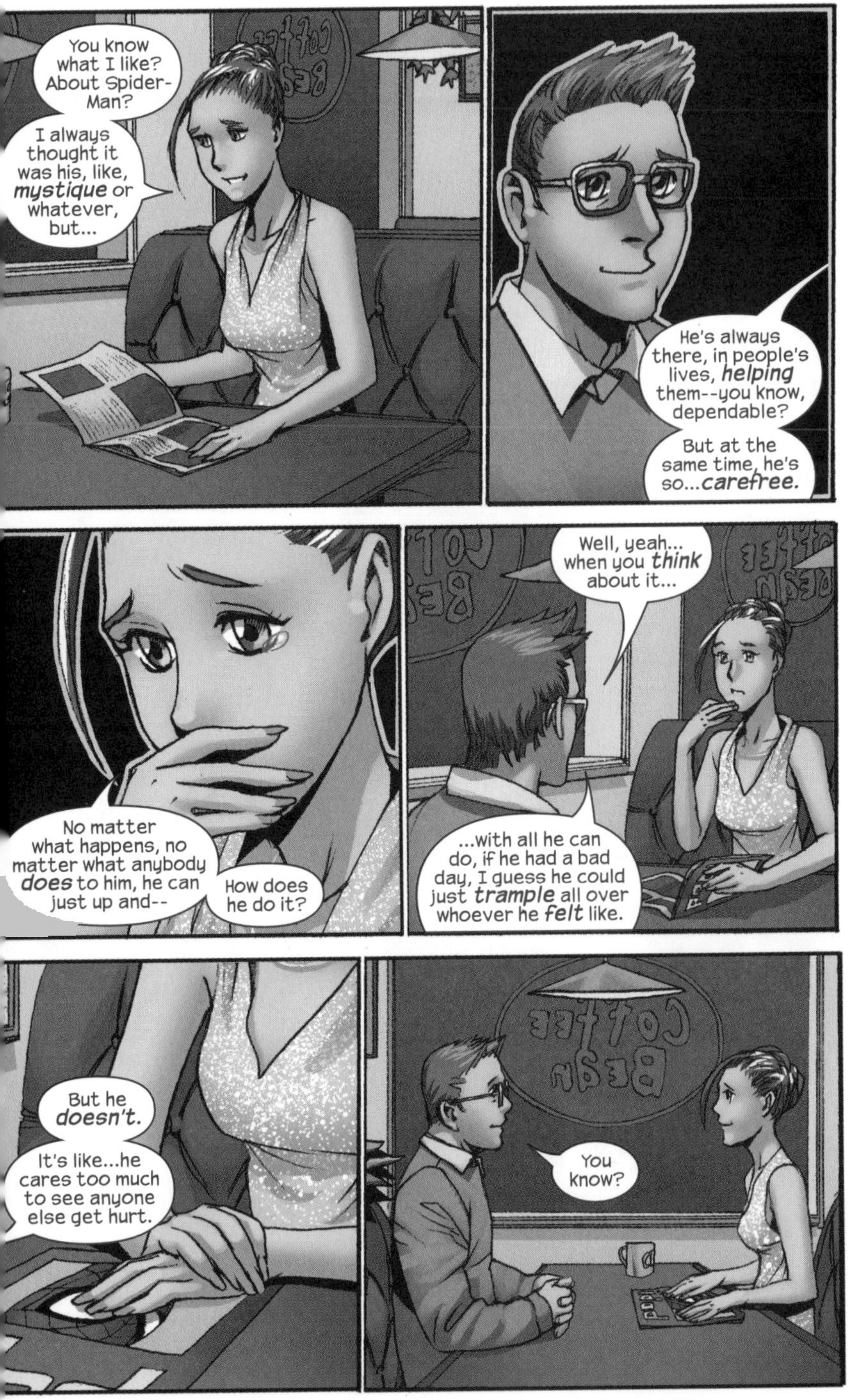
You know what I like? About Spider-Man?
I always thought it was his, like, mystique or whatever, but...
He's always there, in people's lives, helping them--you know, dependable?
But at the same time, he's so...carefree.
No matter what happens, no matter what anybody does to him, he can just up and--
How does he do it?
Well, yeah... when you think about it...
...with all he can do, if he had a bad day, I guess he could just trample all over whoever he felt like.
But he doesn't.
It's like...he cares too much to see anyone else get hurt.
You know?

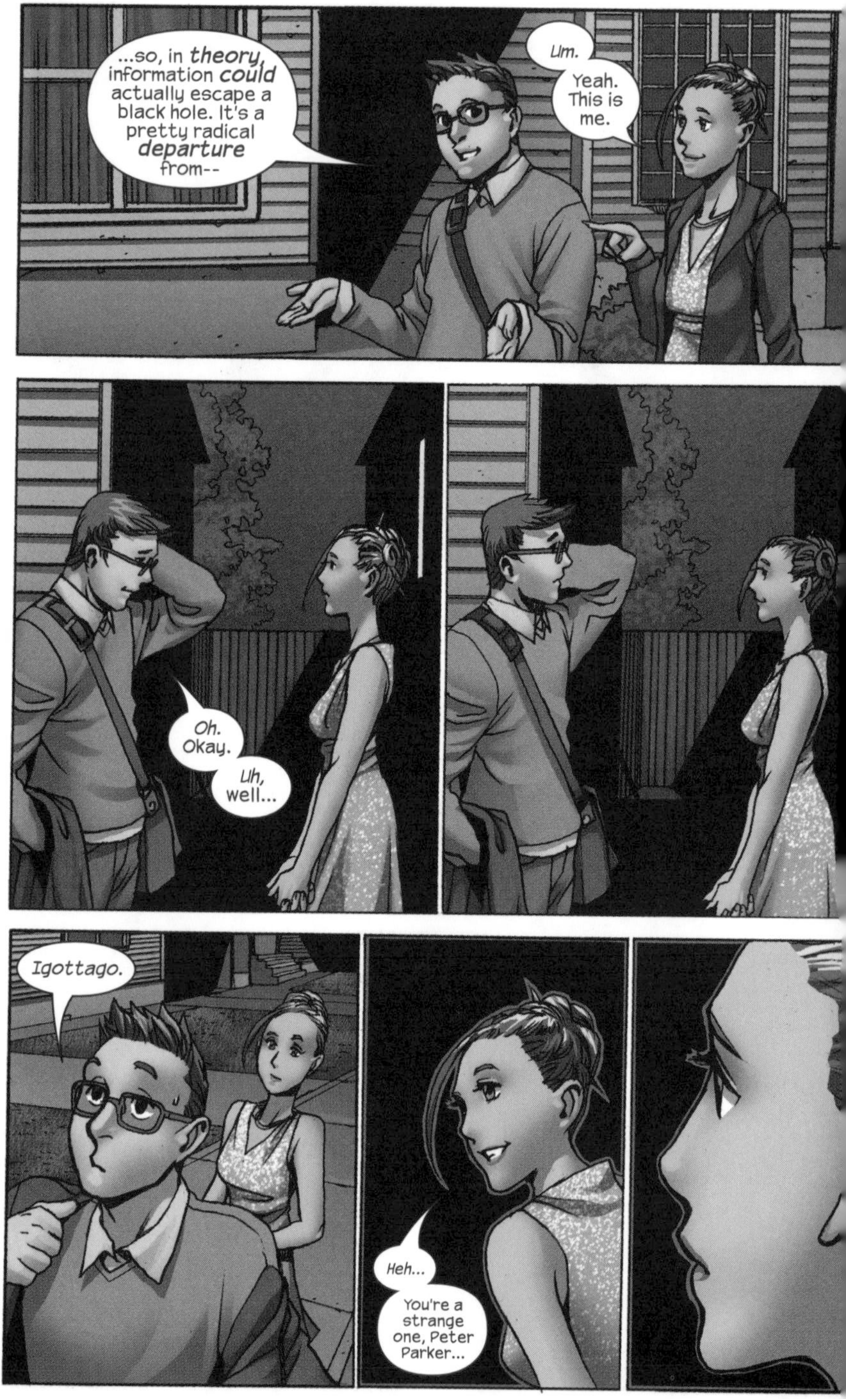
...so, in theory, information could actually escape a black hole. It's a pretty radical departure from--
Um.
Yeah. This is me.
Oh. Okay.
Uh, well...
Igottago.
Heh...
You're a strange one, Peter Parker...

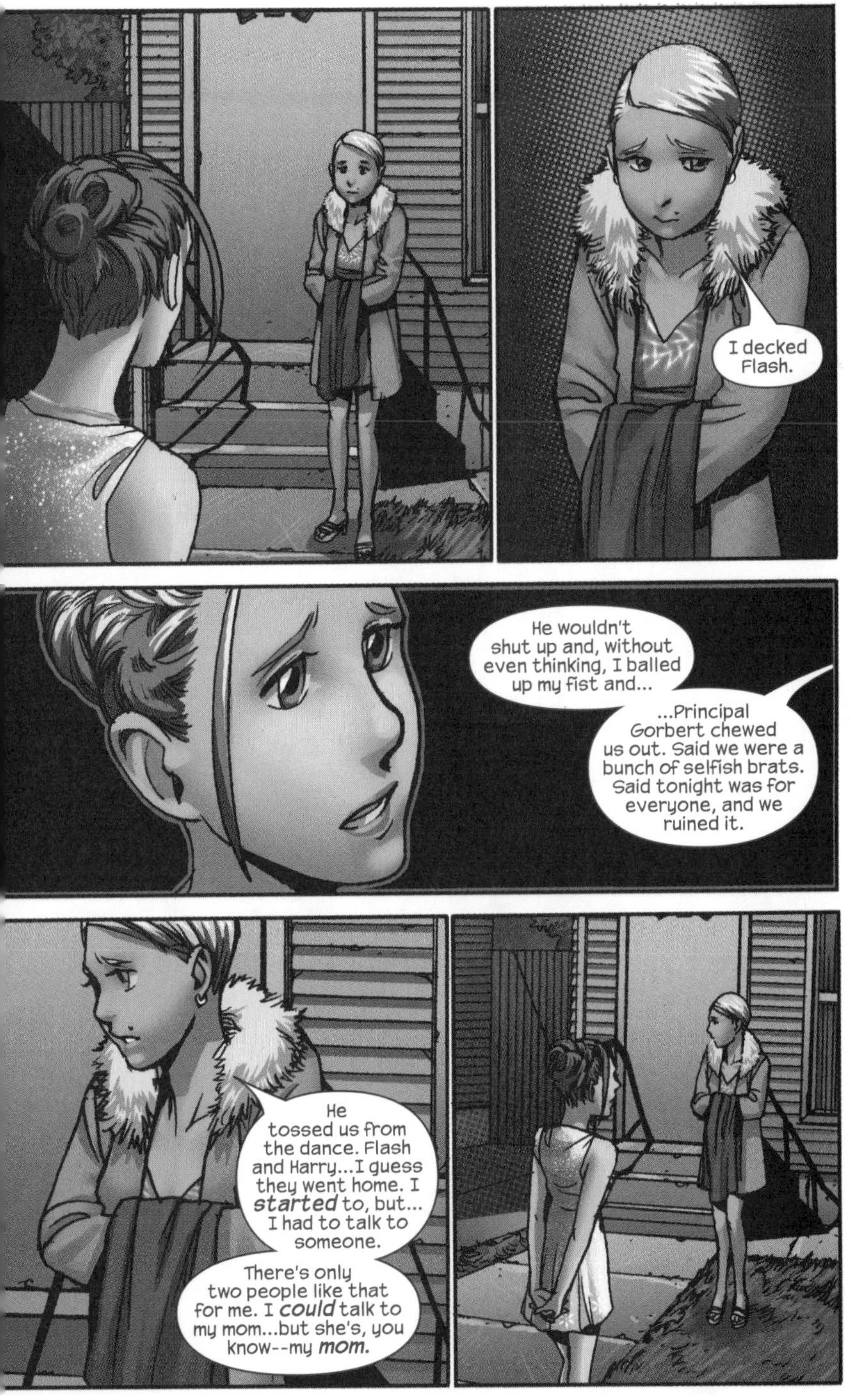
I decked Flash.
He wouldn't shut up and, without even thinking, I balled up my fist and...
...Principal Gorbert chewed us out. Said we were a bunch of selfish brats. Said tonight was for everyone, and we ruined it.
He tossed us from the dance. Flash and Harry...I guess they went home. I *started* to, but... I had to talk to someone.
There's only two people like that for me. I *could* talk to my mom...but she's, you know--my *mom.*

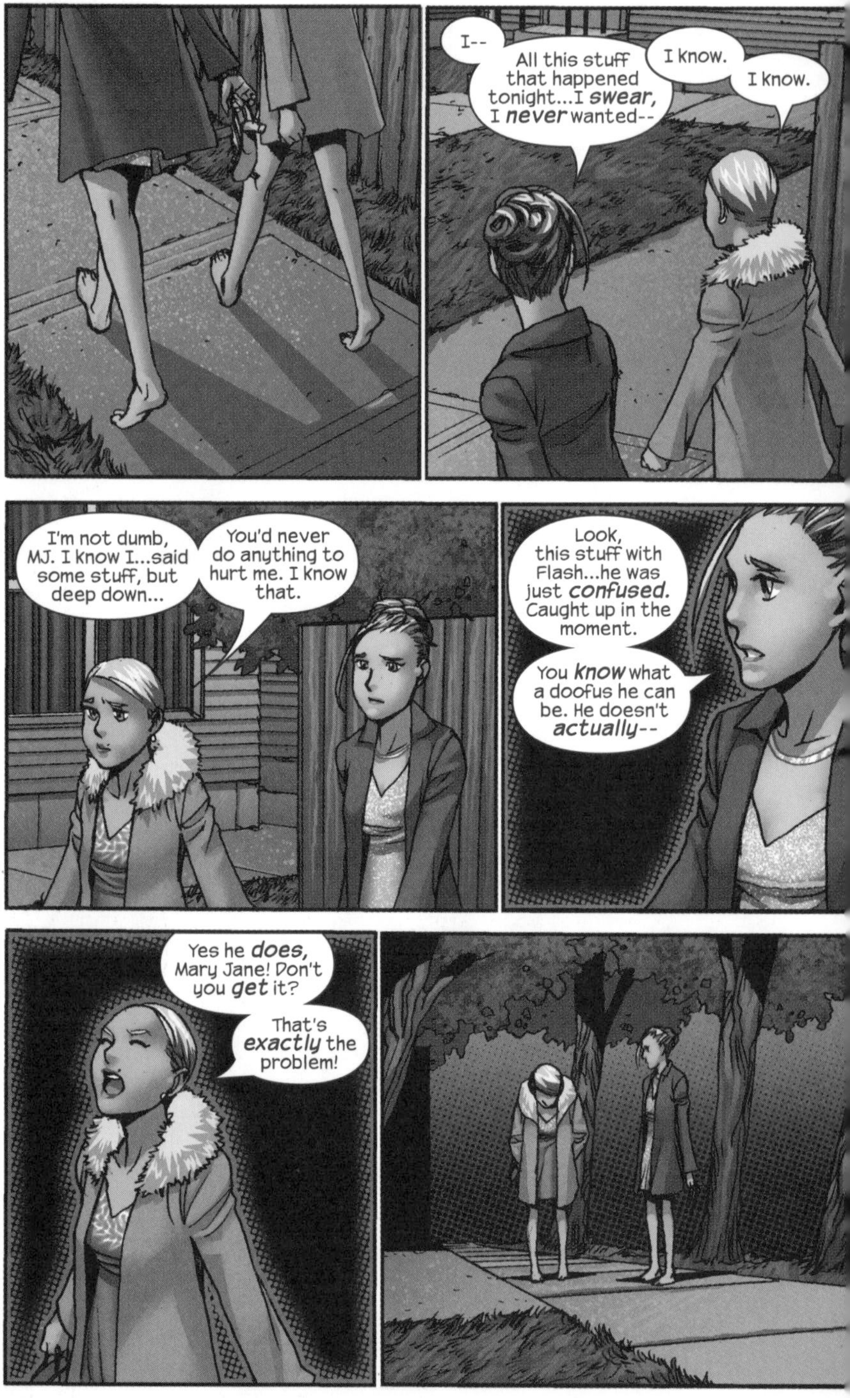
I--
All this stuff that happened tonight...I swear, I never wanted--
I know.
I know.
I'm not dumb, MJ. I know I...said some stuff, but deep down...
You'd never do anything to hurt me. I know that.
Look, this stuff with Flash...he was just confused. Caught up in the moment.
You know what a doofus he can be. He doesn't actually--
Yes he does, Mary Jane! Don't you get it?
That's exactly the problem!

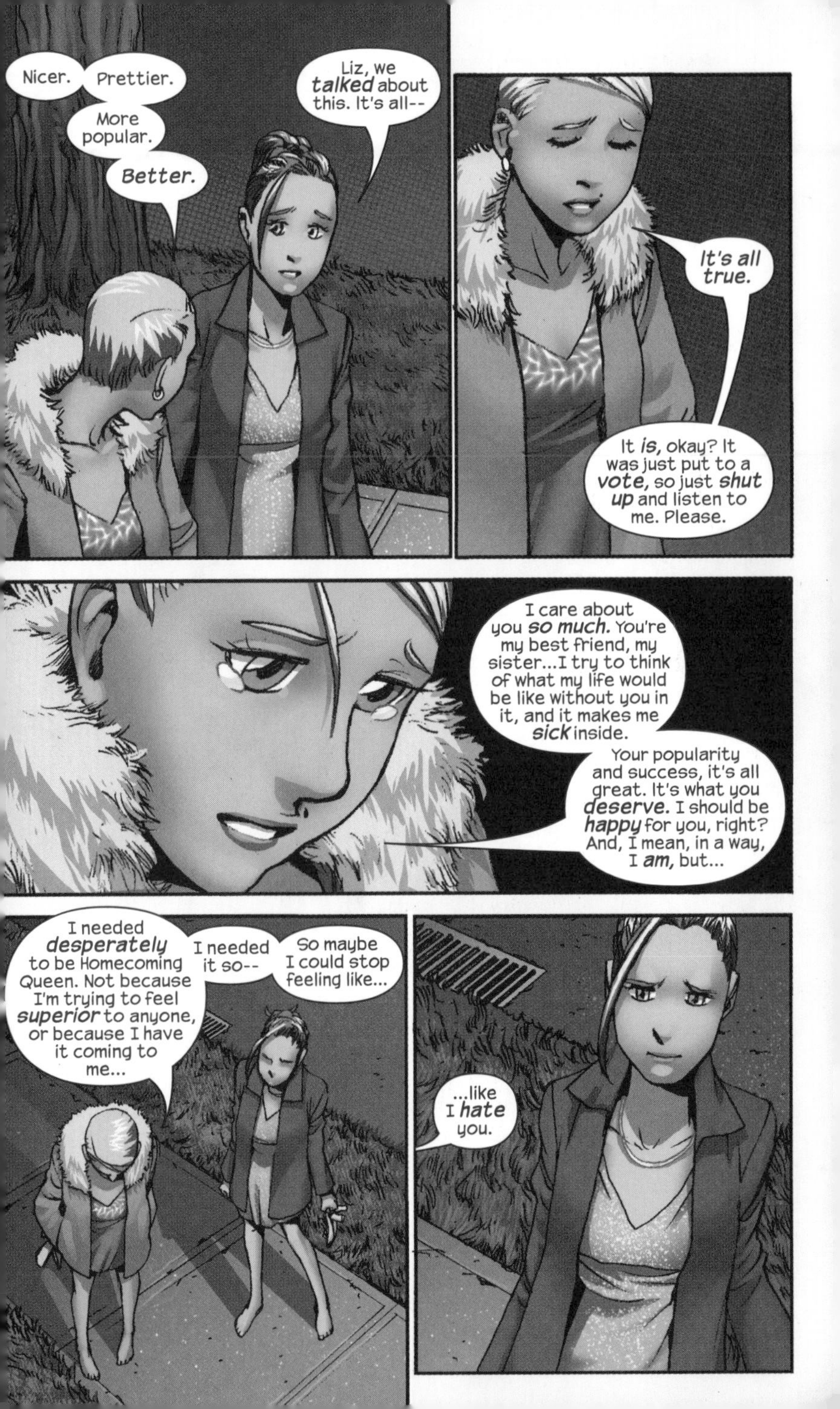
Nicer.
Prettier.
More popular.
Better.
Liz, we talked about this. It's all--
It's all true.
It is, okay? It was just put to a vote, so just shut up and listen to me. Please.
I care about you so much. You're my best friend, my sister...I try to think of what my life would be like without you in it, and it makes me sick inside.
Your popularity and success, it's all great. It's what you deserve. I should be happy for you, right? And, I mean, in a way, I am, but...
I needed desperately to be Homecoming Queen. Not because I'm trying to feel superior to anyone, or because I have it coming to me...
I needed it so--
So maybe I could stop feeling like...
...like I hate you.

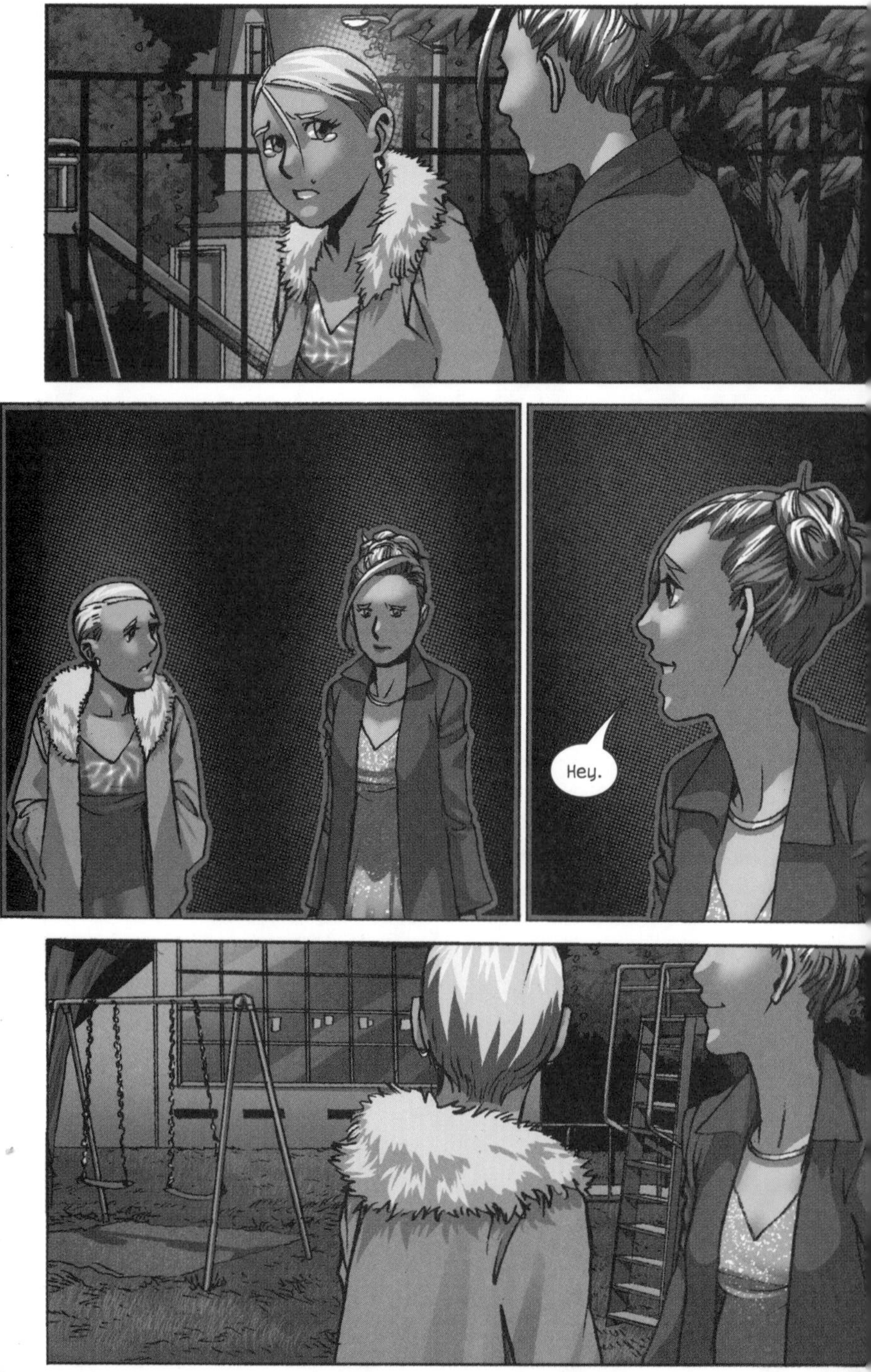
Hey.

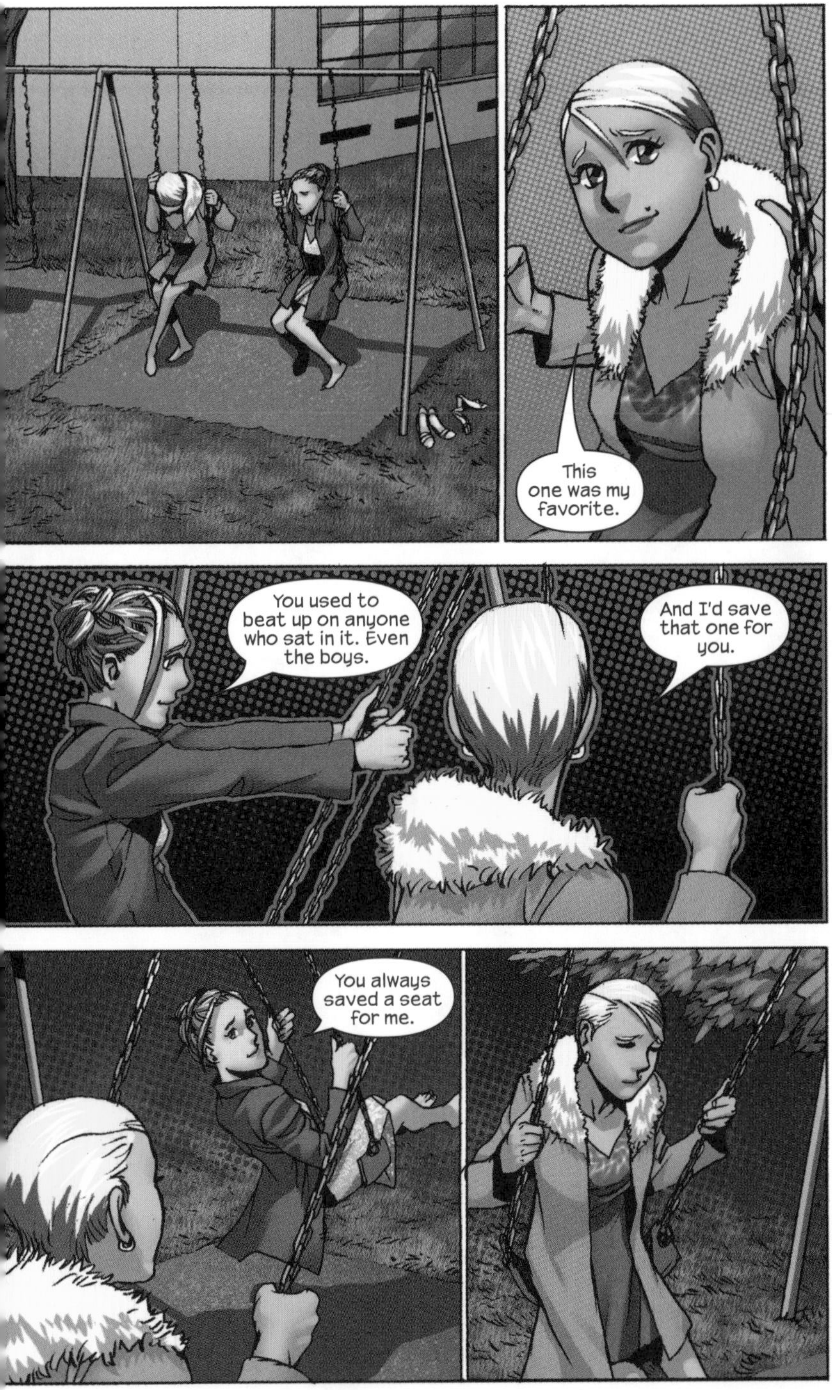
This one was my favorite.
You used to beat up on anyone who sat in it. Even the boys.
And I'd save that one for you.
You always saved a seat for me.

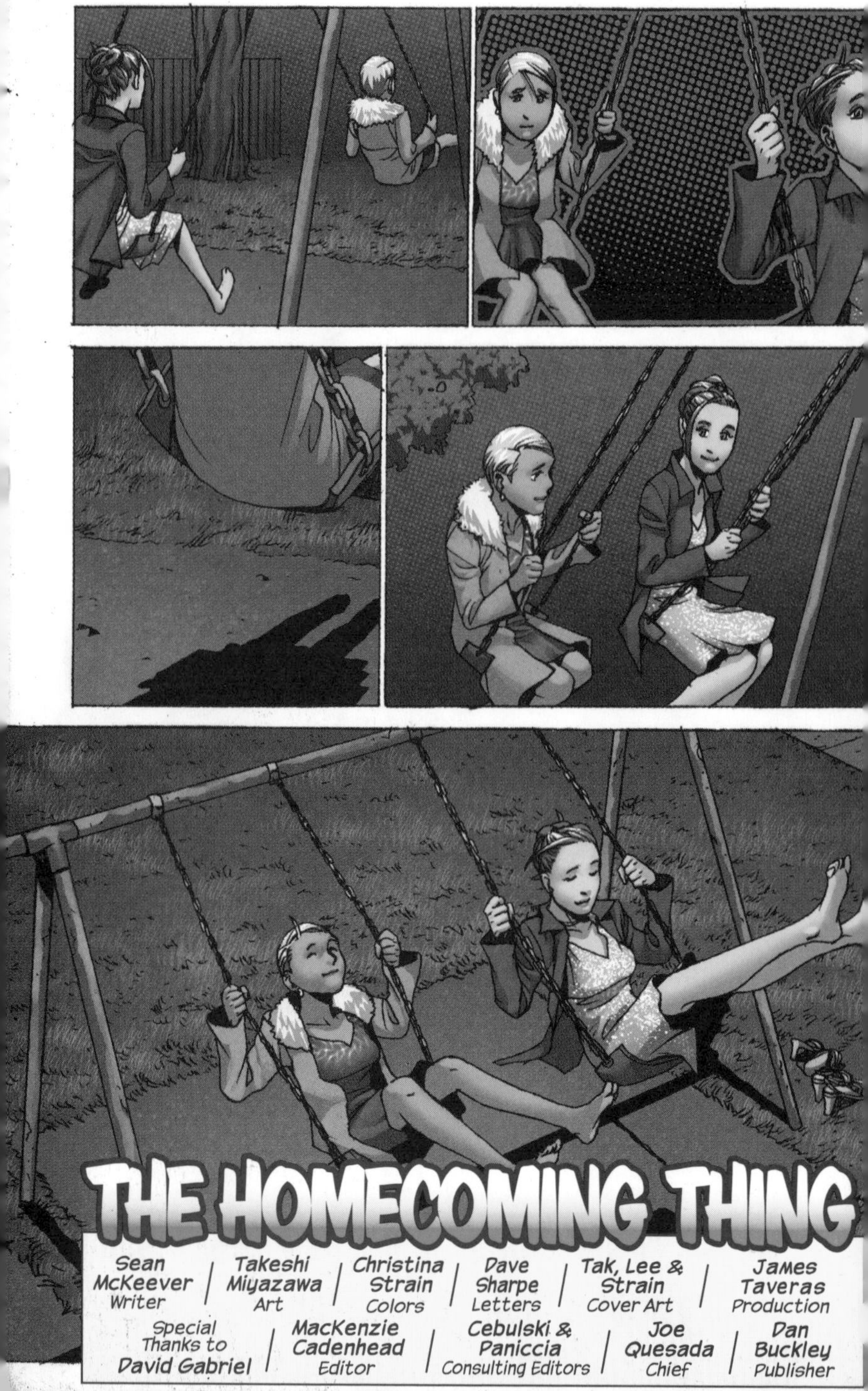
THE HOMECOMING THING
Sean McKeever Writer
Takeshi Miyazawa Art
Christina Strain Colors
Dave Sharpe Letters
Tak, Lee & Strain Cover Art
James Taveras Production
Special Thanks to David Gabriel
MacKenzie Cadenhead Editor
Cebulski & Paniccia Consulting Editors
Joe Quesada Chief
Dan Buckley Publisher